The Passionate Learner

Also by Robert L. Fried

The Passionate Teacher

9/26/03

For Arlene
with best wishes
Rob Fried

The

Passionate

Learner

How Teachers and Parents

Can Help Children Reclaim the

Joy of Discovery

ROBERT L. FRIED

BEACON PRESS   BOSTON

Beacon Press
25 Beacon Street
Boston, Massachusetts 02108-2892
www.beacon.org

Beacon Press books
are published under the auspices of
the Unitarian Universalist Association of Congregations.

Printed in the United States of America

05 04 03 02 01   8 7 6 5 4 3 2 1

This book is printed on acid-free paper
that meets the uncoated paper ANSI/NISO
specifications for permanence as revised in 1992.

Design and Composition by Wilsted & Taylor Publishing Services

Library of Congress Cataloging-in-Publication Data

Fried, Robert L.
The passionate learner: how teachers and parents can
help children reclaim the joy of discovery / Robert L. Fried.
p. cm.
Includes bibliographical references (p.) and index.
ISBN 0-8070-3144-5
1. Motivation in education. 2. Education—Parent participation.
3. Effective teaching. I. Title.
LB1065 .F73 2001
370.15'4—dc21   2001002987

For my sons,
Zachary and Peter,
who have taught me so much
about learning

and for my mother,
Celia Paisner Fried,
who was a devoted teacher

Contents

Foreword by Seymour Sarason   ix

Prelude: Of Passionate Learning, Food Fights,
and Who Needs Soccer?   1

Part One: The Promise of
Passionate Learning

1. The Promise   17

2. The Chasm: How the Promise Gets Broken   28

Part Two: Reclaiming the Promise

3. What Teachers Can Do to
Reclaim the Promise   41

4. Revisiting the Chasm:
Misbehaving Kids, Boredom,
and Wasting Time   57

5. What Parents Can Do to
Reclaim the Promise   73

6. What Schools and Systems Can Do to
Reclaim the Promise   86

**Part Three: The Practice of
Passionate Learning**

7. Curriculum as Relationships   *101*

8. Curriculum? Who *Cares?*   *115*

9. Parents and Curriculum:
A Partnership with Students and Teachers   *131*

10. Words of Power   *137*

11. A "Good Enough" Literacy Program   *159*

12. Lift Every Voice   *176*

**Part Four: Passionate Teaching and Learning
in an Era of Standardization**

13. A Passion for Excellence—
and How We Undermine It   *197*

14. Celebrating "Inconsistent Excellence"   *216*

15. Education at the Millennium:
The Bad and the Good   *232*

16. Passionate Teaching and Learning
in an Era of Standardization   *245*

Finale: Unsung Heroes   262

Notes   271

A Few Thoughts and Acknowledgments   279

Index   283

Foreword

There are people who, when they see the word *passion* in a book's title, may not open its cover because that word conjures up imagery of excessive feeling that shortcuts clear and dispassionate thinking. Though the relationship between the word and the imagery is understandable, it would be a grievous mistake to pass this book by.

The Passionate Learner is about many things, and at the top of that list is the bedrock importance of capitalizing on and sustaining the satisfaction and joy a student experiences when his or her *thinking* about the social and natural world has broadened and deepened. This is a book about *intellectual* development, about why and how the curiosity and puzzlements so evident in the earliest months and years of life can either be fertilized and blossom in school or be blunted near to the point of extinction.

I got to know Rob Fried after I read his first book, *The Passionate Teacher.* I was more than impressed by the book, in several ways. First, he is a gifted writer. Unlike most writers in education, he does not resort to concepts and jargon that sound (and usually are) important in the abstract, only to deny us the concrete examples that would help us understand the substance and scope of the concepts. He knows schools, especially urban schools.

Second, Fried knows that what he advocates runs against conventional thinking and practice. But he is no polemicist, let alone a satirist, who judges others who disagree with him as misguided fools. He sympathetically presents opposing views at the same time he is pulling the rug out from under them. They are not villains, after all, but people who by their school experience (and, if they are educators, by their training) have been socialized to see students, teachers, administrators, parents in the counterproductive ways they do.

Third, Fried exploits his experience as a school board member, teacher, principal, and school consultant. And now—by virtue of being in the university, with the time and obligation to make sense of his past—he has creatively organized his experience. All of these virtues, and more, are compellingly evident in the present book.

There is good research evidence that, as students go from elementary to middle to high school, their interest in and motivation for school learning steadily decrease. When I have pointed this out to secondary teachers, they are not surprised. They experience its consequences daily with most of their students, urban or suburban. From the standpoint of passionate learning, urban and suburban schools are not dramatically different. As Professor Fried correctly points out, colleges and universities (which draw largely, of course, from the suburbs) have in recent decades created programs for the many students who cannot write a term paper or are incapable of independent thinking.

Why this should surprise no one is explained in this book, especially in the chapters on literacy. Literacy is one of those words that means different things to different people. In the hands of Rob Fried, it takes on features, scope, and obligations that are compellingly creative and instructive. He does not just lightly touch upon these aspects—he describes what they look like in actual school contexts. And he accomplishes here what so few education writers have even attempted—he speaks to parents in the same clear, nonjargon prose he offers to teachers, with the intended effect of forging a true partnership on behalf of the passionate learner in every child.

When I finished reading this book, I had the fantasy that someone asked me why I am so enthusiastic about it and would I pick out a few pages he could read that would provide, in a nutshell, one of its major themes. I would tell him to begin with Rob Fried's story about his lack of appetite for food, as a boy, and his love of politics, in both of which his father was the decisive factor. I found it hilarious, and at the same time it so beautifully shows the difference between productive and unproductive learning.

On Broadway, critics always fear (and rightly so) that good first acts are rarely followed by equally good second acts. *The Passionate Learner,* coming five years after *The Passionate Teacher,* is Rob Fried's second act, and it is as stimulating and rewarding as the first. May it have as long a run.

The Passionate Learner

Of Passionate Learning,

Food Fights, and

Who Needs Soccer?

Thou little Child, yet glorious in the might
Of heaven-born freedom on thy being's height,
Why with such earnest pains dost thou provoke
The years to bring the inevitable yoke?

WILLIAM WORDSWORTH

Every child is a passionate learner. Children come into the world with a desire to learn that is as natural as the desire to eat and move and be loved, their hunger for knowledge, for skills, for the feeling of mastery as strong as any other appetite. They learn an amazing variety of things in the years before they enter school, including, miraculously, how to talk fluently in their native language. And they continue learning at a terrifically high rate throughout their childhood.

I

We are less likely to see this same passion when we look at kids in school. Something happens to a child when learning is replaced by schooling. Of course, some children do hold on to a dynamic interest in learning while they are students. Others get support at home for their own individual passions (music, hobbies, reading, sports) and thus can more easily weather any disappointments with school-based learning.

But despite the wonderful efforts of individual teachers who promote and celebrate intense and exuberant learning by students of every stripe and circumstance, too many young people, when they enter formal schooling, feel the passionate learning of their early years begin to decline, often with permanent results.

Something gets in the way. And that something is what this book will examine in the attempt to discuss actions that teachers, parents, and students can take to remove the roadblocks to passionate learning.

A few years ago, in an elementary school in Hartford, Connecticut, I asked a group of third grade students to tell me what were the most important things they were learning in school. They said, "not to run in the halls," "no pushing or fighting," "don't throw stuff on the floor." I agreed with them that these were, indeed, important things, and I wrote them on the board under the heading "Good *Behavior.*" But next to that I wrote "Good *Learning*" and asked them what important things they felt they needed to *learn.* After a few moments, two children raised their hands. One said, "to listen to the teacher." The other said, "to be good."

Already, as third graders, learning had become a world of "good children" and "bad children." Good children listen to their teacher. The bad children don't. Thus far in their lives, these urban third graders still consider it *good* to "be good." For many of their older brothers and sisters, it has already become *cool* to "be bad."

Lots of kids become disenfranchised as learners, become victims of traditional school culture, once they encounter formal schooling:

- independent-minded, strong-willed, high-energy, creative-thinking kids

- those who crave opportunities to learn through physical movement and practical hands-on application or who need the steady presence of a highly skilled adult mentor

- children with greater emotional needs and those with a variety of learning disabilities

- kids "in the middle" of the academic range, whose learning potential is so often undervalued or ignored because they present few problems for the teacher or because they do not impress their teachers as especially gifted or bright

A high percentage of children from poor and working-class families, kids from under-resourced neighborhoods, acquire the distinct impression as they move up through the grades that success in school is meant for other people, not for them. This is particularly true for those who do not come from family backgrounds with a strong emphasis on reading, writing, and conversation about issues and ideas. For too many of them, school is just not a game they feel destined to win. So they stop trying and begin to "blow off" school.

Nobody conspires to deny these children their birthright as passionate learners. Students, teachers, parents fall victim, too often, to a system of education that readily substitutes a kind of hum-drum, low-energy, task-oriented compliance for the intensity, enthusiasm, and joyfulness we see in the infant learner grasping at the world.

In the small New England city where I live with my family and where both of our sons went through the local public schools, the potential threat to learning shouldn't seem nearly as severe as it is for at-risk children from urban or rural neighborhoods. But parents around here, and in suburbia, seem to worry just as much. The stakes seem so high; the doubts and fears so prevalent. It's as though by the time our children are ready for school, the very notion that every child is a natural-born learner has evaporated from the scene, like morning mist, replaced by the harsh glare of a competitive and not easily forgiving educational landscape.

How strange! The same parents who gleefully note each new word, phrase, question, insight, or physical skill that their infants and toddlers acquire from birth onward often begin to lose confidence in their child's inherent enthusiasm and strength as a learner as soon as the shadow of schooling is cast. Little kids who are celebrated, by parents everywhere, for their inquisitiveness, their sense of wonder, their dogged determination to master complex skills of movement and of language, now seem—as students—so vulnerable, so susceptible to inadequacy or maladjustment.

The children of middle-class, professional, well-educated parents are *supposed* to do well in our nation's public schools. But anxieties among parents of preschoolers, or of kids facing the legendary horrors of middle school or the competitive pressures of college preparation, lead many concerned parents to actively consider private schools or home-schooling to shield their children from what they perceive as threats to their well-being as learners. As the mother of a three-year-old told me,

> I remember when she was just born, and I was carrying her past one of the big public high schools just as school was letting out for the day. And I saw all the same cliques; I recognized myself—you know, the shy, quiet girl carrying too many books, with her one friend next to her—and the other girls with a lot of makeup and cigarettes, looking kind of scornful. I saw all of

those familiar kinds, and it gave me a chill to think that my baby is going to be in there, and that I'm going to be unleashing that on her. I want her not to wake up with that dread in her stomach that she has to go to school—which has nothing to do with not wanting to learn—I want her to be in a place where kids are not allowed to be cruel.

By some accounts, our nation's public schools have never been better: reading scores are up, higher standards are in place, accountability on the part of teachers and schools is much more in focus, state curriculum frameworks and standardized tests have been developed to provide for more consistency among schools, violence and vandalism are on the wane, and our political leaders, from both parties, have put improved education at or near the top of their priorities. But try telling that to parents, of all cultures and backgrounds, who know how essential a good education is to their children's future and who recognize how vulnerable their children are to discouragement or outright failure. They want to know how well the schools will serve *their* kids. And they worry.

As for the urban third graders I visited in Hartford, when teachers and children define "learning good things" as learning how to "be good," we set up a potential booby trap that may go off as soon as children begin to question their faith in the consistency and benevolence of adult authority, or when the influences of peer culture begin to militate against individual striving for academic success.

For so many children, urban, suburban, rural, the light of learning that burns so brightly in them as little kids begins to dim once they start school, replaced by a deep ambivalence about learning. This is why, by fourth or fifth grade (or even earlier), many teachers feel their students need "behavior management." This is why few people want to teach middle school, where they would have to deal with "kids whose hormones are running wild," or why high school teachers with years of seniority elect to teach juniors and seniors, those who've remained when the unworthy have found their way (or been pushed) out the back door of the schoolhouse.

A former high school student put it this way: "High school was like a penance imposed for some unknown sin. Everything I ever learned that was important to me was learned outside of school. So I never thought to associate schools with learning."[1]

Does it have to be this way? No.

Are success in learning, achievement in learning, joy and fulfillment in learning scarce commodities, reserved for the few, the motivated, the gifted; for those with competitive, success-oriented parents or those enrolled in elite private institutions?

Again, no (though it may sometimes seem so). Learning is exciting and rewarding for all of us. As various scholars remind us, we evolved as human beings precisely because we were all able to learn—with enthusiasm![2] And, despite our often-frustrating experiences of school, learning is as natural and continuous an activity as anything else we do.[3]

So what has happened for so many children, along the way, to transform the joy of learning that every toddler displays into the resistance and ennui we see too often in the classroom? Why do so many young learners—kids with limitless promise—turn out to be reluctant scholars?

That question is at the heart of this book. I'll raise and try to respond to a number of related questions that underlie the challenge—and the obstacles—of maintaining passionate learning for children. But perhaps the central question for you, the reader, is, *What can parents and teachers do, as individuals, as colleagues, and as partners, to transform our children's classrooms and schools into places of powerful, sustained, and enthusiastic learning for every child?*

I believe that the era of the isolated classroom, like that of the solitary teacher, must end. We can't do the job of teaching all by ourselves if we hope to engage children in the magnificence of their potential for learning. The loneliness of the solitary educator and the isolated parent, the school cut off from a vital connection to its neighborhood, the home and classroom that feel like totally other worlds to the child—these things must change if we are to raise a generation of passionate learners.

Seymour Sarason tells us that we cannot hope to create contexts of sustained and positive learning for children if we do not also create such contexts for teachers [4] This is truer than most administrators are willing to admit. Likewise, we cannot hope to create successful schools if we allow ourselves to rationalize the absence of parents as full partners in our enterprise. We've heard the labels that get flung around: "burned-out teachers," "broken homes," "single moms," "mindless bureaucrats," "self-indulgent boomers," "indifferent administrators," "parents working two jobs to make ends meet," "teachers who dig in their heels and resist change," "dropouts having babies," "parents who don't speak English" or who "don't read to their kids" or who "just don't care." Those epithets do an injustice to the great majority of parents and educators of all cultural and economic backgrounds. Parents and educators alike recognize that lasting partnerships must be developed among and between them if we expect a lot more of our children to achieve to the high standards that everyone is calling for.

We must remind ourselves: *learning is one of the most fascinating and rewarding activities for human beings.* The desire to learn, to discover, to figure something out, to be able to do something well enough to proclaim it as one's own, must surely be as strong as any impulse within the human soul.

Children cannot *not* learn. If they lose their appetite for school learning, it's because somebody, or something, has turned a natural, joyous, life-sustaining activity into a form of drudgery, a theater of the absurd, or—worse—a chamber of abuse.

Dinner in the Fried Household: A Cautionary Tale

Let me introduce a personal anecdote from my childhood that may serve as a gentle warning, as we search for ways to keep passionate learning alive once kids hit school. It's about how, under my father's tutelage, I "learned" to resist eating—and to love politics.

When I was a child, my father, who in certain other respects was a loving parent, held fast to the belief that unless he intervened each night at the dinner table my brothers and I would starve to death. Or, if we didn't actually starve, we'd suffer malnutrition or grow up with weak minds and crooked bones. My mother went along with this, but she didn't seem to make such an issue of it.

My father felt he had to personally supervise our eating to avoid his dire predictions. We kids naturally resisted, trying to eat as little as we could get away with. We would argue, vociferously, about whether the piece of meat on our plate was good protein, as he claimed, or riddled with fat and therefore rejectable. The refrain "Eat it! It's *meat!*" with its answer, "No! It's *fat!*" rings in our ears to this day.

My father was limited in his ability to punish us for our rebelliousness by the child-rearing practices of his middle-class, Jewish social group. Beating us for poor table behavior was not an option, nor was making us sit at the table for hours until we had finished, nor was serving us the remains of last night's supper for breakfast the next morning.

Since his avowed goals were to make sure we were well fed, rather than to crush our rebellious spirit, he avoided the more coercive techniques. He preferred to cajole, to bluster, to harass, even to negotiate with us ("Well, at least eat *half* of your string beans." "Which half, Dad, the bigger half or the smaller half?") Or else try to outargue or outsmart us—a dangerous tack for a father, as I have learned with my own children. To the pronouncement that hungry millions elsewhere on the earth made it unconscionable for us to leave food on our plates, we offered up our meager allowance to pay the postage for sending our uneaten meal anywhere he liked.

And if my father had a loud voice and domineering presence to bring to bear on the dinner table conflict, we kids were not defenseless. We used any weapons allowed under the Geneva Convention on Family Mealtime Warfare: denial (*"Cauliflower?* You *know* I never eat *cauliflower*—we've already *been* through that"); delay ("I'm not *finished* yet; I'll *get* to it"); evasion ("What are you *looking* at? *I* can't see any meat loaf"); distrust ("There's something a little *funny* about this lamb chop"). We might appeal to reason: ("You *really* think I'll *starve to death* if I don't finish this lousy little carrot?"), or amazement ("How did you find *that*? I *already* ate it. Did somebody *put* it there while I was in the bathroom?"), or ruse ("I gotta go and do my home-work; she's giving a test tomorrow"). The struggle was joined.

In reflection, that confrontation resembled nothing so much as the daily struggle that goes on, in classroom after classroom, and in all too many homes, over whether or not adults can force kids to "*learn* what's good for them."

Once, for a few weeks, when I was eight, my father even tried bribing us to eat. (Nobody outside the family believes this, but it really happened.) He offered us five cents per meal if we ate our dinner reasonably and acted with civilized decorum. It was like working for an A or a happy face sticker as a reward for good table manners. When bribing did not work, my father was moved to threaten us. He announced one night a system of "demerits" to punish us for not eating. The parallel to "detentions" is obvious—I was occasionally hit with a "suspension" from the dinner table for my antics.

The result of his "behavior management" at mealtime was that I grew up skinny and unhungry. I was well into my teenage years before I knew there was anything called appetite. I was healthy enough. I just was never hungry. Only when I began to cook for myself did I begin to anticipate the pleasure of eating.

I will argue in this book that, just as we all are born with a hunger for food, so all children come into this world with an appetite for learning. It's there. It just happens. As humans, if we don't learn, we die; if we don't receive the stimuli that can come only from learning, we withdraw into a vegetative state; we starve to death, spiritually.

My father was not a tyrant, despite wanting to dominate and manipulate our food intake. He was in other respects very supportive of many of our interests and pursuits. He discovered, when I was ten, that I was interested in politics, and he adopted what I still consider a perfect teaching role in promoting my learning—a role completely opposite to that at the dinner table. When he put me to bed, I could ask any question about politics that came into my head, and he would oblige me by answering as best he could. He'd stand at my bedroom door, with his finger on the light switch, and as long as I had good questions to pose, the light would stay on. When I had exhausted all inquiries for the evening, he would switch off the light, and I would enter into slumber with visions of becoming a civil rights lawyer.

Without planning it that way, my father let *me* be in charge of my political education, even as he had tried to be the czar of my eating. It was ironic: I ate as little as possible, because he badgered me about eating. I learned a great deal about politics because I wanted to, because I had the power to direct my studies, and because he was there to support me with facts and insights.

My appetite for politics was the inversion of my indifference to food—one activity empowered me; the other humiliated me. It is curious to reflect that my father was central to both activities.

School is like my family dinner table for too many kids. It's the place where someone else sets the rules and decides what's good for you, how much of which kinds of knowledge stuff you've got to ingest—it assumes that most students have little natural appetite of their own. School can be a place where table manners are more valued than good nutrition, where the only food that counts is consumed under the watchful eye of the teacher, who usually works from a standard cookbook that is more about categorizing the ingredients than producing tasteful meals. You prove your worth by how willingly you consume (and "give back up").

But enough about the dinner table. Let us investigate the world of children, who are naturally born learners—passionate learners—in that they learn with gusto, with intensity, with pride, with originality, and they do it all the time. They don't need bribes, and they don't need threats.[5] No child ever learned to speak by being threatened with sanctions for not speaking; no child began walking because somebody offered her gold stars if she would cross the kitchen floor on two feet.

Who Needs Soccer?
Here, at the beginning, I want to address the most common criticism this book is likely to encounter, namely, that the purpose of our schools—flawed though they may be—continues to be to produce a sufficient number of well-trained young people, people who continue on to college and good jobs. If anything, some critics have suggested, we need to return to a more tightly structured, more traditionally content-focused ap-

proach to curriculum, rather than to pursue a "child-centered" approach often associated with what they see as the discredited tenets of progressive education. Why, they ask, push our already overcommitted teachers, schools, and students to undertake so seemingly esoteric a task as promoting "passionate learning" when they can hardly fulfill the more basic tasks we depend on them to accomplish?

I was musing over just this question, a week or so ago, while walking in our neighborhood park on an early-fall afternoon. The baseball fields had been rechalked into large rectangles, with nets placed at either end. It was the start of the local kids' soccer league, and the grounds were a swirling mass of kids running, pell-mell, trying to kick a leather ball somewhere they wanted it to go.

The scene, so familiar in almost every town and village all over the world, is for us Americans a rather recent phenomenon. Back in the 1950s, when I was a boy, it was only baseball, basketball, and in bigger towns and schools, football (with field hockey and cheerleading for the girls). Those (and hockey, here in the north) were the only sports that "counted." Now, suddenly, soccer has taken over as the most popular game.

Soccer has some terrific aspects to it that, in retrospect, were missing during my boyhood. You don't need to be very big and strong to play it; height offers no special advantage, nor do you need to have good hand coordination. Everyone on the field gets to play all the time (unlike baseball and football, which involve lots of waiting around). Soccer is a sport for teams, not just for stars—there's no pitcher or quarterback to shoulder most of the pressure and get most of the glory. It's a great sport for girls as well as for boys and, up until fourth or fifth grade, many teams are of mixed gender. You need very little equipment, just some sort of footwear and a ball. You don't need a big

field or full team to have fun (it's like basketball, in that respect). Two, three, or more people can play anywhere they find
a level spot of ground. In an era of globalization, soccer is a universal language, revered on all continents.

And, perhaps most desirable for less-than-stellar athletes
like I was, soccer offers a wonderful chance to get in there, play
hard, and gradually get better without facing the very public
display (and humiliation) of striking out or failing to catch a
pass. You can (for a while, at least) hide your inexperience, your
lack of confidence or skill, and just play along with the rest of
the field, hoping to improve over time and with practice.

I want school-based learning to offer more kinds of opportunities to a more diverse group of young scholars, as soccer does.
I want there to be lots of ways for kids who aren't especially
"gifted and talented" to become good players and valuable
team members. I want kids who haven't been endowed with
highly educated parents to have a chance to get in there and run
with the pack, without repeatedly striking out and feeling humiliated and stigmatized by their minor-league status. And I
want our classroom coaches to plan better how to make sure
everyone gets out there to play.

Some, undoubtedly, will point out that, in soccer as in all
sports, "you have to get the basics down first," which calls for
discipline, motivation, and following the coach's directions. I
agree, but watching the kids on the playing fields, this doesn't
seem to pose a problem. Skill differences among players are
evident, but the opportunities for full-scale participation are
abundant. The team works together. The enthusiasm is infectious.

I could keep pushing this analogy for a while, but my real
goal is to see our classrooms evolve until they become fields of
play where no one is sidelined, where all are challenged, where

excellence is valued as both an individual and a team goal, and where all can develop confidence and skill amid the diversity of their dreams.

The Passionate Learner is all around us, within us. It is the child who questions, who daydreams, who invents problems and tries to solve them. It's the child who winces at injustice and wants to know how to make life more fair. It's the child who acts and then steps back to wonder why things turned out that way, who reads and then links the universe of the book, seamlessly, with that of her own imagination.

Let us find ways to celebrate the eternal promise of the passionate learners that we are.

PART ONE

The Promise of

Passionate Learning

CHAPTER ONE

The Promise

The child, awakening to the world. A world of light and sensa-
tion—of touch, of taste, of sounds familiar and unfamiliar. The
human embrace that allows the child to reach out with confidence and encompass the world with her senses. Learning that
happens continuously, joyously, both arduously and effortlessly.
Crawling that leads to pulling oneself up to stand or lean against
a chair, that leads to cruising along while holding onto the living
room furniture, that leads to walking and then to running. The
babbling that becomes "Mama" and "Dada," that grows by a
slow accretion of sounds and words, cadenced by rapid explo-
sions of new phrases and sentences, when circumstances and
the child's own spontaneity call for them.

Our son Peter, as a baby, running to his mother to warn that
a friend's dog has grabbed hold of his brother Zach's favorite toy
lamb. In panic, Peter forms his first sentence: *"Ma Ma! No No!
Woof Woof, Baa Baa!"*

The toddler who runs ahead of—away from—his mother,
turning back every so often to make sure she is following
closely; who dares to take on the world so long as the protecting
arms will be there. The early years, so full of learning and the
increase of skills, awarenesses, words, questions, that their ve-

locity and abundance cannot be captured by even the most ar-
dent of parent chroniclers. Songs and rhymes sung and learned
by heart, then proudly performed at church and family gather-
ings. Stories told. Books reread until their bindings wear out.
Obstacles of every kind encountered and surmounted. The discovery of science, via the spider climbing down from the bathroom ceiling or the earliest dandelion pushing up in the yard.
The world of the child is nothing but eating, sleeping, growing,
loving—and *learning*.

Andrew Meltzoff, coauthor of *The Scientist in the Crib: Minds,
Brains, and How Children Learn* (1999), says that "cognitive developmental psychologists are now actually looking into the
crib to study the development of the mind early on, even before
children develop language. And what we find there is very interesting. We find a little scientist peering back at us—a child
who is desperately interested in making sense of the people,
the objects, and the language around him or her, a child doing
mini-experiments to try to sort everything out."[1]

A very small Asian girl, about two or three years old and accompanied by her American adoptive mom, gets on my commuter
bus and sits in the row across from me. The girl begins to speak
at once, and there follows an almost continuous stream of
words:

"Oh, *look,* Mommy! There are no seat belts, here. This is
just like a plane, but there are no seat belts. How come there
are no seat belts? Aren't we *supposed* to use seat belts?" She
bounces up and down, to demonstrate her freedom and her
danger, then peers out the window.

"Oh, we're up *so high*! The cars look little. Are they little?
Or are we *big*?"

There is a pause, while she sits down and starts to suck her
thumb. Her mom nestles her, inviting her to take a nap, but in
a moment, she is up again.

"Mommy, I'm scared. I'm scared about aliens. I don't want them to get me!"

She looks to her mom for reassurance. Her mom tells her there are no aliens.

"But I'm still scared of them. What will they do if they get me?" Patiently, her mom repeats that there are no such things as aliens.

"But they may be just out there, and we can't see them. Do you think they know I'm here?" Her eyes twinkle as she says this, as if she knows she is being playful about her fears. She hides beneath her mother's arm, while her mother carefully explains to her why she shouldn't be afraid.

"Okay," she says quietly.

There is a moment's pause, as though the little girl is trying to decide which is more real, her fantasies or her mother's solace.

"But what about vampires!"

Her mother tries to head this one off, asking, a bit sternly: "Now, what do we *know* about vampires?" Soberly, the girl answers, in a tone of voice that lets everyone listening (she has drawn the attention of a number of the commuters) know that she knows what the right answer is— or ought to be.

"There are no real vampires. They don't exist."

"That's right," her mother tells her.

"I *know* they don't exist, Mommy, but what do they *look* like?"

Scientist, philosopher, observer of social phenomena, safety engineer, fantasist—the girl astounds us with her vocabulary, her energy, her intellect. Her mother tells me that she was adopted a little over a year ago and that for months she wouldn't say a word. "Then, one morning she woke up talking and hasn't stopped talking since." Meltzoff comments that "there seems to be a deep kinship between adults doing science and children learning. Some of the principles are the same: forming hypotheses, making predictions, doing experiments to test ideas. Even babies have theories of the world, very simple theories, but cognitive structures about how people, things, and language work."[2] Author Frank Smith puts it this way: "Children spend the first years of life solving problems all the time. They are born learning; if there is nothing to learn, they are bored and their attention is distracted. We don't have to train children to learn, or even account for their learning; we have to avoid interfering with it."[3]

This is the promise of the preschool child. A born learner, proud and proficient, gaining mastery of the known world within the embrace of home and family.

And then. School. Play group to day care center to preschool to kindergarten. Growth. Adventure. Relationships. Anxiety, too. What parent does not face the prospect of school without awe, anxiety, hope, and foreboding mixed together to form a knot in one's stomach? Who among us, as parents, has not seen our child off to school without the fear that others—classmates, teachers, school staff—may not understand this child the way we do, love her as we love her, treasure the things we treasure, avoid what we try to avoid, and above all protect this child from too much of the world happening too quickly?

On separate occasions I interviewed some parents of preschool children about questions like these. Here are excerpts from two of those interviews. One is with Mary, an editor who has taken several years off from work to spend at home with her daughter, Kate, who is three. The other is Opal, a native of Jamaica and a school nurse, whose three-year-old daughter, Sydney, is currently enrolled in a multicultural preschool. Mary talks about Kate:

She's ready to start preschool. In the fall, she'll be going to two preschools, for two mornings each. I feel like I can't give her more than I've given her up 'til now, and I need other people to give her I don't know what. And the point is, I don't know what! I'm starting to get a little nervous that I'm producing a little clone, and that she's going to share my strengths— which are getting As at school and being a quiet little spelling champ—but also come out with my weaknesses, such as a lack of initiative. I want her to learn the tools to become a confident investigator and to set her own goals and figure out how to get there, even if she makes some mistakes along the way.

Maybe my own school actually was a safer place to make mistakes than I imagined, but to my mind, school was about *not* making mistakes. So, I'm hoping she won't repeat that. But *how* to not repeat that is a really open question for me. Her involvement with books has really enlarged her vicarious experience —she knows about a lot of things, different kinds of lives, from books—books are great! But, given an open-ended essay question—will she be capable of taking the ball and running with it? Or will she wonder, "What's the right answer? What's the answer the teacher is fishing for?"

I ask Kate what she will be learning in school, and she says, "I am going to learn that wild animals can *EAT YOU UP!*" And then adds, "That's if you get too close."

Opal looks ahead to kindergarten for Sydney:

One of the biggest things that I'm hoping for her from kindergarten, wherever we decide to send her, private or public, is that energy, that enthusiasm that she has now, that they will be able to understand that and to use it as a motivational tool. I mean, I understand that in any school, a child must be able to conform, to sit down and do what's appropriate. But when you see a child who's just such a spitfire, so full of energy, you wonder, in a year and a half, is she going to have to sit somewhere,

regimented? At a desk? For hours and hours? So I want a school
for her where her energy won't be squelched, even though I
know that it has to be, well, channeled.

Sydney starts to bang on a piano. Her mom shushes her, and I invite her over for an explanation. I tell Sydney, "The reason we
want you to be quiet is that your mommy is telling me about
you. She is saying some *very* interesting things about you, and I
want to be sure that I can hear them. But if you make too much
noise, then I won't be able to hear your mommy talk about
you. Okay?"

And Sydney puts her lips up to the microphone and says, "*I*
want to talk about *me*. And I want to talk about my Dada." And
she tells us a little story before trotting away. Her mother
continues:

> I see children all the time in kindergarten who are like Sydney.
> You see them running in in the morning. They're so excited.
> They are *ready*! And then, all of a sudden, I hear someone shout-
> ing at them: "You have to line up *straight* in line! No talking
> when you're walking in the corridor!" It's order, order, order,
> order. I almost cringe when I hear a teacher speaking that way
> to the children. Now, that may be just this one teacher's style,
> but I think it's indicative of school. When they walk into my
> office, they're almost becoming stoics. That fire, that energy
> is gone! They have to do everything in order. It's so *orderly*.

I ask Mary, "What about going beyond preschool? You seem
to think that in a traditional elementary school, Kate'll be a
star."

> That's a scary thing. I mean, it's not on my agenda for her to be
> a star. Her father and I were both academic "stars," and I think,
> where did that get me? Kind of nowhere, in the sense that it
> didn't serve me well in the real world. I developed this un-
> canny, intuitive ability to produce work that would please my

mentor figures. And that was my whole goal. That was what it was about for me. Finding an advisor I revered and then making her approve of me. So I want Kate to have a good time in school. And I want her to learn everything she's interested in, without impediment, or being frustrated, or being slapped on the wrist.

We talk for a while about different kinds of schools—public and private, traditional and experimental:

I think in a traditional setting, she would do beautifully—an all-A student, a teacher-pleaser. That's not necessarily what I want for her. Of course, I want her to be successful. But I think what I'm hoping we'll be able to find is a setting where she will be pushed to find her stride in other ways, ways she doesn't get from me. We're very academic, bookish people. She's sort of all set to go in there and get all the spelling words right and raise her hand for everything. That's sort of a natural result of three years full-time at home with me, talking and talking and talking.

What I want her to learn is other stuff that's even hard for me to name. Working with people, with spatial relationships—it's not stuff I was ever trained in—learning in other ways, integrating things that you learn, so that you can move from one realm to another realm. There's a whole box of blocks here, which she ignores for their 3-D properties; she uses them to make walls for houses, within which she can make fantasies for little people. I play along—it's what I would have done as a child. It doesn't occur to either of us to build elaborate bridges or structures.

Opal, too, wonders where to send Sydney after preschool. She is attracted to the low student/teacher ratios of private schools, but she has other concerns:

There are a number of highly regarded private schools in our area. But in most cases, their commitment to diversity is lim-

ited. Right now, Sydney has a very good sense of who she is as a
little girl. She doesn't really talk "color," she doesn't really understand "color." Because—look at the rainbow of kids in her
preschool class. We're very fortunate that it's not an issue. And
in our own family, we have an incredible mixture of people. I
don't know what it would do to her self-esteem if I put her in a
school that was predominately white, and where there are few
teachers of color. Now, I'm sure that independent schools do
recognize the benefits of diversity in the classroom. But I also
think public schooling has a lot of merit. And our son, Grant,
seems to be doing well in public school, here in Cambridge.

I ask Mary, "If Kate were entering public school, say, as a first
grader, what would be the most important thing that you would
like to be able to count on from that school?"

That's exactly the question I wish I knew how to answer. One
thing is that all, or virtually all, of the teachers seem enthusiastic and engaged. It almost doesn't matter what you learn, if
you're learning from a teacher who is enthusiastic, that enthusiasm is contagious and you will find excitement and joy in that
subject. I'm looking for an absence of burned-out, resentful
teachers, who feel that they're not paid enough, they're not
listened to by the administration, they've got too many kids,
they're spending all their time on paperwork. I'd like, instead,
to find teachers who feel that they're supported in what they
feel eager and excited to do with kids. They're backed by resources and by a principal who respects what they're doing
and wants them to keep doing it.

That's really what I'm looking for. If she can't get algebra at
the right age, my husband will teach her. And if she's not getting quite enough history, then we'll go to a library. I'm not so
worried about her reaching x, y, or z level of knowledge. I'm
worried about her losing this natural bent she has for just suck-
ing up knowledge as if it were play, with that same eager joy-
ousness. She wakes up in the morning and she wants to go

learn! I don't want that to be killed. The school doesn't need to provide people who know the Encyclopedia Britannica; it needs to provide people who are going to share her excitement and help her continue it.

I invite Opal to say more about her daughter's learning:

What's incredible to me about Sydney's learning is that when we talk about something, or she asks a question about something and I explain it, within a matter of seconds she gets the concept, she understands it right away. And from what I've heard from her preschool teacher, she will actually go to school and process it with her classmates. So the other day, she asked me to explain what I meant when I said something was "all in God's hands." And she wanted to know, "Does God have hands?" We talked about it, and when she went to school that day, she kept saying to her classmates, periodically, "Do you know that God has hands? And His hands are strong and will protect you from bad things?"

There are few apathetic kids in preschool or kindergarten. When the teacher asks a question, every hand goes up. Curiosity is everywhere. Questions abound. Pride and delight in learning are everyday occurrences. The children draw and paint seemingly without inhibition (although they are often intensely curious as to what their friends think); they make up rhymes and chant slogans; they seem fascinated to be part of a community of kids their own age. They build stuff out of blocks of wood, Styrofoam, or cardboard, only to knock it all down and build again. They wonder constantly about why things are the way they are.

They're "just typical little kids," of course. But each, in her or his own way, is an artist, a poet, a citizen of a new and intriguing community of people their own age, an architect—with blocks and with imagination—of internal and external edifices, a questioner of natural and social phenomena.

The challenge facing those of us who view all children as passionate learners is this: How much of this spirit of learning, so abundantly visible in the young children we see in preschool and kindergarten, can extend up through the grades, even into high school?

What might happen if as teachers and parents we were able to hold on to the notion that each child has a natural capacity to remain an eager and enthusiastic learner? What if we were convinced that the spirit of learning could be reawakened in every child, under the right circumstances, and that it is our highest duty to discover those right circumstances?

I maintain that the *promise*—of limitless potential through learning—is a renewable warranty. It's not just a matter of holding on to the naive zest of the young child, but of reigniting the fire at any stage of a young person's life. That is possible, but only if we remind ourselves of what children are like, what knowledge is really about, and what learning can do for people of any age who are open to its challenges and its joys.[4]

Let us journey together into the uncertain, complex world of young learners and their varied reactions to the world of school. Let us see if our investigation of whether we can extend the enthusiasm for learning that young children evince up through the grades of formal schooling leads us toward the discovery of dispositions, approaches, and collective actions that might keep learning alive for a lot more children than at present.

William Butler Yeats, who was a school official as well as a poet, admonishes us that "education is not about filling a pail, it's about lighting a fire." In a world where standards of pail filling seem to have overwhelmed efforts at fire lighting, Yeats's injunction burns.

For psychologist and author Robert Coles, education is about "awareness":

Again and again I have come to realize that even preschool children are constantly trying to comprehend how they should think about this gift of life given them, what they should do with it. People like me, trained in medicine, often emphasize the psychological aspects of such a phenomenon and, not rarely, throw around reductionist labels. . . . In fact, moral exploration, not to mention wonder about this life's various mysteries, its ironies and ambiguities, its complexities and paradoxes—such activity of the mind and heart make for the experience of what a human being is: the creature of awareness who, through language, our distinctive capability, probes for patterns and themes, for the significance of things.[5]

Let us adjust to and accommodate "the way things are" in other matters if we must, but not in advocating for the right of every child to be cherished as a passionate learner. It requires no legislation, no huge funding schemes, no complex physical reorganization of classrooms or entire schools. At its simplest and most elemental, our duty to every new generation should be thus: to celebrate with each child the wonder of learning that is his or her birthright, the capacity for learning that is so naturally and so abundantly apparent in a child's mastery of speech and movement.

Let us, with the ancient doctors, vow first to do no harm, and promise to resist measures that deprive children of their natural enthusiasm and exuberance as learners, their impulse to ask questions, to figure things out, to wonder, to express, to investigate, to construct, to imagine. Let us commit to a quiet contemplation of the idea that children are universally passionate learners.

CHAPTER TWO

The Chasm

How the Promise Gets Broken

I am in the chair, settling in for an hour-long stint as my dentist prepares an old, battle-scarred molar for a crown. My jaw numbed by novocaine, my teeth clamped on impression putty, I can only listen as the dental assistant (who has learned that I am working on this book) fills my ears with her woes over her ten-year-old. "He hates school," she says through her blue gauze mask. "He'd much rather be outside, hunting, fishing, camping—doing anything physical. It's a daily struggle to get Scott to do his homework."

I ask, through clenched teeth, whether he reads. "Oh yes, but only the stuff he likes—you know, outdoors magazines and, of course, all the Harry Potter books. He can't stand the books that his teacher makes him read."

I learn, in the course of the next half-hour, while she shapes my temporary crown into a nice replica of what my molar will look like, that Scott is in every other respect a normal, healthy child, with lots of interests and many friends. His mother eagerly accepts my suggestions of Richard Adams's *Watership Down* and Philip Pullman's *The Golden Compass* trilogy, along with Canadian novelist Farley Mowat. "They sound like the kind of books he'd like," she says, adding, "But I don't know *what* we're going to do about school." The dentist returns and both are soon very busy working inside my mouth.

I know very little about Scott, but the symptoms seem clear—a kid whose learning passions are largely out of sync with his classroom obligations. A kid likely to be headed for years of frustration and conflict, along with the possibility that learning will be forever associated with other people's notions of what's good for him.

There are far too many kids like Scott. They begin school and, imperceptibly at first (it's not yet visible in kindergarten), this passion begins to ebb. It is replaced with a hesitancy, a reluctance, a frustration, and a growing aversion to schoolwork. Learning becomes a chore, a burden, an unpleasant obligation. It stops being something that all children want to do on their own or with those they love (family members, playmates), as was true in their early childhood years, and becomes identified in their minds as work. And in our culture, the less *work* you have to do, the more time you have to pursue your own interests.

When many kids reach their early teenage years, if not before, school learning also takes on characteristics of a "kids versus grown-ups" struggle, in which students ally with one another to resist adult (teacher) authority. Their teachers, in turn, may reach for behavior management techniques that assume that some students don't want to learn and must be cajoled or coerced into doing what should be, after all, in the students' self-interest. In response, many kids just naturally begin to see school as the enemy of what's interesting, fun, and worthwhile.

We accept it as normal for students to select less challenging books, to avoid researching complex historical issues or tackling intricate math problems, and that it is only a minority (generally children from well-educated families) who are confident and willing to challenge themselves intellectually. Likewise, most students resent homework, except for a minority eager to do whatever their teachers tell them. But there is, in fact, nothing normal about it—I maintain that it is a child's wholly understandable response to an environment in which submissiveness and lack of power are the norm. More on this later.

Faced with resistance, some teachers reduce the complexity of the tasks they assign so that unmotivated students will believe that they, too, can be successful. But easier does not equal more interesting, and the process spirals downward, with learning becoming equated, in too many children's minds, with boredom and drudgery.

Our point of departure is to remind ourselves that we wouldn't exist, as a human race, unless we had evolved as the most effective lifelong learners in the history of the planet. And no child born today is without resources to continue that tradition. As human beings, we are makers and users of tools. We just have to make sure that the tool we have invented, called "school," has a handle that can fit every child's grasp.

Notwithstanding their innate love of learning, all children are susceptible to factors within the classroom, school, neighborhood, and home that can cripple them as passionate learners. The "culture of the school" and of the school's environment (playground, lunchroom, hallways), which Seymour Sarason describes, affects how kids view learning. The personality, sensitivity, skillfulness, and philosophy of their teachers also play a huge role, as do school policies regarding grading, sorting, labeling children. Elementary teachers tell me that enthusiasm begins to fade, for many children, when they get their first "real" letter grades, and they feel that they have now been officially classified as second-rate learners.

But other factors deserve scrutiny. Lots of "good kids" become indifferent or irregular scholars in the presence of dutiful teachers who feel compelled to deliver instruction and to monitor obedience in keeping with school regularities. Other kids, goaded by parental anxiety and ambition, repress their negative experiences of school because they have accepted the notion of "success in school" as a necessity, as something one must achieve regardless of one's private thoughts on the matter.

As a society, we accept that a certain distaste for learning is a universal human experience. "You say school is boring? Big deal! So is much of life. And you'd better get used to it! Get your homework done, and keep those grades up!" A tough skin forms, a psychic insensitivity to the assaults on one's love of learning, which can easily transform that early love into a passionless duty to achieve.

Thus, in many ways, and to differing degrees, a chasm begins to open up for many a growing child, a gulf between the natural and joyful pursuit of skills and knowledge with which the young child is imbued and the child's experience as student. Our literature is full of heroes who abandon school in order to "get a real education," from Huck Finn to Holden Caulfield. We take an almost perverse pleasure in celebrating the learning we do *despite* our teachers' efforts to make us conform to their agendas: "*She* thought I was doing trigonometry, while I was *really* working on a racing form."

Is this chasm—between a child's natural zest for learning and what Wordsworth called the "shades of the prison-house" —unavoidable? Is it part of growing up, a necessary stage of development? Or is it, as I claim, a largely *preventable* phenomenon, a process that can be reversed, a pattern that can be redefined?

I believe that parents and teachers can help children avoid falling into the chasm of boredom, perfunctory effort, teacher-pleasing (or the obverse: disillusionment, resistance, teacher-bashing). I am convinced that children can continue to be passionate learners as they grow more sophisticated, more able to tolerate the mundane provisions of life.

How can we keep the chasm from developing? How can we bring our children and those we teach back from the brink? How can we guide them to successful academic experiences without exacting from them, as a price of academic success, the surrender of their spirit of passionate learning?

Signs and Origins of the Chasm

There are many causes of the chasm that opens up between a continuation of wonder, of openness, of energy in children's learning and the reality of school. They fall into various categories and affect diverse children in similar and dissimilar ways. We can't address all of them in this book, but perhaps a quick summary will alert readers to fifteen common fault lines that children we know are vulnerable to. No child faces all of these, some children easily overcome those they face, and others appear to glide through their school years relatively untouched by disaffection. Nevertheless, all children are affected by the struggles of their classmates.

We become aware of what I'm calling the "chasm" when students react negatively to certain aspects of their school experience. We may notice it in their *attitudes:*

1. They get discouraged after first receiving low grades on tests and report cards; they don't seem to be able to catch up and "make the grade"; they begin to think, "I will never be a good student."

2. They are easily distracted from schoolwork; they say they're "bored"—either because they think "I already

know this stuff" or because "this stuff" doesn't seem worth knowing at all.

3. They decide that they are just not interested in school subjects; they feel their real interests lie elsewhere; they see themselves as people who "learn by doing"; they resent the amount of time spent in "seat work" and develop a real distaste for it.[1]

We may observe another set of rifts among students for whom the joy of learning has turned into a race to be at the head of the class:

4. They are too focused on their teachers or parents, instead of on learning for its own sake; inner motivation is replaced by working for the grade.

5. They become obsessed by the competition in school and fear being seen as unsuccessful or as a failure; they try to be perfectionists—the best in their class.[2]

6. They see themselves ahead of most of their peers, academically, and worry that "the teacher always has to slow down and go over the same old stuff for other kids who haven't yet got it;" they are bored by how easy schoolwork is.

7. They become disheartened by not being placed in the very "top" groups in class for reading and math; they begin to see themselves as less smart than they may have been led to believe by their supportive parents and family.

Conversely, other students may get the impression that the school is a place where "kids like me aren't expected to do well":

8. They react negatively to "remedial" instruction, to being placed in what kids call the "dummy" group or class; they sense that others have labeled them as "losers."

9. If they are members of ethnic or cultural minorities, they might feel that they are the targets of racism or cultural hostility from teachers and from other school staff and students; they don't trust that the adults around them are really interested in them as persons; the school seems geared for the kids in the mainstream culture —not for them.

10. They begin to feel that kids of their gender are being treated unfairly, or that peer pressures are making it "uncool" for girls or boys to excel in certain subjects.[3]

11. They think they are being picked on by hostile or un-friendly staff; they believe some of their teachers are "unfair" or "mean"; they see themselves as bullied by adult authority.

Some students may become overly concerned about the way other kids at school look at them, to the detriment of their impulse to remain active learners:

12. They come under the sway of negative peer pressure; they feel they have to choose between being "in" with their antischool friends or siding with the teachers.

13. They face teasing or ostracism by other students for being different and withdraw into themselves socially, intellectually, and emotionally so that they will appear to be less of a target.

There are background causes that derive from a child's family situation—problems that may be only temporary. Although such causes precede the child's school experience, they can easily deter learning in school:

14. They are thrown off balance by the difference between the language or dialect spoken at home and the "standard En-

glish" practiced in schools, and thus feel at a disadvantage in keeping up with other children in reading, writing, speaking, and interpreting what they hear.

15. They become aware that they are entering an environment that other children are well prepared for—but that they are not; they don't know how to "play by the rules" (e.g., ask permission, share toys, or respond to teacher directions).

There are also causes related to developmental disabilities, as well as those deriving from divorce, death of a family member, family violence, loss of home, or frequent migration. Unfortunately, the scope of this book does not permit me to address these.

But as my experiences in schools have affirmed, many of these factors soon manifest themselves as *a profound negative shift in the child's attitudes toward learning*—a shift that may draw teachers, parents, and students into conflict. Certain teachers who encounter too many students displaying the attitudes listed above find that the enthusiasm they originally brought to the profession is eroded by "children with problems." If they do survive as teachers, some may, over time, adopt a cynical view of certain types of children and their learning that can last an entire career. I can still hear a middle school teacher in Chelsea, Massachusetts, protesting: "Some of these kids think this whole school is built around them!"

The chasm opens when students start to view learning as an onerous chore, interrupted once in a while by a field trip, an in-class movie, or a pizza party. They come to see learning as a burden to be avoided, if possible. Before they know it, students and teachers have become adversaries: teachers want kids to do their homework; kids want to get out of doing it. Teachers want kids to study for tests and quizzes; kids hope for easy questions.

Teachers want to pose challenging questions in class; kids wait till somebody else answers them. Day in, day out, the mind-set grows that students and teachers are locked in a power struggle.

A Parent's Predicament

For parents, the appearance in their child's demeanor and school behavior of any of the fifteen factors listed above causes alarm. I know as a parent that nothing is quite as frustrating as a child's problems with school. You run through the cycle: blame your kid; blame the teacher or school; blame yourself—and then focus your anxieties, again, on your kid. For parents who were themselves successful at school, a child's apparent failure to achieve to the expected family norm is at very least an embarrassment. It is likely to call down a whole shelf of proposed remedies: change teachers, hire a tutor, yank out the video game machine, monitor the Internet hookup, pull the cell phone or the extension from the kid's bedroom, cook up a diet of homework supervision to force-feed the child at breakfast, lunch, and dinner.

For those who had bad school experiences of their own, add the shame and humiliation of seeing your own sad school history repeating itself in your child's life. It's not a pretty picture, any way you look at it: threats, bribes, groundings, all accompanied by shouts, tears, doors slamming, plus interminable and highly emotional conversations about whose fault it all is.

Parents' natural tendency to overreact to what may, after all, be only a temporary impasse or misunderstanding between your child and her or his teacher is undergirded by the real fear of the awful consequences of school failure for anyone's child in our information age. There is no way what I am going to say now will erase that fear.

But I would ask any parent faced with the reality, the prospect, or even the remotest inclination that one's child "has begun to hate school" to take a few deep breaths and ask yourself, "Is my child still an active learner *outside* of school (if not, right now, in the classroom)?"

If the answer is yes, then your child may be having a difficult time reconciling his or her innate love of learning with the way learning is now being defined in the school situation. There is hope—not only that your child will, with or without your help, resolve the immediate problem that is causing frustration or failure in the academic setting, but also that your child has the inner resources and family support to continue to grow as a learner.

None of this is meant to suggest that you, as a parent, are off the hook (again, nobody could convince you of that). It is just that our world is full of highly talented and successful people for whom learning has always meant more than schooling, people (like my own kids, now in and beyond college) who have maintained a passion for learning even in the face of disaffection with school. In following chapters, we will talk about practical ways teachers and parents, in partnership, can cope with these factors and reclaim the promise of passionate learning.

To anticipate this, I want to signal my inclination to view these fifteen aspects of the chasm through a lens that focuses on certain shared characteristics:

- ❧ The factors are experienced primarily as problems of *attitude,* rather than of resources or forces beyond the influence of the school. When the attitudes of students and those adults who work with them improve, these factors diminish or disappear.

- ❧ While a single teacher can do much to help students overcome many of these difficulties, there is a much greater chance of progress if teachers work together to confront them.

❧ Children greatly benefit from parent/teacher collaboration in facing any obstacle. As parent/teacher trust grows, these factors become much less threatening and disruptive.

❧ Students need to become full partners in problem solving, along with teachers and parents. To bridge the chasm, students must play a major role in discussing, analyzing, and combating these fifteen potentially divisive factors.

But let us reflect, for a moment, just how painful and discouraging it can be for a parent, a teacher, or a child to experience any child's "failure to thrive" in the school environment. It is, indeed, heartbreaking—whether such a chasm is something new to the family or a repetition of the parents' own school experience. It is also unnecessary. The chasm doesn't have to be there. Or, if it does open up, it can be bridged. Let us explore how.

PART TWO

Reclaiming the Promise

CHAPTER THREE

What Teachers Can Do
to Reclaim the Promise

For Susan Cooney Hagner, who runs the Ralph Waldo Emerson preschool in my hometown of Concord, New Hampshire, a vision of passionate learning is the organizing principle in working with young children.

When I visited the preschool, I noticed sunflowers everywhere—living ones planted in large pots, cut sunflowers in a vase, kids' drawings of sunflowers on the walls, paper cutouts hanging from the ceiling and waving gently. I asked Susan where the sunflower theme had come from:

> On the very first day of school, one of the boys brought a bouquet of sunflowers, as a gift. He picked them from his garden. And they were beautiful. So we thought we would put them out at the drawing table the next day. And it just evolved from that.
>
> Most schools have themes that are chosen by the teachers. Our curriculum emerges from the ideas of the children. We try to take something that we feel has a lot of potential for learning, and we focus on it for a long time so the children can explore it, let it sit, revisit it, and come up with new ideas. Or

41

maybe provoke them to think a bit further. We do a lot of photo taking, recording conversations with the children and playing the conversations back to them. Otherwise they can forget— they forget how smart they are.

The other day they were painting with colors, and I was just reading some things we had jotted down from a previous conversation, and I read aloud to them what one of them had said, "It is red, and it is orange, and sometimes green." It was almost like a riddle. And so I asked them, "What is it? What were you talking about?" And they all had to think, and they were talking about colors, and I kept reading them these little quotes. And you could see their eyes getting so big, and they were wondering, "What *is* it we were talking about?" And all of a sudden someone said, "I know, I *know*! It was the *sunflower petals*!"

We were studying sunflowers, and the children were asking, "Where are the sunflower seeds?" and your temptation is just to answer them and to say, "They're right here, in the flower. See them?" But when they finally get into the flower and begin to take it apart—*the discovery of finding the seeds within the sunflower is just magical for the children!* And they find more and more, hundreds of them. And they're just fascinated. Most adults would just answer for the child. But then you've really stolen away their opportunity to discover, that opportunity to anticipate the answer to their question. But that emphasis on *telling* is so prevalent. It's the power of *not* telling that needs to be explored.

It's trusting that learning will come from what the children are interested in. A very skillful teacher can include our goals —what we want children to come away with—in a lot of different curriculum ideas. If it's helping a child build his vocabulary, there's vocabulary around sunflowers. If our concern is with math, there's *lots* you can do around sunflowers—we counted all the petals, and compared one kind of sunflower with another. We want children to learn to see their world in a way that is deeper than just "math" or "vocabulary."

As I listen to Susan speak, I walk around the busy classrooms full of students making choices about what they want to learn, and whom they want to work with, and how they want the grown-ups to assist them (if at all). And I wish it were in my power to allow all kids to go to school at places like this. There is something almost sacred about the exquisite care that the staff of the Emerson school take in nurturing—but not directing, or prescribing, or managing—the learning of children there. They do, of course, intervene. They are busy all the time, talking with children, recording their conversations, meeting with them in ever-changing groups; as well as talking with parents.

> We had gotten parents involved, and we asked them if they had sunflowers at home. And we had people digging up these huge sunflowers and bringing them in trucks to school. One sunflower was so tall that we provided a stepladder for the children to climb up to the top of the ladder to look at the sunflower.
>
> Now, if I had just put the sunflower on a table, they might just look at it and go on. But the *ladder*! It was so motivating for them to climb up and really look at it. That's when the counting of the petals took place, and the counting of the leaves.
>
> We're watching the death of the sunflowers right now. Death is something that has a lot of religious implications, and that's something we're a bit uncomfortable with—exploring that directly. But we are going to look at the death of the sunflower and relate it to the changes that are happening in the fall, outside our classroom window. And wonder, with the child, about what's happening.
>
> The other day, when we finally found the seeds, there was this joy among the children: "Well, we could plant the seed. And grow a new sunflower." So I think we will do that.

I reflect on Susan's notion of "the power of *not* telling" as a salient feature of the school's philosophy. Discovery is valued over performance; initiative over compliance; thoughtfulness over management. There are rules, of course, but these evolve, wherever possible, in conversation with the children. Somebody who is big is always there to watch out for safety, for fairness, for the little ones who need a prompt, a referee, a shoe tied, or a lap.

It strikes me that these *pre*school children exhibit far more intellectual and interactional freedom in learning than their older siblings do in school. A curious inversion of the normal social process of people gaining responsibility as they age.

A story at the other end of the educational spectrum—involving my college students—may be useful here, to complement the preschool story. In the course I am teaching to undergraduates on children's literature, I require them to write a children's book of their own, alone, with a coauthor or illustrator, or in collaboration with young children. In past years, I have been largely disappointed with the results—moralistic stories about bunnies or turtles who learn lessons on how not to be selfish or how to accept the limitations of their life situations.

This year, I ask them to reach back for inspiration to an aspect of their own childhood that has remained particularly vivid in their memory—something that speaks to their unique life experience, something they know more about than anyone else. Many are stumped at first; they don't believe they have such memories, or that anyone else would be interested. But we go around the room and each person shares something special about their childhood. They spark one another's recall. Students who pass the first time around suddenly discover an incident that has powerfully affected them and reclaim their turn to share.

Among the stories that students eventually turn into books are these: a girl whose mom left her alone with her dad, and whose dad did everything a mom should do (except learn how to do her hair right); another girl who was the tallest in her elementary school (she also had the biggest feet) and who had to stand in the back row with the boys for the class picture each year "while all the other girls got to sit in their pretty little dresses in the front row" (she has since become a star athlete on the college crew team); a first-time sleepover that was loads of fun until it was time for "lights out" (when homesickness took over); a child, certain that her parents were planning to desert her and her brother, who would wake her younger brother so that the two of them, unseen, could keep vigil until the parents went to bed. The quality of the stories was higher than I had ever received.

What does all of this have to do with the recovery of promise in passionate learning? Only this, that the potential exists for teachers to connect students of any age with the power of their own life experiences as a force for engaged and enthusiastic learning. The promise is out there to be reclaimed, even though it may not seem that way for too many teachers, too much of the time, as we watch students struggling in our classrooms.

Is there anything worse for a teacher, after all, than kids who don't or won't learn? The emergence in a classroom of a few students who resist academic learning—kids who refuse to do homework or other assignments; who aren't attentive, don't seem interested, or "just don't care"; who come to school unprepared; who disrupt the learning of others—can drive conscientious teachers crazy.

Some teachers also get upset by students who are willing to do what they are told but who don't put much thought into their work—they don't disobey, but they do only the minimum, or they try to please the teacher but invest little of their own initiative.

There are lots of handbooks around that tell us how to solve problems involving students and school, with recommenda-

tions ranging from behaviorist notions of "positive reinforce-
ment" to an emphasis on no-nonsense discipline. My focus here
is different. Without for a moment minimizing the severity of
such student behaviors and attitudes, or offering sure-fire
cures, I want to say to all teachers facing such challenges: Stop
and reflect for a moment. Are these problems that you caused?
Or do they come from years of disengaged learning, from a failure in earlier grades to celebrate this child for who he or she is,
from the absence of a dynamic home/school partnership?

Consider the options that become available to us once we accept the notion of each child as a passionate learner despite past
or current difficulties. When children feel *the vital connection between classroom learning and their own worth and growth as persons,*
learning in school becomes a shared undertaking rather than
one in which a teacher issues orders and students decide
whether or not to obey.

We cannot trick students into learning, no more than we can
bribe or threaten them (except in the very short term). Students must, in the end, *want* to learn—and each does. Viewing
them as naturally passionate learners makes us look for and encourage the will to learn that resides within each child. Visualize the passionate learner locked up inside the reluctant scholar,
like Rodin's sculpture of a figure emerging from its marble con-
finement.

We can become so habituated to sorting out students along
a spectrum, from "bright" to "slow," from "cooperative" to
"unruly," from "college-bound" to "potential dropout," that
we fail to remember that these are the same kids who impressed
us as such eager learners in kindergarten.[1] These are the kids
whose learning outside of school—in jobs, hobbies, music,
sports, or volunteer activities in church and community agencies—displays greater levels of maturity and discipline than
anything we get to see. Some claim that these are just extracurricular activities that young people *choose* to participate in.

But achieving academically is also a matter of choice. Students *choose* to absorb, or to repel, the instruction we offer them.

We know what students look like when they are busy or bored, compliant or resistant, cheerful or unruly—but what does passionate learning look like, and how can we create conditions for it to flourish, both in school and outside? Not as a special thing, a rarity, a gift granted only to the bright student engaged with the talented teacher, but as a common aspect of humankind, a universal trait we hope to nurture and sustain for most kids on a regular basis? I will point, throughout the rest of the book, to examples of passionate learning in specific areas, particularly literacy. But let me make a few generalizations.

I believe that passionate learning, for children in school and elsewhere, is mostly a function of *relationships*. Our storied view of "the scholar" as a lonely figure hunched over a pile of books, working far into the night with nobody around, is more fantasy than fact. Human learning has for eons been largely a social and interactional activity. Relationships among and between teachers, students, family, and community members have great power to affect the child's pride, persistence, and learning performance.

This is a crucial, often missing part of our vision of schooling, especially when we are tempted to isolate, diagnose, and try to cure an individual student's learning difficulties. When the relationships go wrong, the chasm opens up, the fault lines widen and threaten to engulf the child as a learner. When the relationships are right, children may struggle for a time, but they bridge the gaps and emerge as proud and confident learners both in school and on their own. I have, this year, seen both responses from similar groups of students within a school. The contrast is astounding.

As we look for practical ways to overcome various causes for the chasm that emerges in the school experiences of many children, let's revisit four characteristics:

1. The problems we encounter are primarily problems of *attitude*—*our* attitudes, not just the kids'.

2. There is much that each of us as individual teachers can do, but so much more can happen if teachers work together.

3. Parent/teacher collaboration helps resolve many impediments.

4. We must include students in recognizing, analyzing, and combating any obstacle.

This is not to say that societal, systemic, and bureaucratic forces don't play a large role in creating the conditions for school success or failure. They certainly do (and chapter 6 will propose systemic and organizational remedies). But this is a book for adults who believe that they can make a difference working within the teacher/student/parent triangle, even while the rest of the system remains embedded in a culture that hinders passionate learning and teaching.

Though this chapter is directed primarily to teachers, I would ask parents to pay attention to any among the following suggestions that makes particular sense for your child, since successful implementation often depends on parental support. You should also feel free to initiate a discussion of any of these ideas with your child's teacher.

The best thing we as teachers can do is to get together with our colleagues and ask, What can we do to help students in our classes feel that we, their teachers, are interested in them as whole people, as lifelong learners? Also, how can we engage our students, and their families, in a celebration of *who these kids are* and how much they can achieve if we work together on goals that matter to us all?

These are questions that, in the hurly-burly of our daily tasks in school, we rarely ask ourselves. There's so much to do, so much stuff that we're obliged to "cover," that posing such questions must seem like a luxury. But I have a very practical reason for posing them, namely, that students perform much better on school tasks if they feel appreciated and respected for who they are *outside* of school. Teachers say they must spend so much time trying to keep students "on track" with school lessons that they have "no time left to waste on nonessentials." But when kids feel unconnected, unappreciated, unmotivated, and unknown, their attention span decreases, their conduct deteriorates, and their teachers have to spend more time haranguing them to do their work.

Education is *about* relationships. They are the key to learning success.

We, as educators, must know and respect our students and help them know and respect one another as fellow learners. Here are some ways to go about it:

1. **Showcasing children's in-school and out-of-school learning**

   a. *Celebrate each child's in-school learning* (e.g., gains in skills, in knowledge, in social growth or citizenship) via daily, in-class, informal ceremonies (circle discussions, kids recognizing other kids who have been helpful to them,[2] teacher observations), as well as displays of student work. We ought to recognize students' genuine accomplishments in ways that don't embarrass them. Kids should help design these rituals so they are more authentic.

   b. *Celebrate each child's out-of-school learning* achievements through topics such as "Learning from My Family," "Things I've Learned How to Do on My Own," "Stuff I'm Really Good At," "Books I'm Reading That Nobody Assigned." These are accomplishments that we will mostly learn about from the kids, since we may not see a lot of evidence of them in class. But students need their teachers to acknowledge such learning. Making a third or half of each week's homework focus on learning that the student initiates may at first seem hard to organize or assess, but it is crucial to helping create a balance of ownership and initiative.

c. *Balance daily activities to allow different kinds of learners to showcase their abilities and talents* (e.g., rotate classroom chores and roles, incorporate more of what happens at recess into daily lessons). Drawing on lessons from Howard Gardner's concept of "multiple intelligences," teachers might schedule reading lessons followed by group conversations, followed by art activities, where "good readers" share the spotlight, by turns, with the "good talkers," "good artists," "good role-players," and so on.

2. Building or enhancing a sense of community within the class

A fearful child becomes a withdrawn and inhibited learner. A confident child brings an infectious spontaneity and goodwill into the classroom environment. The difference is striking between classrooms where a sense of community prevails, based on mutual respect and norms of behavior established with student input, and classrooms that seem like gathering places of random individuals, each trying to get what he or she wants, with a teacher yelling in the background.[3] Too often—especially for beginning teachers—"behavior management" translates to "teacher control."

Of course, control is preferable to chaos in the classroom. But to achieve a more collaborative and positive climate, teachers might try the following:

a. *Hold regular "circles" in class to discuss behavior and to help make and uphold rules that children understand and support* (e.g., "You *can't* say '*you can't play!*'" "*You can't do or say things that hurt other people's feelings*"). Some children come to school from a family background that is traditionally authoritative in nature: the parent is the boss and the child is expected to obey without argument. Other children come from families in which negotiating and questioning regarding adult directives are allowed or even encouraged. But every child wants to be a citizen of a society in which individuals have rights but also have responsibilities; where they can find safety, order, and justice; where "meanness" is as out-of-bounds as is "hitting."

Teachers should be "reminders" and "mediators" rather than lawmakers and enforcers. Experienced teachers maintain more control with a nod, a look, a touch on the shoulder than with yelling or threatening. Establish class procedures for the inevitable disruptions (kids who seek help or want to go to the bathroom).[4] Help children become better listeners ("What did you hear Sara say, Michael?" "Is that what other people heard her say?" "Why should we really listen to each other before getting angry or feeling bad?" "What's the difference between saying 'I'm sorry' and *meaning* it, and saying 'I'm sorry' just to get it over with?").

b. *Kids may not know the U.S. Constitution and the Bill of Rights, but they are experts in distinguishing what's "fair" and "unfair."* Help them learn how to be peer mediators and problem solvers in ways appropriate to their maturity. Challenge them to deal with teasing and disrespect among peers. Help them learn to resolve conflicts without violence. Let them exercise their minds and their hearts to help make their school a better place.

c. *Use music, storytelling, games, projects, to teach mutual respect and to help children create a sense of community.* But find materials that don't insult kids' intelligence in an effort to teach them good values. Let the suggestions come from the kids.

   d. *Increase the adult-to-child ratio in a class by inviting in parents, grandparents, senior volunteers, interns, and so on.* As Deborah Meier often reminds us, the sharp loss in frequency of meaningful, sustained contact between kids and competent adults is one of the more tragic byproducts of modern society. Children need to interact with adults in positive, affirming ways. Left to their own, exclusive society, children can easily make the wrong choices or are vulnerable to being bullied.

   e. *Use pairings, groupings, partnerships among children to carry out projects,* to reinforce collaborative skills, and to allow children to pick up important insights from one another. Using older students as tutors, mentors, big brothers and sisters is another underutilized resource in most schools. It was one of the best features of the old one-room schoolhouse.[5] If teachers or administrators don't trust younger kids being with older ones, under supervision by adults, then something very serious is wrong with that school.

   What the above suggestions have in common is that they require teachers—of whatever grade or subject—to pay attention to the culture they are helping to create in the classroom and to the impact of that culture on the child's openness to learning in school.

   3. Linking the classroom to a wider, supportive community
Almost all schools are surrounded by a neighborhood, yet too rarely do educators find ways to bring neighborhood resources into the daily and weekly learning activities of the classroom. Our schools are isolated from neighborhood elders—people with wisdom, good will, and a sense of the community's history. Here, too, it often helps to have several teachers working

together, so that resources can be shared and experiences compared. An overwhelmed, isolated teacher has no time to look for helping hands out in the neighborhood, even when that is just what might make the role of teacher a manageable one. Here are some ideas:

a. *Invite parents and representatives of various ethnic and cultural groups* (including people who earn their living through manual skills, music, art, small business, police, clergy, etc.) to reinforce the idea that "there are lots of ways to be 'smart.' "[6] Special neighborhood friends and parent volunteers can work with individuals and small groups of children to demonstrate the continuity of learning across the ages.

b. *Display students' work in accessible neighborhood locations* (storefronts, libraries, places of worship, neighborhood centers), so that local residents get to see what children are learning, and so that students can know they are producing for a "real" audience.

c. *Ask students to conduct interviews of local residents regarding* local and national history and culture, or by conducting neighborhood surveys on improving the community environment.

d. *Invite panels of local citizens to "judge" classroom performances or to respond to student questions on key topics.* When students see their teachers showing respect to area residents by inviting them to share their wisdom, it helps build trust between school and community, particularly where most of the teachers are white and most students are people of color.

e. *In the higher grades, develop vital community internships for students with local adults who can work alongside them as mentors and role models.* This may be very demanding for individual teachers to arrange and supervise, in addition to regular classroom duties.[7] Staff may need to be hired to supervise such efforts. But,

on a smaller scale, teachers can inquire whether any students
have jobs or hobby experience that relate to in-school lessons.
Unless we ask, we'll never know how our students' outside
learning connects with what we do.

4. Communicating to parents about a child's academic and social progress

Nothing seems more crucial between parents and teachers than
report card time. This is when it comes together or falls apart.
Parents, teachers, and children need to feel confident about
how student learning is assessed. It is well worth a teacher's
time to work with as many parents as possible to develop strong
lines of communication and trust. Teachers should communicate regularly with parents—via phone calls, notes, personal
contact when possible[8]—so that there are few surprises about a
child's progress.

In a visit to a summer enrichment program at an elementary
school in Hartford, I had a conversation with the combined
third and fourth grade class. I drew a big triangle on the board
and labeled it the "Triangle of Partners." I asked the children
if they knew who partners were, and they told me they were
"people who help each other, people who work together." I
then invited them to guess: "Who are the partners in *your*
learning triangle?" They quickly identified "The Teacher" and
"The Student," but then they were stumped. They suggested,
by turns, the principal, the librarian, the custodian. It was only
with much hinting that someone finally said "my mom." It was
as though they were saying, "*This* is the world of school, and
Mom has no place in it." Without such a bond of shared engagement in the learning process, the chasm opens up, with potentially tragic consequences for the child.

Years of isolation and distrust have led some parents to say,
"Look, my job is to feed 'em, clothe 'em, and bring 'em to

school on time. Your job is to teach 'em! That's what you get paid for." Here are some suggestions for how teachers can repair the damage:

a. *Invite parents to document growing responsibility, skills, and knowledge in their child that take place outside of school.* How often are a child's achievements in church or temple shared with the teacher? Yet such activities—doing volunteer work, teaching Sunday school, helping in the soup kitchen—may play a very large role in a child's developing sense of self and citizenship. If we don't know about that part of her life, we don't know the child.

b. *Use substitute or supplementary "report cards" that don't compare kids to one another,* but that reassure parents that we take their children's progress (or lack of it) seriously. There are lots of model report cards to select from, and they work best when both teacher and parent see them as part of a pattern of communication between partners in the education of the child.

c. *Bring children into the conversation, in joint parent/ teacher/student conferences,* so that students have a chance to articulate their sense of progress and problems and can help set goals for improvement. It is a lot easier for parents to hear criticism about their child's efforts when it comes from their child, accompanied by promises to do better next time. It takes the heat out of the interchange, because the child is seen as "part of the solution."

These are only a few of the many possible initiatives that teachers can take to help students avoid discouragement and failure that can occur when a child's early vision of herself as someone who's always growing, gaining, learning, mastering runs up against the redefinition of learning that occurs in school. We educators must remember that formal education is only a very recent addition to a process of learning that has taken place over hundreds of thousands of years of human evolution. We must look for ways to connect learning as we see it with those much older roots.

To visit a well-run and inviting preschool or kindergarten is to remind ourselves of the magic of childhood and the spontaneity of learning. Many great educators, Deborah Meier among them, began their careers as kindergarten teachers and then did their best to recapture that magic up through the grades. There is life after kindergarten—it's just that not enough of us believe in magic.

CHAPTER FOUR

Revisiting the Chasm

Misbehaving Kids, Boredom, and Wasting Time

If you ask teachers for the one thing that undermines their ability to teach, most will point to "a handful of troublemakers who spoil things for the whole class." If you ask school kids what is the one thing that they dislike most about school, most will complain that too much of what goes on is just plain boring. If you ask educators of all types what keeps them from implementing the reforms they already believe in, most will say, "There's just not enough time to do all that—we can't do half the things we're supposed to do now." No discussion of the struggle to reclaim the promise of passionate learning can avoid these three seemingly indelible features of school life. Before moving on to speak of the things parents and school systems can do to attain that goal, I want to acknowledge some of the unpleasant realities of life in school.

When Kids Misbehave in Class

In the School of Education where I teach, the charge that is most often leveled at us by student teachers and recent graduates is that we haven't prepared them well (or at all) in the area they call "behavior management." And while I bristle every time I hear that phrase, I cannot deny that a lack of training in techniques or approaches to help teachers respond to disruptive behavior is a serious obstacle to teaching and learning.

Bad behavior affects everyone in the classroom. I find it a difficult topic to get my hands around, since it is so often complicated by issues of gender, race, culture, and social class; by factors of teacher inexperience, administrative error, and poorly conceived school policy—as well as by deficiencies in teacher preparation.

Although the challenge of misbehaving kids is one that many experienced teachers manage to handle with admirable expertise, the problem cannot be solved—in the sense of a lasting, positive change of attitude—without a partnership involving students, parents, teachers, and school administrators. Skilled teachers can keep bad behavior in check, but without real collaboration, it will reappear as soon as those students move on to someone else's class.

In a typical situation, several students, often led by one or more charismatic kid, "take on" the teacher and other school staff as "the adversary." They regularly disrupt the classroom in pursuit of their own needs for attention, or out of a desire to see how far they can go in challenging authority without getting kicked out of school, or as a way of dealing with their anger and lack of trust in teachers. Children who are labeled as troublemakers or ringleaders may have crises within their families— some may be victims of abuse and neglect—and school may be the safest place to express their rage and sense of betrayal by adults in their life.

These children are often highly intelligent and charismatic. Their virtuosity at challenging adults gets them into trouble. Their early run-ins with school authorities lead these children to be labeled as problem kids, and they are quite aware that their reputations precede them as they move from teacher to teacher, which only adds to their distrust.

We should not overlook the impact of racism and cultural prejudice on the negative attitudes that certain children and teachers can bring with them into the classroom. In schools where most teachers are white and most students are of color, or where changing demographics have given some teachers the impression that "this school population has gone downhill" or that "few of their parents even care about education," problems with student behaviors are likely to be interpreted as validating such views.

Parents try to avoid placing their children in classes with too many "problem kids." They fear that their own children will suffer because "the teacher spends so much time on the troublemakers." Those who can afford to, buy homes in neighborhoods where there are likely to be fewer children from disadvantaged backgrounds. Others place their children in private or parochial schools where, they believe, rules are more rigorously enforced and school officials have more leeway in disciplining or expelling students who regularly disrupt the learning of others. Homeschooling has also become an alternative for some families. Public schools serving low-income neighborhoods are often viewed as "dumping grounds," where problems and "problem children" have to go because there is no place else for them.

For a new teacher, experiencing constant disruptions is disheartening. More than one teacher has come into a classroom full of high expectations, only to be upended by a small group of students who try to do whatever outrageous things they think they can get away with. The shock of finding a knot of kids who not only appear uninterested in learning but act as if they have a license to pull pranks of one kind or another is humiliating and exhausting. The thought that a majority of their classmates might be silently rooting for the "troublemakers"—enjoying their bravado vicariously while avoiding their punishment—increases a teacher's frustration and dismay.

For the veteran teacher, the response may be all too simple —come down hard on these kids, early and often, until they learn who's boss. Threaten them with whatever punishments you think you can impose, isolate them from their coconspirators, and eventually they will toe the mark. Other teachers may elect to try to be for these children what other adults have not been—a kind and loving friend, a steady and affirming presence —however much effort that takes. Whatever the approach, teachers regularly confide that such children take up half or more of their attention and energy. And even when a particular teacher manages to make headway with these children, the next teacher may face the same disruptive behaviors. The problem cannot be solved until the child himself begins to take responsibility his behavior. Easy to say, tough to make happen.

Today's *New York Times* (September 28, 2000) has a front-page story about Donna Moffett, who left a well-paying job as a legal secretary to become a teacher in a public elementary school in Brooklyn, at a one-third cut in salary. Her motives could hardly be more praiseworthy: "I was leading a pleasant life with very little risk. This school and these children, they may take everything I have. But there's a really deep well in me, and it's time to draw on it."

As a new teacher in a first grade class, Moffett received a summer of intensive training, but "in her first month as a teacher," according to the *Times,* she is "learning she must spend far more time on 'classroom management,' as veteran teachers call it, than on lessons." The *Times* gives the following example of what happened during her first week:

Ms. Moffett promised her students a party at the end of the first week if they behaved nicely. Whenever the whole class followed a rule, she wrote another letter from the word "party" on the board.

But on Day 4, plenty of rules were still being broken. Students lingered at the pencil sharpener and fooled around as Ms. Moffett took attendance. Some straggled in as late as 8:40 [school begins at 8:00]. As Ms. Moffett, still smiling, went over the months of the year, Daysha, a restless, bright-eyed girl, raced to the front of the room and grabbed the chalk, ignoring Ms. Moffett's command to sit down.

As the teacher dealt with the disruption, her aide, Ruth Baptiste, asked Larry, the sullen boy, what month came after May.

"Do you want to guess?" Ms. Baptiste asked.

"No!" Larry replied.

"Why?" the aide persisted as horns honked incessantly outside.

"Because it's stupid," the boy grumbled, pounding his fist on his desk.

This scene is emblematic of the way small events combine to throw a teacher off course.

After I had experienced a day or two of just this kind of situation, as a fill-in teacher for study hall and a temporary substitute for art classes for a group of sixth graders in a Boston pilot middle school where I had been assigned as a consultant, I was quite ready to get advice, and I went to my good friend Deborah Meier to get some. Deborah Meier is principal of Mission Hill Elementary School in a Roxbury neighborhood. She was previously the principal and founder of Central Park East Secondary School, in New York, and was the first public school educator awarded the MacArthur Foundation's "Genius" prize. What she told me gave me hope, but only in the context of a systemic view of behavior change via collaborative problem solving.

Some background: Mission Hill is a K–8 pilot school, which

is similar to a charter school except that it is sanctioned by the Boston Teacher's Union and operates within the union contract as part of the Boston public school system. Like a charter school, faculty and staff are free to adjust working conditions to suit the school's philosophy. Mission Hill accepts its students by lottery, with preference given to children whose siblings are or have been students there. Much effort is expended by the staff in forming relationships with parents and families, and this, for Deborah Meier, is the starting point. I asked her how people at her school think about issues of bad behavior, especially for middle school kids:

> We had a situation this year in which several middle school children became leaders in challenging the rules and defying their teachers. Most were newcomers to the school who had no history with us and thus really had no reason for trusting that the adults here are on their side. These kids were adept at disrupting the class and attracting several other children as allies in that effort. After speaking with the students and determining that they had little interest in modifying their own behavior—they rather liked their image as "tough kids"—we called the parents to tell them what we saw going on and to ask for their support as we tried to cope with the situation.
>
> Our approach is not to blame the child, in such situations, but rather to say to the parent something like this: "Your kid *can* learn; we're convinced of that. But right now, your child is *not* learning, because of how things are going in class. And we're not going to let your kid go down the drain this way. Right now, your child's behavior is preventing her from learning. So we need your cooperation in taking some measures that your child may not like, at first, but that we think will help your child begin to trust that the adults here truly want her to succeed."
>
> It was six months of a lot of frustration before we got to this point. What we said to the kids in question was basically this:

"You are breaking the two fundamental rules of the school—
the rule against treating other people disrespectfully and the
rule against preventing other kids from learning. Because
you've broken these rules, you can't be with other kids until
things change. So we are going to remove you from class and
teach you ourselves (the assistant principal and I). We don't see
this as punishment—it's just a matter of you not learning as
things stand now. You can spend from now till June, if necessary, under our supervision, apart from your classmates, until
you find a way to convince us that you can learn with other kids
around."

I wondered if this was merely a variation on the standard administrative response of removing disruptive students from the
classroom (however it may be voiced to the offending kids), but
Meier emphasized that there were some distinctive features
here:

The school has to be set up to accommodate this. We're not
talking about a special room for these kids—not some in-
school suspension room, some "bad kids room" where they
get to be with other kids who have the same problem, with
somebody there as prison guard. We have to view this as an opportunity for these kids to develop a relationship with people
in authority and have some success in learning until they feel
capable of returning to their peers.

The assistant principal, the school secretary, and I set up a
desk for each of the kids in different corners of our spacious
and busy office, and we made sure that they had books to read
and schoolwork to do. We coached them and taught them. We
tried to develop a friendship with them, under the banner of
helping them learn how to learn successfully—as individuals—before returning to class.

Meier was at pains to explain that this was a particular response
to a particular challenge and not a procedure that's automati-

cally invoked whenever student resistance shows itself. She indicated that she understood the reluctance of the students in question to merely accommodate themselves to the wishes of (friendly) adults:

> Some of these kids are afraid to be seen as backing down in the face of teacher disapproval—and of losing their audience, among their friends, for their rebelliousness. We try our best, in all our dealings with troublesome kids, to avoid humiliating them. We want a relationship, not a temporary truce.
>
> Again, it's extremely important to have the parents supporting us. We reiterated that "your kid has been preventing himself from getting an education, and we are committed to every kid getting an education." We try always to inquire of the parents what seems to work for them, at home, and we often find that the parents are as frustrated as the teachers. So they are usually very committed to our finding a solution. With these students, the parents' support for what we were doing never wavered—we convinced them that we were on the kids' side.

I asked Meier how the situation with these students managed to resolve itself:

> It took several weeks. In the end, the children even felt a bit ambivalent about going back to class, since they had allowed themselves to do good work under our individualized supervision. We wanted them to go back to class with the confidence that they could distinguish themselves in other ways than by preventing other kids from learning. And when they did go back, they knew we were here, in the office, to support them as they tried to continue their success in the classroom.

What made Mission Hill's approach to these kids who were considered troublemakers so intriguing is not just that it *worked*—that it seemed to "solve the problem" and "get kids back on the right track"—but that it kept on working, because of the children's acceptance of responsibility for their behavior.

Various other approaches also appear to "work" in overcoming the obstacle to learning presented by chronically disruptive students. Kicking the offenders out of school "works," as does setting up an in-school suspension room with a firm but fair taskmaster who has zero tolerance for misbehavior. I have visited urban middle schools where students were marched, single-file, from one classroom to another, as well as to the bathroom and back to class. That, also, seemed to work.

But these other solutions are temporary; they shift the problem elsewhere without addressing the needs of the child for a self-respecting pathway to becoming a successful in-school learner. We can understand the frustration that such students can cause— —a frustration that can try the patience of a saint— but they are still our children, and we need to help them gain control of their own behavior. Urban students are often much more strictly disciplined than their suburban counterparts, and the results of such strictness are often mixed. Certainly, order is preferable to disorder, and kids need to feel confident that the grown-ups are there to protect them from the potential danger of undisciplined classmates. But learning is too often sacrificed when behavior management is the top priority. I remember a high school principal in Hartford telling me, "Well, I've finally got this school in order. But they're not yet learning."

Most public schools are challenged by disruptive children, and all need to cope with the threat they pose to their own learning and that of their schoolmates. But we will only solve the problem of misbehaving kids when we view it in the context of a school philosophy that is clearly focused on self-respect, personal responsibility, and response to the diverse needs of learners, one that is based on a school/home partnership and a collaborative ethos within the school. Otherwise, it's the age-old struggle of "teachers versus bad kids," a struggle that regularly consumes most of the little time allotted to conversation, planning, and decision making within a school.

A Fascination with "Boredom"

Adults rarely pay enough attention to boredom in classroom life. We see it as a "typical schoolboy excuse" for not doing one's work. We hear kids say, "It's bor-r-r-ing!" and we are inclined to respond, "So what? Not everything can be as interesting as video games. Sometimes you have to do things that are a little boring, you know! And anyway, it wouldn't be boring if you put a little effort into what you're doing. So stop making excuses and get on with it!"

But boredom is serious stuff. A huge entertainment industry earns billions from our obsession with avoiding boredom. As adults, free from the confines of school, we subscribe to 125-channel cable television, so that at the slightest affront to our attention span we can switch to something else.

Shouldn't we treat boredom as seriously as we do disruptive students, tardiness, or failure to hand in homework? Ah, but boredom has always been the students' nemesis—we contend it's not *our* problem, as adults—not in the same category as kids who misbehave or won't do their assigned work.

Frank Smith advises that one can discover whether or not students are bored very simply:

> You don't need a test to discover whether individuals are learning, just look at their faces. If they look confused or bored, they aren't learning (or rather, all they're learning is that whatever they are doing is confusing and boring). But if they *don't* look confused or bored, if they're just getting on with whatever they're doing with interest and understanding, then you *know* they must be learning.[1]

I define educational boredom as the separation of a learner from a sense of purpose, anticipation, curiosity, or investment in a particular activity; the disaffection or restlessness that settles in when one decides that an activity or goal is no longer worthy of interest or energy.

Surely there are few activities that are inherently boring. There is *repetitiveness*—but that describes most video games; there is the *forced attention to detail*—but that's what putting together a jigsaw puzzle entails. There is almost nothing that one person finds boring that is not deeply engrossing to someone else. Practicing how to write the letter G is potentially no more or less boring than practicing how to kick a soccer ball or play a chord on a guitar.

When students in a classroom decide, alone or collectively, that a teacher-sponsored activity is boring, it may represent a breakdown in the relationship between students, teacher, and the task at hand. Completing a task or activity is no longer linked to becoming a more skilled and powerful person (if, indeed, it ever was)—thus it is removed from the category of *passionate learning*. And that's the critical break, for it separates the willing learner from the merely obedient or the rebellious.

It's easy to say that teachers and students need to communicate better about the reasons behind the activity and how it relates to some goal that the student understands is worth achieving. But that assumes that it is the student's *right* to be consulted about the purpose of a particular activity or assignment, and there are many teachers and parents who believe that young people have no such inherent right. This is the critical point of friction between conflicting philosophies of how adults and children should relate to one another. We cannot deal with the phenomenon of boredom without invoking the principle of mutuality and power sharing among adults and children.

This does not necessarily mean that every teacher and parent must first gain permission from a child before setting forth the lessons, or chores, that the child is expected to perform. It does mean, however, that parents and teachers have a duty to explain the value and purpose of the proposed task (or risk having to rely on coercion or bribery to get it done).

A story from my own parenting experiences may illustrate this point: We were camping with friends one summer, and when we arrived first at the campsite, I told my oldest son (then about eleven) that I expected him to do his share of unpacking the car before he went off to explore the woods and pond. He had other plans in mind, however, and soon disappeared, leaving the whole task to me. When our friends showed up, I complained about my son's behavior—his refusal to "do his rightful share" of the work. The response I got from my friend (who happens to be a child psychiatrist) surprised me. He said, "Either he's a totally irresponsible kid, rotten to the core—or you didn't ask him in the right way."

"What are you talking about!" I protested. "He's eleven years old—he should be expected to help out a little. I was asking him for five, maybe ten minutes of work! Don't I have a right to that much cooperation from him?"

My friend repeated: "Either he's a no-good kid, a despicable human being, or you didn't figure out the right way to ask him for help."

In reflection (after my temper had cooled), I had to agree. I had no inherent right to my son's labor. I had every right to ask him, to point out the rationale and purpose of all of us pitching in, even (if he resisted) to warn that there may be things he would later want me to do for him that I might not agree to if he refused to give me a hand now. But I had no right, as his father, to *command* his obedience. It's not the way we've raised our kids (although my wife and I were raised that way, and I'm sure a great many other families adhere to other principles which *do* include such parental rights to command).

As teachers in school, we often find ourselves on the boundaries of this issue—coercion versus cooperation and consent.

And there are few of us who don't have mixed feelings about it. We feel we'd be lost without the authority to require students to perform the tasks we assign. But a voice within us cautions that every learner must, in the end, find his or her own reasons and rewards for learning—or else little is gained.

So with the issue of boredom. There is always the risk that the complaint "It's so boring"—were we to take it seriously in our dealings with students—might be abused by them. Students could claim to be bored as an excuse not to challenge themselves or not to complete their learning tasks. And few teachers would want to place themselves in the position of being forced into a debate at the whim of any student who lost interest in whatever was going on. Still, there is something very important about the whole question of boredom. It's something educators should be fascinated about.

Can we not create a climate in a classroom that treats boredom as a serious matter, but one that also requires students to take responsibility in how they react to being bored? "It's boring" should not be a condition that only the teacher must cure. The culture of a learner-friendly class should include a student-developed list of "What to Do When I Feel Bored" that could illuminate ways of coping with such a feeling when it is experienced by one, a few, or most of the class.

As just one example, a class might agree on the rule that "if you feel bored and want to stop doing something that other people (including the teacher) think is important, then you must take responsibility for coming up with an activity at least as challenging as the one you want to stop working on." Another rule might state, "If at least half of the class feels that an activity is boring (after trying it for a while), the teacher should ask for suggestions from the kids on how to make it more interesting and worthwhile."

Education writer Evans Clinchy, who reviewed an early draft

of this book, has this to say about classroom boredom: "I think boredom is most often the result of a teacher expecting the whole class to do something that only a few are likely to find interesting. I've never understood the necessity for most 'whole class' activities."[2]

In any case, we need to help our students analyze boredom and understand why and when it occurs and how to cope with it. Students need to be assured that we, too, want to avoid boredom whenever possible (and it usually *is* possible), but that we expect to have the "final say" in whether an activity should be continued, altered, or ended.

The balance of powers operates here as elsewhere: if the adults *always* have things their way, kids will soon stop believing that we truly care about their input, and they will refuse to be part of the discussion except to mock or disrupt it. If the adults *never* hold sway, then kids will soon stop respecting that the adults care about anything more than avoiding hassles with kids at any cost.

Where Will We Find the Time?

In responding to the varied impediments to passionate learning, the issue of time inevitably arises. If we are to act boldly on behalf of passionate learners, we will have to stop wasting so much time in school.

To open up the issue, I will make an outrageous claim: Most teachers and students waste 50 percent or more of their time in school. I say this with no disrespect. I start from an assumption that both teachers and students are right when they complain either about misbehaving kids or boredom: "Your fooling around is *wasting valuable learning time* for the rest of the class!" warns a teacher. "I don't know why we have to *waste our time* with this stuff that doesn't mean anything" is the unspoken complaint of bored students.

Sometimes, the school bureaucracy wastes time for both teachers and students, with intrusions, bells, weeks of standardized testing, and test-preparation exercises. But most of the waste is in things we bring on ourselves. We waste time so consistently that we often do not consider it a waste of time at all but an inevitable part of a normal day at school. Like getting stuck in traffic while commuting to work, it's just part of the job. There are, of course, various ways of wasting time we all acknowledge as such:

- teachers trying to get the class to settle down so the lesson can begin
- teachers having to deal with kids who are disrupting the learning of others
- students talking or daydreaming instead of doing their work
- students who come to class without pencil, textbook, paper, or homework

But there are other manifestations of wasting time that we may have never even considered:

- students having to listen to things that they either already know or can't understand
- teachers obliged to "cover" material that's required by the school or district but whose value and relevance they deeply question
- students not caring about what's being taught, seeing no connection to their lives
- students who just don't learn well by sitting still and who decide not to pay attention
- teachers handing out "busy work" to keep students occupied and in their seats

 ∽ teachers grading assignments that have been carelessly
   or sloppily prepared

 ∽ students who cram for the test but then forget
   everything as soon as the exam is over

The second list differs from the first primarily in that the
"time wasted" results from negative attitudes toward the
learning opportunities presented. Here, too, *attitude* is the obstacle to passionate learning. The antidote to wasted time (the
second list) is time spent in passionate teaching and learning.

We so often choose to waste potentially productive time by
doing less intense, less engaging, less interesting things because
we feel like prisoners of our surroundings. I don't want to mini-
mize the quandary we find ourselves in. When we feel power-
less, the "law of survival" tells us to operate at minimal energy.
And so we waste time. And feel even more depleted.

Combating the wasting of time in school is a constant challenge, requiring us to remind ourselves, daily, that passionate
learning *is* possible, that it is *the* alternative to wasting time. It's
obviously idealistic, but imagine asking yourself every class
hour: *How regularly do students come to school anticipating that they
will be discovering valuable information, practicing useful skills, and
engaging in interesting activities and challenging conversations?* And
imagine viewing everything that hinders or prevents these
kinds of engagements as potential time wasters.

CHAPTER FIVE

What Parents Can Do
to Reclaim the Promise

Parents have a crucial role to play in helping children feel se-
cure, valued, and competent as learners—no matter how they
are "doing" in school at this moment. You play a key part in
helping your child and his or her teacher keep the spirit of learning alive.

It's so easy to forget, when faced with a child who's not doing
well in school, or who is doing "okay" but not enjoying school
all that much, that this child, too, is at heart a passionate
learner—someone who thinks, feels, questions; who aspires,
makes critical judgments; who experiments and learns from
making mistakes; and who strives for mastery—even if, currently, little of this seems to result in academic success, even if
she is making trouble for herself and others, even if she resists
the help of teachers or parents. She remains a passionate learner.

I speak, here, of a variety of children whose in-school attitudes and performance may be problematic: the undermoti-
vated and the underchallenged; the child who seems so far "behind" and the child who already "knows it all"; the rebellious

and the resistant; the social butterfly who just wants to "hang out" with peers, and the child with a book from home hidden under the desk that seems much more interesting than what's being put on the blackboard.

I speak, also, for learners who seem *not* to be a problem, who do their homework, who arrive in school with pencils sharp and homework complete, who sit quietly at their desks and do their work. Are they excited by what's happening? Have they preserved the enthusiasm and delight for learning they showed in kindergarten? If not, they too are at risk of falling into the chasm that threatens passionate learning.

If we allow ourselves to overlook the passionate learner in any of our children, if we focus only on their school problems or successes, we may succumb to the "medical model," wherein any deviation in a child's academic path is viewed as if it were some sort of condition or dysfunction, to be treated with a dose of this or that, gold stars or Ritalin. Unless we keep the image of the child as passionate learner before us, we may find ourselves equating a good report card or proficiency on some standardized test with a zest for learning.

I need hardly reiterate that, for your child and mine, success in school is a highly desirable goal and that high achievement in school often leads to successful learning beyond school. As a father, I want my kids to do well in school, and I get upset when that seems not to be happening. But I am convinced that we owe it to our children to look beyond their report cards and test scores to see how healthy the spirit of *independent* learning is within them, and to see to it that that spirit is mirrored *in* the child's school experience rather than eclipsed *by* it. That's the promise we must reclaim.

Agendas in Conflict: Learning to
Recognize Passionate Learning

Here's the critical point: When your child is having some difficulties in school, it's so easy to respond by trying either to increase the pressure on your child to "do what the teacher asks"
(by threatening to take away some privilege or to restrict your
child from following his favorite pastimes) or to criticize the
teacher for not being sensitive to your child's uniqueness. But
consider that a child may be experiencing a *disconnect* between
his customary approach to learning—how he encounters new
situations, new skills, new knowledge—and the way the
school defines learning.

For example, one child may be a *cautious* learner, someone
who likes to poke around quietly at a new challenge before ex-
perimenting with something new; another may be an *impulsive*
learner, who likes to dive right in and see what happens; or an
analytic learner, one who likes to ask a lot of questions before
taking on a new skill or concept; or a *social* learner, who works
most productively in an atmosphere of lively conversation with
other students; or a *visual* learner, who wants to picture the task
rather than just listen to verbal instructions. Any and all such
approaches to learning may be quite appropriate and adaptive
in life.

But most schools don't allow these differing modes to operate freely. The kid who "pokes around" may be accused of stall-
ing. The one who "dives right in" may be faulted for lack of impulse control or not waiting his turn. The analytical kid may be
chided for wasting everyone's time by "asking too many questions." The social learner may be admonished to "sit down and
do your own work!" while the visual learner may be told to
"listen more carefully" to instructions.

The result may be a child who feels that his natural way of

learning is somehow "wrong" or "bad"; that what has always served him well as a learner in the world is now getting him "in trouble" with his teacher in school. Nor is it necessarily true, in the above examples, that the teacher is being insensitive or demanding undue conformity. Children may well need to acquire some new approaches to learning, particularly if they are part of a large classroom group, as opposed to being with pals or playing alone in their room.

The real issue is that no one is helping your child understand that school learning and learning on her own are not always the same and that both are good and useful in life. A parent can say, for example, "You don't go to school in pajamas or go to church in your ballet costume. Different activities call for different clothes. Just so, learning in different places (school, home, outdoors, etc.) or with different people (alone, with a friend or two, on a team, in a class) call for different ways of going about things." This should be discussed in a loving and affirming manner, so that your child comes to see that he or she is not "wrong" or "bad" or "dumb," but rather has not yet adjusted to the school's way of learning important things.

As a parent, you also have a right and a duty to *help the school adjust to your child,* to help a teacher accommodate your child's preferred style of learning. This need not be confrontational; it may be just a question of sharing with your child's teacher the fact that your child may benefit from some personal attention or some flexibility in accomplishing tasks. Usually, when approached in a friendly manner, a teacher is happy to make such adjustments, ones that may benefit other learners as well.

But most of all, you want to assure your child that his or her own style of learning—of *independent* learning—is something very much to be valued, not discarded, since it is a key to maintaining your child's own learning spirit.

Your task—working as part of the team of parent, child,

and teacher—is to help the student adjust to the new kinds of learning without abandoning the old. It is a daunting but necessary task, because when a child abandons the passionate learner within, in an effort to "be a good student," it may be very hard to regain that independent spirit later in life. I see far too many college students, graduates and undergraduates, who lost their independent initiative as learners in school. They did well enough to get into college or graduate school, but they have been transformed into students who now read and write almost nothing but what teachers require and who flinch from any assignment that moves them "outside the box."

I see this spirit of independent learning, this passionate engagement in ideas, not as icing on the cake of traditional school success but as *the cake itself,* the core of how each child engages with life as a learner. I want us to value school success and growth of the child's independent learning spirit as *equal* goals. As parents or teachers, we want to foster academic achievement and independent learning at one and the same time for those children in our care, not only because that is what is in the child's best interests, now and in the future, but because these goals are mutually supportive. We get a better student when we tap into a young person's sense of personal ownership of the task at hand, and success in school can build in young people the confidence to continue as independent learners once they have left school behind.

Faced with a child who wants to go to the local library for a new book, or take apart an old clock to see how it works, or build ever more intricate structures out of Lego blocks, or visit the ducks at a nearby pond—instead of completing a much less interesting homework assignment, I'd like us as parents to at least acknowledge the problem. The father in me wants to say, "*First,* do your homework. Then, if there's time left, you can do those other things." And I am certain that I have used much the

same words with my own children. But I have some reservations about my impulsive response (although admittedly fewer
reservations about restraining a child who appears addicted
to television, video games, or some media-driven fad or who
shrinks from schoolwork because the gratification isn't immediate). There is something about a child whose independent
learning interests focus on ideas, skills, literature, community,
nature that would make me hesitate to pull that child back to an
admittedly boring homework assignment.

In his remarkable work *The Book of Learning and Forgetting*,
Frank Smith reminds us that "people learn from the company
they keep."[1] If they keep company with books, they learn different things than if they keep company with video games. If
they keep company with kids whose values and basic human
qualities we admire or approve of (even if we sometimes find
their styles of dress or speech not to our liking), we can rest easier than if the kids they hang out with enjoy shoplifting or bul-
lying others. Let us spend what influence we have, then, helping
our children choose the company of other learners, rather than
pressuring them to conform, in every respect, to the conventions of school.

Here are a few hypothetical cases: Your second grader
doesn't like her reading group. She says there are some bossy
kids in it and "the Reader is dumb." As a result, she doesn't participate in group activities as much as she normally does, and
the teacher has given her lower grades on reading. But she continues to read a lot on her own and gets books each week from
the library. Should you be concerned about her reading? No.

You have a fourth grader who won't do his writing assignments because his teacher corrects each error and hands him
back papers full of red marks. But he writes letters via e-mail to
his grandfather in Texas and his friends from summer camp,
and he has shown you some of the science fiction stories he has

written on his computer. Should you be concerned about his writing? Again, no.

Your seventh grader, who has always loved science, despises her science class because of all the teasing that goes on in the lab and because the teacher is "boring." Her science grades have fallen from As to Bs. But she is a member of a local environmental group that tries to influence town decisions, and she volunteers on weekends at the SPCA (Society for the Prevention of Cruelty to Animals), working with animals there. Should you worry about her science education?

The commonality in all these admittedly oversimplified cases is that the child is vigorously pursuing outside of school the same areas of skill and knowledge that she or he finds frustrating in school. Of course, most parents will try to work things out with the teachers involved (even though the seventh grader doesn't want her parents to "make a fuss and embarrass me," the fourth grader tells you, "There's no way she's gonna change the way she grades just because you complain," and the second grader says that they will be switching reading groups and reading new books in two weeks).

Most parents are rightly concerned when their children's school experiences are less than satisfactory, and most become especially worried when their kids' report cards show lower grades. I do not advocate a blasé attitude toward school by parents. It's a question of where to put one's limited energies. The best strategy might be to keep an eye on the school situation, make sure that it does not continue to deteriorate, but devote more energy to supporting your children's *independent* learning—through hobbies, trips to libraries and museums, discussions about science and politics around the dinner table, encouraging appropriate use of the Internet, and so on. Here are a few positive signs to keep looking for, regarding a child who seems temporarily turned off from school:

&. Is my child reading on her own and does she like to
write stories?

&. Does he still ask lots of questions about why things are
the way they are?

&. Does she enjoy making predictions, estimating things,
and solving puzzles or problems that involve
mathematical thinking?

&. Is he interested in music, in drawing, in making (or
taking apart) mechanical stuff?

&. Does she participate enthusiastically in sports and other
team or group activities that are offered in your
neighborhood?

&. Does he prefer the computer to the television, and is he
making connections to topics and ideas on the Internet
that seem interesting and appropriate?

If you see several of these indicators, you can feel confident
that your child is a healthy, active learner, engaging in pursuits
that build a strong foundation for future academic success, despite the frustrations or setbacks of his or her current school
situation. This is especially true if your child is an avid reader,
someone naturally curious who thinks books are a great way to
go exploring.

Among the most important things you can do is to show your
child that you, too, are an independent learner who maintains
an interest in important ideas and issues, who reads for pleasure
and information—even when you are not being graded.

One way of putting this in context is to reverse the cases,
such that all these children do well in school but refuse to do
anything that sounds educational on their own initiative—
your second grader and fourth grader now consider *all* reading
and writing to be homework (and, therefore, stuff to do and get

over with); your seventh grader associates science with school and willingly does what the teacher demands but has stopped pursuing her outside interests in the field. Do you comfort yourself with the thought that, after all, his or her grades are pretty good, even if your child is noticeably less inquisitive, less adventurous, less motivated to read, write, draw, question, explore? Or do you worry that something vital in your child's imagination, curiosity, intensity has been at least temporarily lost because of school-related issues? Even while acknowledging that children's interests often change as they develop (particularly when they come under the influence of their peer group's styles and priorities), it remains important for parents to be as conscious of out-of-school learning as of in-school learning.

I want to urge parents, as well as teachers, to become advocates for that independent spirit of engagement that I call passionate learning—even as we go to work on preventing, or lessening the impact of, the various causes and factors listed in chapter 2.

What Parents Can Do When Children
Feel Defeated as Learners

At the first signs that a child may be unhappy or unsuccessful in school, many parents become very concerned. Whether it's the strangeness of being away from home that comes with kindergarten,[2] or the reaction to a new second grade teacher who seems less kindly than last year's, or getting teased by kids on the playground, or finding out that you're in the "dumb reading group," or bringing home that first report card with less-than-satisfactory marks—a child's responses to school can be a great source of anxiety for a parent.

We feel that it is we who are being judged by the experiences of our children. We are apt, as normal, concerned parents, to worry that unless we intervene—with our child, with the teacher, with the school—our child will "fall behind" as a learner and may not easily recover. In an era in which school success is deemed so crucial to life success, parents often feel they must "get on top of the situation" early.

And certainly there are circumstances and situations that call for such intervention: matters of personal safety for our child, a desire to let a teacher know something about our child's individual nature that may help her forestall or resolve some problem, a suggestion to the principal regarding our child's placement or teacher for next year, a request for a conference about a report card. Every parent should bring such concerns to the attention of school staff, if only to establish a personal level of acquaintance and communication that may prove useful later on.

But I would invite parents to think about ways of talking with their children about matters that influence their child's *learning*—not just *schooling.* Let me say again, it's not that issues surrounding a child's success in school are any less important than we, as parents, think they are. It's that a child's attitudes and actions regarding independent learning are much *more* important than many parents are likely to realize. It's not an either/or situation. If a child is having difficulty in school, the parent's response should be to ask whether there is any conflict or problem that he or she feels is causing that difficulty. Here are some of the things parents can do, depending on their circumstances and inclinations:

> ◦ Parents can come to school and spend time there—
> before any real indication of a problem—to familiarize
> themselves with the classroom procedures and goals and
> therefore help their child interpret what's being asked of
> him in a way that he can feel comfortable with.

∽ Parents can make a point of getting to know some key
people in school—the secretary, nurse, principal, guidance counselor—so as to get a better feel of whom to go
to, aside from the teacher, should a problem arise.

∽ Parents should show support for teachers as colleagues
working on behalf of all children, via Teacher Appreciation Week, helping out with projects or field trips, and
so on, so as to become known as someone who is a
"friend of the school."

∽ By enrolling in community classes at school, parents
can share with their children the experience of being
a student, having homework, and the like.

∽ Parents can make a point of doing homework assignments *alongside* their child (not doing it *for* her), and
thus they can share the experience of coping with
frustration or finding amusing ways to tackle a boring assignment.

∽ Parents can plan a learning outing to a child's favorite
place, as antidote to schoolwork that seems, or is, boring. Or offer a "mental health day" break from school,
on occasion, when the stresses are getting a bit too
much, just to reaffirm that there's more to life than
school.

Having lived through the K–12 experiences of two boys who
had their ups and downs with public schooling, I have the luxury of some perspective. Among the experiences we went
through, during these years, were battles with a third grade
teacher over disciplinary practices; the refusal of one son, during grades seven through nine, to allow himself to excel in any
school activity; the social life of another son that threatened, at
times, to overwhelm all other concerns; the studious avoidance

of all high school "advanced placement" courses by one; the other's lack of desire to push himself to achieve "ivy league" eligibility scholastically. Neither tried to be a star athlete or a class officer or a prizewinner, academically or otherwise.

Both boys graduated from high school (one took off in the middle of his senior year and headed for a semester in Mexico, once he discovered that he had enough credits to graduate). Both were accepted by a very good college, despite not having a stellar school record, and both have very positive feelings about their college experiences. One has since graduated; the other is enjoying the intellectual adventure at college that seemed to have eluded him in high school.

I know parents who are experiencing much more traumatic conflicts involving their kids and school. I know parents who push their kids to achieve competitively, both in class and on the playing field, with mixed results. I do not offer our experiences in support of any of the theories or recommendations made on these pages.

I do offer one reflection, though, and that is that each of our sons had to find within himself the motivation to be a true learner and not merely an obedient student. It was their independence of thought, expressed primarily in the college essays they wrote, that made them attractive applicants, despite just okay SATs and few extracurricular embellishments. I think now that it is this independence that has made their college experience more than a stepping-stone to a career or a four-year holiday from home.

Each in his own way brought to college a quiet determination to be his own person, as a learner—to explore subjects he had no previous experience with; to take chances in signing up for courses that seemed especially challenging; to change majors several times without panicking. I am very proud of them for that, and it has reaffirmed for me the value of a parent's backing off and waiting for the child's own sense of self, as a learner, to emerge. Backing off was rarely an easy choice.

To other parents, I say this: celebrate your children's sense of themselves as learners; keep a watchful eye on school achievement (or lack thereof); get involved with the school before problems occur; join with your child and his or her teachers to keep the spirit of independent learning alive; intervene when it seems that there is some conflict that the child and the teacher cannot easily resolve themselves; and look for indicators that your child is maintaining a zest for learning regardless of the latest report card grades.

Above all, try not to forget that your child was a powerful and successful learner during those years before entering school (largely through your nurturance and delight) and will in all likelihood be a powerful and successful learner once she or he leaves home. School is only a part of that picture.

CHAPTER SIX

What Schools and Systems
Can Do to Reclaim the Promise

It's going to take some doing to convince most parents and teachers that we can expect those who run our school systems to make passionate learning a priority. With most school administrators worrying about perennial budget shortfalls, racing to keep up with changing demographics in elementary and secondary schools, coping with special education, locked in struggles with politicians and bureaucrats over standardized test results, and trying to recruit qualified teachers to replace those who are now retiring—how much time does that leave for nurturing an independent spirit of learning within each child? And, even if a principal or superintendent can find a moment to think about quality learning for kids, will he or she stick around long enough to begin changing the culture of schools so that passionate learning will thrive in more than a few classrooms?

Please don't ask me to answer these questions. Let me, instead, identify specific actions that a principal or district administrator can take that will make a significant difference for young learners. Although no wise administrator would take such actions alone, genuine and lasting reform requires strong administrative leadership.

Still skeptical? I don't blame you. But let's look at some proposals for how systemic change—or whole-school change—can benefit kids.

Three Teachers Working Together for Three Years

I believe the single best way to help young children maintain a spirit of passionate learning is to have them stay with their teachers for three years. Such a reform is within our means, fiscally and organizationally, and it will change the climate of isolation and of transience that occurs in almost every elementary classroom every year. It will end the upheaval that undermines the quality of children's learning and leaves teachers vulnerable to exhaustion and professional paralysis.

To do this, we must radically rethink how elementary school teachers relate to each other, to their students, and to their families. Instead of a teacher getting a new class of kids each year, three teachers would work as a team with sixty to seventy children over a three-year period, in grades one through three, two through four, three through five, and so on. The teachers would take responsibility, together, for three regular-size classes of children, say twenty to twenty-five kids, and would agree to move up with those kids from grade to grade to grade. The teachers would coordinate their teaching so that the strengths of each could be shared with all the kids. If one were stronger in math, another in reading, a third in arts or science, each would spend some time in one another's classes teaching to their area of strength. Each student would be known by three teachers, and each teacher would have two close colleagues. This is an extension of the fairly common practice of "looping" (having a teacher remain with the same class for two years), or of having two grades in the same classroom. What I'm adding here is the concept of a supportive team of three teachers.

Our schools traditionally require teachers to create a new classroom "family" each September and then subject that family to a divorce in June. This can seriously damage the quality of human relationships. Our classrooms become for children a perpetually "broken home." Kids worry, "Who will I get in September?" or "Will she like me?" Too many parents to fail to sustain contact with their child's current teacher, since "my daughter will have a new one in September."

Under my plan, parents would know that they had a three-year commitment with a primary teacher, so the energy they put into developing mutual understanding between parent and teacher would be rewarded over time. Parents would be encouraged to get to know their child's teacher, and also to join a parent support group for the class, knowing that such supportive relationships would not be dismantled each June. Parents would also know two other teachers who could help solve problems, if needed, and teachers would have each other's impressions of a child to help them find the best approach. If the relations between a particular child and a particular teacher were not working out well, then there could be some switching of students within the team.

How would such a structure promote passionate learning? We've seen how the chasm between the promise of passionate learning and the reality of school is caused by factors that have a lot to do with relationships between and among teachers, students, and parents. Most of these potential pitfalls open up around grading, competitiveness, peer relations, and student behavior. Having three years to work out those relationships, with a supportive team behind each teacher and student, offers vulnerable children of all types more stability, more support, a greater chance to attain and reinforce positive attitudes and behaviors toward learning.

Nobody, of course, wants a "bad teacher" for one year, let alone three. The team concept would lead to more conscientious evaluation of teachers by principals and to ineffective teachers being avoided by their peers, encouraging them to seek professional improvement, transfer, or retirement. Inexperienced teachers would find support and mentoring as they adjust to their roles. Superior teachers would be able to influence team members and to share their expertise with more children.

Develop a One-Page, Parent-Friendly Curriculum Guide

The curriculum cannot remain the private reserve of professionals. I am appalled by how rarely parents and students are invited into the conversation about what teachers should teach and what kids need to learn. The field of "curriculum" (which I treat in much greater depth in the next part of the book) is assumed to be the private matter of professional educators. I cannot think of a more dysfunctional way to set the stage for learning. For children from under-resourced neighborhoods, the lack of clear, understandable learning goals—*goals that rely on the active participation of the family*—is a tremendous impediment to learning success of any kind.[1]

Absent such a guide, academic learning remains something for teachers alone to understand and articulate; behaving well and "coming to school prepared" are seen as the most we can expect of such "at-risk" kids. Maintaining curriculum as the domain of academic professionals can lead to that awful dichotomy of "good children" (who obey their teacher) and "bad children" (who don't).

A clear curriculum statement, in child- and parent-friendly language, is vital for learners of all social strata, for it allows younger children to connect their hobbies and family activities with the larger purposes of learning—for example, to read and write well, to ask good questions, to take responsibility for doing one's best. Most kids hear that message at home, in their place of worship, in community-sponsored youth activities—as well as in school—but the voices rarely become a harmonious chorus; there is no common songbook that celebrates children's learning.

We need a district-wide effort to translate the most important aspects of the curriculum into language that all parents and children can understand and become conversant with. Over several years, in the mid-1990s, I worked with teachers, parent leaders, and curriculum specialists in Hartford, Connecticut, to design such a curriculum statement—the "I Can Do It!" or, in Spanish, "¡Sí, Puedo!"—document (see page 91), defining some curriculum goals for Hartford kids in grades one through three. I wish I could say that this experiment was well received by the central school administration and that it brought about a new level of understanding among Hartford parents, teachers, and students. That didn't happen, for largely political reasons. But a number of those who used the "I Can Do It!" list on an experimental basis found it quite useful. Teachers would give kids a copy to take home and post in their kitchens or bedrooms; teachers would have one in the classroom. The potential was there for parent/teacher conferences to revolve around the question, How well is this child learning the most important stuff?—with parents contributing their experiences (e.g., the reading they do at bedtime, kids coming to the grocery store and helping figure out how to calculate the food purchases) related to the items listed on the "I Can Do It" list. A citywide group of paraprofessional parent-liaison workers, who spend much of their time trying to interpret the city's two-inch-thick curriculum document to parents, called for its adoption—also unsuccessfully, also for political reasons.

I recently led a workshop on parent and community involvement for an urban school district in New Jersey. The response

"I Can Do It!"

Dear Students:

Here are Some **Important Things** You Will Be Learning

Can You Do These Things? **That's Great!**

Not Yet? Ask Your Teacher and Your Family for Help.

✔ CHECK THE ☐ BOX THAT SHOWS HOW WELL YOU CAN DO IT *NOW*

"¡Sí, Puedo!"

What Every Student Will Be Learning Through 3rd Grade

Reading, Writing, Speaking, Listening:	Beginner	Sometimes	Pretty Good	Expert
★ I read on my own, every day, at home and in school.	☐	☐	☐	☐
★ I find books I like in the library and at home.	☐	☐	☐	☐
★ I can read longer and harder books than I did before.	☐	☐	☐	☐
★ I know where to find the books I need to do research.	☐	☐	☐	☐
★ When I read, I find out what the main idea is.	☐	☐	☐	☐
★ I can write about what I read and tell how I like it.	☐	☐	☐	☐
★ I write stories about people and things I care about.	☐	☐	☐	☐
★ I write about ideas and feelings important to me.	☐	☐	☐	☐

Science:				
★ I can tell who a scientist is and what a scientist does.	☐	☐	☐	☐
★ I can ask why things are the way they are.	☐	☐	☐	☐
★ I know how living and non-living things are different.	☐	☐	☐	☐
★ I know why animals, plants & people need each other.	☐	☐	☐	☐
★ I can draw and talk about changes in the weather.	☐	☐	☐	☐
★ I can talk about different kinds of energy in our world.	☐	☐	☐	☐
★ I can explain problems in my neighborhood.	☐	☐	☐	☐
★ I help my family improve our environment at home.	☐	☐	☐	☐

Social Studies:

	Beginner	Sometimes	Pretty Good	Expert
★ I can speak and write about what it means to be me.	☐	☐	☐	☐
★ I can explain where my family comes from.	☐	☐	☐	☐
★ I can describe the city, state, and nation that I live in.	☐	☐	☐	☐
★ I know what voting is and how people get elected.	☐	☐	☐	☐
★ I know how to be a good citizen in my school.	☐	☐	☐	☐
★ I know how to be a helpful member of my family.	☐	☐	☐	☐
★ I can read and make maps of places I like to go to.	☐	☐	☐	☐

HIGH Challenge

HIGH Performance

Math:

	Beginner	Sometimes	Pretty Good	Expert
★ I can add numbers up to 9,999.	☐	☐	☐	☐
★ I can subtract numbers up to 9,999.	☐	☐	☐	☐
★ I can multiply whole numbers by 2, 5, and 10.	☐	☐	☐	☐
★ I understand the fractions: quarters, half, and thirds.	☐	☐	☐	☐
★ I can estimate how big or small something is.	☐	☐	☐	☐
★ I can predict what the answer to a problem might be.	☐	☐	☐	☐
★ I can tell time on a clock with hands and numbers.	☐	☐	☐	☐
★ I can use a ruler to measure how long things are.	☐	☐	☐	☐

to the "I Can Do It!" model among K–12 teachers was very positive, with many teachers reiterating that the lack of parent access to and understanding of the curriculum is a serious impediment to their teaching, and several sharing projects they had done that were successful only because parents were able to understand and participate in the work. I remain convinced that a family-friendly curriculum statement is necessary and doable, one that highlights the most important areas of skills and knowledge without relying on jargon. We cannot expect parents and family members who were themselves poorly served by the school system to become active players on behalf of their children's learning if we continue to construct a language barrier around our profession.

Hire as Teachers Only Those
Who Can Communicate Well with Parents

Schools should hire as new or replacement teachers only those who are ready and willing to work consistently with students' parents, people who view parents as essential, active partners in their children's learning, regardless of how much or how little formal education those parents have themselves received.

Any teacher, especially in elementary school, who believes that she or he can provide an adequate education within the classroom with only occasional contact with parents is tragically unprepared for the task at hand. Such teachers oblige their students to view the world of school and the world of home as two unconnected realities, driving a wedge between the child's loyalties to family and the desire to succeed in school.

How can we change this if parents and teachers spend so little time in one another's company? How can this partnership exist if the child is included in the conversation only when he or she has done something wrong, and Mom or Dad must come to school to deal with it?

People complain of being stressed out. Parents work two jobs to stay ahead. Teachers have families of their own; they can't hang around until the late shift lets out to meet with parents. They have meetings after school, and sometimes before school, too. So what do we do to make this partnership work? Here are three suggestions:

1. *Voice mail for teachers:* Equip teachers, in their classrooms, with phones and voice mail that can record a message at the beginning and end of each week, informing parents what the class will be doing and what they can do at home to reinforce the child's learning. Encourage parents to leave a message when they have questions and to tell the teacher when it's best to call with the answers.

2. *Make time for parents:* At least twice a month, the school should plan a special program in the auditorium for the children—a visiting artist, a favorite movie, a puppet show—supervised by paraprofessionals and volunteers so that teachers will have two to three hours to meet with parents individually or to have planning meetings and thus free up after-school hours to meet with parents.

3. *Time off for parents to get involved:* Have the legislature pass a law, or get area corporate and business support, to give every parent one or two days a year, as paid leave, to spend in their child's school seeing what and how their child is learning.

Adopt a Constructivist Approach to Learning

The classroom should be an environment where meaning is *constructed* rather than imparted or delivered. Skills are acquired through a combination of direct instruction, student exploration, and peer coaching, in a blend that is based on the teacher's guidance, planning, and role modeling. Every child has an opportunity to help another child learn, either in the same class or where a younger child buddies up with an older student.

For example, fifth grade kids each pick out a favorite story and learn to read it aloud and expressively to a first grade class. The older kids then write a story with and for the little ones. The sense of everyone functioning as both teacher and learner underscores this concept and is reinforced as the students progress through the grades. Students feel that they are giving to the community from early grades, rather than waiting for junior or senior year "community service" projects.

Help Students Become Part
of the Teaching/Learning Continuum

Schools should create more multigrade classrooms, that place students at two grade levels in the same classroom. This approach, already in effect in schools like the Mission Hill Elementary School in Boston, allows students to learn at their own pace, so that a student who is ahead of her cohort in math but a bit less advanced in reading can work with varying groups in subject/skills areas. It also allows students to help one another with skills. Since children vary considerably in terms of physical and emotional development, as well as academic achievements, the age differences within the two grades need not be an obstacle. It wouldn't have the same stigma of a child being held back and forced to repeat a grade.

The value, for passionate learning, lies in a reduction of the anxiety and stress that often accompanies too-frequent change for kids. With more security the child develops more confidence as an independent learner.

Link Schools and Their Faculties within a District

No school is an island. Schools cannot be islands unto themselves, nor can classrooms be isolated places where teachers do their work alone, cut off from other classrooms and grade levels.

This builds on the idea of multiyear relationships and teaming, but it also pertains to the transition from elementary to middle school and from middle to high school. Some kids can't swim well from one "island" to another, especially when some of the adults who rule this new school are suspicious or contemptuous of the adults who run the school the kids are coming from (e.g., "What did they give you kids back in middle school—five hours of 'self-esteem' per day, along with fifteen minutes of proper English usage?") Kids need to feel confident that their new school is allied to the school they just came from.

Many children also need familiar and trusted teachers to come with them for their first year in a new school. For example, if middle school begins with grade six, then the team of teachers who has been with the students in grades four and five can go with them to middle school for grade six. The same is true for grade eight teachers moving with their students to grade nine in high school. We need our teachers to be able to work comfortably in more than just one school. We need to build those bridges.

Create Networks for New Teachers
We must help new teachers create a supportive network for themselves upon entering a school system. This is one of the most woefully undeveloped aspects both of teacher preservice education and of teacher orientation to first or new jobs. By leaving new teachers alone and isolated, we weaken their ability to support passionate learning.

I often ask my education students, senior or grad students preparing themselves for their first job, "What will you do, once you've been hired, to prepare yourself for the school year ahead? Say you land a job in June, and the principal or superintendent tells you that you are due to report on August 24. What do you then ask for?" Often the answer is "a copy of the curriculum," or "a copy of the textbooks I'll be using," or "a list of the kids, so I can write each one a little note."

But there are four things they need that are even more important:

1. a list of other new teachers who've been hired in the district (to get to know and form supportive friendships with at least some of them)

2. the name and phone number of a teacher whose teaching effectiveness the principal is most excited about, and another teacher who is most highly respected by colleagues

3. phone numbers and addresses of the parents of the students, so that the new teacher can make informal contact with them before the school year begins

4. introductions to people, businesses, and organizations in the neighborhood surrounding the school, so that new teachers can begin to know the community

The importance of building a network of advice and support for new teachers cannot be overemphasized. Lack of such support probably contributes more to the isolation and early discouragement of teachers than any other factor. My graduate students, those with a few years of teaching under their belts, talk about the "messages" they received from certain veteran teachers upon entering the profession, most of which, sadly, were some version of "Look, honey, just forget all that philosophy stuff they taught you in college about teaching. All the 'new methods' are bull. You're in the trenches now—where those professors have *never* been—and the most important thing to keep in mind is to *stay in control—at all times!* Don't be a softie—let the kids know who's boss, or they'll run all over you, sweet thing that you are. And don't worry about the curriculum. Just do what I do, and you'll survive."

Create Partnership Opportunities for All Teachers

Where teachers feel supported by administrators and parents, they are much more willing to take creative risks in trying to get better results in their work with students. By contrast, in schools where teachers do not feel supported by administrators and parents, everyone plays defense. Few teachers are willing to go out on a limb on behalf of their students if they worry that somebody is going to saw off that limb.

Our kids need a solid team of professionals to support their learning, not one big boss at the central office who tells another boss in the principal's office how to boss around the teachers. The most alive and dynamic schools are those in which teachers play a major role in developing new programs, new approaches, new ways of linking what they do in the classroom with the home and the community.

Here's where it's so important to have parent groups for each elementary class—not just a school PTA, but a group for each classroom. That way parents and teachers can talk through ideas and plan together, and the teacher can feel support when she or he goes to the principal with an idea on how to do things better. Change initiatives must build from the classroom up, not just from the central office down.

Creating a Capacity for Initiative and Partnership among Teachers and Parents

The kinds of changes listed above require administrative leadership and initiative. At very least, they require administrative support for teachers and parents who want to try out ideas such as these within the existing structure of the school. Anyone who has ever attempted such an experiment has found that in a traditional school culture teachers who attempt reforms often find themselves ostracized by other teachers who fear changes in the status quo.

But there is some cause for hope, along with much reason for caution. The hope comes from the recent proliferation of charter schools and the breakdown of existing schools into smaller administrative units, with consequently more teacher and parent input in collective decision making.

I see considerable hope in the growing ranks of charter schools and pilot schools as venues for collaborative action within schools, especially for the enhanced role of faculty in policy making and in creating partnerships with families. But even where such schools have not yet been established, their existence as a national phenomenon has loosened up the thinking surrounding the reform process. Teachers and parents are now being recognized as educational resources, as leaders in improving the environment for children.

This means that it should be more possible, in almost any school, for a group of teachers and parents to at least propose experiments such as the three-teacher, three-year team sequence or the "I Can Do It!" curriculum. It will likely take initiative from all sides, from parents and teachers and administrators, for such bold but commonsense steps to be taken. Somebody has to take the lead.

PART THREE

The Practice of
Passionate Learning

CHAPTER SEVEN

Curriculum as Relationships

Mention the word *curriculum* and most of us cringe. People in school see it as a weighty harness that someone *else*—some*where* else—fashions to make them bear. Politicians love to berate it while demanding that it be toughened; for school board members, it's a blackboard upon which they can chalk in their philosophies. Most parents view it as a remote and mystical tool of educators for making kids learn the right stuff, which they as mere parents will probably never understand. Teachers come at curriculum in a bunch of ways, positive, negative, or neutral: as clay they can mold to fit their own artistry, as an idol that the bureaucracy forces them to kneel before, or as a useful mantle that covers them while they "cover" it.

There are, of course, lots of ways to define *curriculum*. I begin a graduate seminar on the subject by asking my students to write a quick, one-paragraph definition, which I collect and sort. I respond with this handout:

Your definitions of *curriculum,* what are we going to do here? You seem to see curriculum from at least forty different viewpoints —and there are only about twenty of you to begin with!!!!

1. Let's start off with the *scope-and-sequence* people, who believe that curriculum is basically a "body of knowledge" made up of "units of instruction" that are developed by teachers, based on district and state guidelines and presented to students one topic at a time, one grade at a time.

2. But then come the *skills-and-performance* people, who believe that curriculum consists primarily of teaching and assessing essential skills and competencies that prepare children for the Information Age. They believe that it is access-to-knowledge skills rather than specific bits of information that should be reinforced as students grow and develop.

3. Then there are the *classical* people, including advocates of "cultural literacy," who believe that our civilization is based upon a basic "core of knowledge": English, history, science, math, plus foreign languages and the arts, and that it is our role, as teachers of this curriculum, to instruct young people in this core and thereby pass on our heritage to a new generation.

4. That position is challenged by the *student-centered* people, who believe that curriculum is a guide for the teacher to help each individual achieve his or her full potential, and who are convinced that a teacher must be free to design lessons around activities and experiences that allow students to motivate themselves, expand their intellects, and enliven their imaginations. Some also think that the curriculum should be student-driven, with students involved in developing lessons with their teachers.

5. But don't forget the *political/pragmatic* people, who believe that "curriculum is politics"—dictated by trends and fashions, with the pendulum swinging between "core knowledge" and "skills," between "tradition" and "innovation," and that teachers have to put up with the popular trend of the time. Curriculum is whatever it takes to prepare young people to "function in society," with enough knowledge to become gainfully employed and to be good citizens.

6. Finally, there are those who believe that curriculum is an *evolving, holistic philosophy and pedagogy,* that teachers—with student and parent input—develop and adjust as they create a whole-school environment for learning that emphasizes their school's vision and goals.

So, who's got it *right???* And don't you dare tell me it's a combination of all of them, *because they don't fit together!*

———•◦•———

We have fun with this. I ask the students to pick the one among these six definitions they most agree with, gather together in a corner of the room with like-minded classmates, and come up with a rationale why *they* have the "right" definition and the rest of us are "wrong."

My favorite definition, however, is not on this list.

I have a problem with these definitions, despite my attraction to parts of each of them. But before I offer my definition, I want to underscore the negative attitudes curriculum so often elicits from students and teachers alike.

For a number of years I have struggled with a feeling that curriculum is not quite real; that it may be something of a myth—a polished shell that obscures a dusky interior, the Emperor's New Clothes—quite invisible to the eye of the common folk, however brazenly it is paraded before us all.

What gives curriculum this "unreal" quality is what I observe in the actions of the middle school students I work with and too often on the faces of students in my own college courses: *The content of the lessons seems to pass through them, much of the time, like an indigestible substance.* Nothing new in that; teachers have complained for ages that "too many of the important things I have to say pass right over—or through—them."

But I worry that our students have been "educated" to view curriculum through a rather narrow band of light. They may see it as "things my teacher wants me to learn," or as "the pathway to getting a good grade," or as "something I should know for college." Or it may be a fog of material to wade through, or a menacing sermon that contains a list of "things I'd better watch out for." This latter view was best expressed to me years ago, when I was teaching a first-year English course, by a student who listened to two days of my introductory lecture on "the value of literature as integral to your life" only to ask, as I finished, "Do we have to worry about 'the hidden meaning' in this course?"

Curriculum, as "instructions for today's work" means one thing to "the boss" and quite another to "the hired hands." The boss sees it as the all-important context for the work to be performed: the scope and sequence of the tasks, the raison d'être for the entire enterprise. To unempowered workers, what's important is to figure out what "counts." What will I be rewarded or punished for? What do I have to do to get through the day?

In our enthusiasm for our subject matter, we teachers often do not understand how what we are saying is being received by our students. That's the Emperor's New Clothes aspect of curriculum: how our lessons appear depends on whose eyes are looking.

For parents, curriculum often remains a mystery, its language remote and foreboding. As described in chapter 6, few school systems help parents understand and play their part in assisting their children to acquire the skills, the knowledge, and the attitudes that make curriculum "real." Here's an example of how school systems confuse parents about curriculum—even when they attempt to communicate with them. In a publication entitled "Kids First," subtitled "What Every Student Will Learn" and distributed to parents several years ago by the New Haven Public Schools, the following objectives for third grade students were listed in the column headed "Language Arts," under the subheading "Word Analysis":

- ❧ Use the various cueing systems (pictures, graphophonics, structural and semantic) in conjunction with one another to determine pronunciation of familiar words and construct meaning

- ❧ Use the graphophonics cues of consonants, double r-controlled and irregular vowels, vowel and syllabication rules, prefixes, suffixes and common word parts

These were some of the most egregious items on this handout, but other items seem similarly unrealistic. Third graders in this under-resourced and underperforming urban school system are expected, for example, to "make judgments about fact and opinion, authority and validity of evidence, consistency, relevance and logical order of statements, sufficiency of support and distinguish between fiction and nonfiction." Imagine how humiliating such a list might be to a parent, how huge the gulf between her desire to help her child learn to read and the demands represented in such language.

In contrast to *how* curriculum is usually defined (i.e., "material"—content knowledge and skills—to be taught *to* students) and *the language* that curriculum is often written in, I now view curriculum as inseparable from the social milieu in which teaching and learning take place.

A curriculum written for educators that is unintelligible to parents and students is an invitation to alienation and failure. Rather than viewing curriculum as a thing apart, a list of content or skills objectives that supposedly stand on their own, I see curriculum as embedded in a series, or web, of relationships that promote or impede the learning process. I have outlined this notion in a chart at the end of the chapter.

Curriculum is not just "stuff"—indeed, from the students'

standpoint, the "stuff" is often an irrelevant component of pleasing, or getting by, the teacher. To find the heart of any curriculum, we must look at the connections that learners make with an area of skill or knowledge. Such a connection is likely to be strong

- ❧ when the thing or skill to be learned makes sense to the learner
- ❧ when the teacher exudes a vibrancy that makes the material exciting and rich
- ❧ when there is a spirit of mutual engagement involving teacher and students
- ❧ when students enjoy learning together and accept the challenge to exhibit what they have learned[1]
- ❧ when "things to be learned" have meaning in the families and neighborhood that surround the school and are expressed in language that is friendly but not demeaning or belittling

If even *one* of these characteristics is present in a child's learning environment, the child will be much more likely to learn and to retain that learning over time. The "material" of the curriculum, the "stuff" and "skills," becomes the *context* for an engaging relationship. The material is the field upon which students actively engage (or disengage) with mind and heart.

Note that I have left off of my list the one item that most popular guides to teaching place at or near the top: The learners' connection with an area of skill or knowledge is likely to be strong "when the teacher has carefully planned the learning task and provided a clear structure for students to complete their work in a timely manner." It's not that such structure and organization are unimportant; but passionate learning requires more than efficiency in carrying out a learning task. It requires a particular *attitude*. And in the rush toward efficiency, both teacher and students often mistake the means for the end. Without a disposition toward learning and understanding, all is soon forgotten.

Thus, curriculum for the passionate learner has everything to do with whether or not the relationships are *right,* whether teachers and learners feel that together they are shaping the learning that goes on. This cooperation is necessary even when teachers feel pressure from external forces, be they the district or the state, to "cover" certain topics that students will be tested on.

Melissa Parent, a third grade teacher, uses just such an approach in constructing her lessons with her students:

> In science, with the topic of "sound," I tell the kids, "We're going to study 'sound' because we're supposed to, but you get to decide what we actually *learn* about." This helps me because it allows me to key my own lesson prep to aspects of sound the kids have identified as most interesting. For them, it was questions like "How do we hear?" or "What makes a sound loud or soft?" "What makes some things sound good and others sound really bad?" I tell them, "*You* are the designers of this unit. We will learn the things that you are interested in." And I often remind them that I am a first-year teacher and I have a lot to learn. They think it's more fun, because then I'm not teaching it *to* them, we're learning it *together.*"[2]

As a university teacher who has been spending time this year at two pilot schools in Boston, I see quite a different picture emerging. What strikes me about the curriculum as I see it evolve with the K–8 students in one school and with the sixth and seventh graders in the other is not so much its stated purposes but its social and interactional qualities.

Curriculum always seems overshadowed by something *else* that is going on in classrooms. When I observe classes in the humanities—language arts and social studies (which in this school are taught by the same teacher in a daily hundred-minute block)—and try to imagine how the children here experience curriculum, what impresses me is that it seems inextricably linked to how they feel about their teachers. If their teacher is excited about what he or she is teaching, it's likely the students will pay attention. If the subject being taught seems remote from the children's experience and interests, many are likely to resist, to fool around, dawdle, or "act out."

It almost doesn't seem to matter what topic the lesson is on. *Something besides the content takes center stage.* I want to expand on this later. For now, consider that for most students of all ages, "curriculum" means "what's going on between me and my teacher, what she or he is making me do."

Committing oneself to get the relationships right usually takes a lot of courage on a teacher's part. And I am in awe of the teachers I've been observing this year who are new to teaching or to teaching urban kids. Rather than cleave to a set of "behavior management" procedures for keeping the kids in line and on task, most have been willing to struggle with these eleven- to thirteen-year-olds, largely from immigrant and low-income neighborhoods, in an attempt to engage the students' hearts and minds with the material at hand.

It has not been easy. There are lots of kids who have had, in prior schooling, "strict" teachers who kept them in line with a firm hand, and some kids who assume that any adult who doesn't discipline them severely is asking to be pushed around and disrespected. And there are kids whose standing with their peers depends, they think, on the amount of back talk and goofing they can get away with.

The courage I witness is of teachers who, instead of "managing," opt to explain, to confer, to negotiate, and even to plead sometimes with these preteenagers in hopes of developing a mutually respectful relationship that will allow the children to absorb the curriculum willingly, not just tolerably or dutifully. These teachers are, to varying degrees, placing the value of a mutually respectful, mutually vulnerable relationship at the heart of the teaching/learning process as an integral part of curriculum. It is a messy, slow, often frustrating, not often triumphant, but heroic process, as I witness it.

To view curriculum as embedded in a web of relationships is to acknowledge that the lasting value of any skill or concept learned depends largely on the state of mind, the disposition of the learner toward the act of acquiring that skill or understanding that concept. It is the spirit in which the learner's encounter with the material takes place. The student who, after struggling with a vexing math problem, or with unexpected results of a chemistry lab, suddenly exclaims, "Wait! *I got it!* I see where I messed up!" bespeaks just such a spirit, even if such diligence and reflection were not originally present when the activity was undertaken.

When we view curriculum as a function of relationships, we bring it to our classrooms and lay it out, like a comfortable and useful garment. We allow ourselves and our students to make it belong to us, to adjust it, to restyle it, to enliven it, to infuse it with meaning. Such ownership increases the likelihood that young people will approach the knowledge and skills to be learned as active, critical, thoughtful investigators, rather than as passive receptors (or rejecters). We will waste less time. We will allow the passionate learning impulses of children to reach outward and challenge them, rather than to shrink back and figure out how to do the minimum.[3] They will work for something other than the grade. They will form learning partnerships with one another, with their teacher, with other learning resources out in the world.

We all recognize the opposite—work that is hurriedly and

carelessly performed for the sake of "getting it done and handing it in"; students who are impatient with anything but "the
right answer," since that's all they think teachers care about;
or students who want to be rewarded just for "being there,"
regardless of whether they have been thoughtfully engaged.
"Why do *you* care how I got the answer—it's *right,* isn't it?" The
drudgery of teaching comes when we feel compelled to labor
over student work that wasn't conscientiously or rigorously undertaken in the first place.[4]

It saddens me that teachers of all grades and subjects expend
so much time and thought developing or refining their curriculum only to find that most students view such a curriculum (if
they think about it at all) mainly as "stuff we gotta do," as a
series of obstacles between them and their true interests. We
are so accustomed to thinking of curriculum as a "body of
knowledge," or a "grouping of concepts and theories," or as
"the scope and sequence of instructional material," that it is
easy to forget that such definitions, absent an active partnership
between teacher and students, are little more than words on a
page.

In his memoir *'Tis,* Frank McCourt describes his struggle
between adhering to the given curriculum and responding to
his students' desire to relate to him as an individual with a curious brogue. It's his first week as a teacher at McKee Vocational
High School, in Staten Island, New York. It is the early 1950s.
McCourt has been hired to replace a teacher who has given up
and retired a few months before the end of the school year. He
has come to school on St. Patrick's Day, much to the chagrin of
his students, who were counting on him taking the day off to
celebrate with his countrymen.

> It is time for teacher intervention, All right, all right, open
> your notebooks, and there are cries of pain, Notebooks, note-

books, Mr. McCourt, why you doin' this to us? An' we don't
want no *Your World an' You* on Paddy's Day. My mother's mother
was Irish an' we should have respect. Why can't you
tell us about school in Ireland, why?

All right.

I'm a new teacher and I've lost the first battle and it's all the
fault of St. Patrick. I tell this class and all my classes the rest of
the day about school in Ireland, about the masters with their
sticks, straps, canes, how we had to memorize everything and
recite, how the masters would kill us if we ever tried to fight in
their classrooms, how we were not allowed to ask questions nor
have discussions, how we left school at fourteen and became
messenger boys or unemployed.

I tell them about Ireland because I have no choice. My students have seized the day and there's nothing I can do about
it. I could threaten them with *Your World and You* and *Silas
Marner* and satisfy myself that I was in control, that I was teaching, but I know there would be a flurry of requests for passes
for the toilets, the nurse, the guidance counselor, and, Can I
have the pass to call my aunt who's dying of cancer in Manhat-
tan? If I insisted on hewing to the curriculum today I'd be talking to myself and my instincts tell me one group of experienced
students in an American classroom can break one inexperienced teacher.

A bit later, McCourt sums up the philosophical and pedagogical
conflict, as he sees it being played out among the faculty at
McKee:

In the teachers' cafeteria there are two schools of thought. The
old-timers tell me, You're young, you're new but don't let
these damn kids ride all over you. Let 'em know who's boss in
the classroom and remember, you are the boss. Control is the
big thing in teaching. No control and you can't teach. You have
the power to pass and fail and they know goddam well if they
fail there's no place for them in this society. They'll be sweep-

ing the streets and washing the dishes and it'll be their own
fault, the little bastards. Just don't take shit. You're the boss,
the man with the red pen . . .

Younger teachers are not so sure. They've taken courses
in Educational Psychology and the Philosophy of Education,
they've read John Dewey, and they tell me these children are
human beings and we have to meet their felt needs.

I don't know what a felt need is and I don't ask for fear of
exposing my ignorance. The younger teachers shake their heads
over the older ones. They tell me the war is over, these children
are not the enemy. They are our children, for God's sakes.[5]

McCourt knows that had he not given way and responded to
his students' "felt needs" to relate to him as a person, his teaching career would have ended. Lacking the confidence and the
philosophical training of his young colleagues, he would likely
have become embittered at the kids' ignorance and at his own
inability to keep them on task. As it was, his career at McKee
did end early, after he bought and distributed copies of *Catcher
in the Rye* in response to his students' rebellion over *Silas Marner*.

In the interest of passionate learning—active, willing, productive, and sustained engagement of learners with skills and
knowledge—I propose that we define curriculum as *skills and
knowledge that are embedded in a web of relationships*. I want us to
view curriculum material as the context for engagement and
collaboration, leading to valued and sustainable results. By
looking at curriculum in this way, we may be able to anticipate
and set the stage for higher-quality student work and more satisfying teaching. But in order to do so, we had better be ready to
rethink our assumptions.

Let us imagine a classroom in which teacher and students
agree, as part of their agenda, to monitor and take the pulse of
the quality of engagement on a given topic, skill, or body of

CURRICULUM EMBEDDED IN A WEB
OF ATTITUDES AND RELATIONSHIPS

A. Relationship of Student to the Material or Academic Task

1	2	3	4	5
Anger, hostility	Indifference, boredom	Mild interest, openness	Active interest, desire to engage	Love of learning, pursuit of mastery

B. Relationship of Teacher to the Material or Academic Task

1	2	3	4	5
Boredom, resentment	Perfunctory transmittal	Getting material across, teaching to the test	Teacher-as-learner, role model for students	Passionate teaching

C. Relationship of Students to the Teacher Regarding Academic Work

1	2	3	4	5
Animosity, indifference	Grudging or minimal compliance	Respectful compliance	Working to make the grade or to please the teacher	True learning partnership

D. Relationship of Teacher to the Students Regarding Academic Work

1	2	3	4	5
Burnout, indifference, "waste of my time"	Defensive monitoring	Hoping for decent results	Interactive coaching, optimism, eagerness	True learning partnership

E. Relationship of Students to Peers Regarding Academic Work

1	2	3	4	5
Hostility, fear	Isolation, passivity	Tolerance, each doing the work	Helpfulness, responsibility	Teamwork, pride, elan

F. Relationship of Students, Parents, and Teacher Regarding Academic Work

1	2	3	4	5
Cynicism, anger, lack of trust	No genuine communication	Acceptance without understanding	Frequent, friendly communication	Cooperating for student progress

knowledge. They agree to make conscious and to analyze, at appropriate intervals, how they are relating to both the material and to each other in their respective roles.

Curriculum Embedded in a
Web of Relationships: Taking the Pulse

Two summers ago, in a graduate curriculum seminar at Northeastern University, I offered students a more detailed model of my theory that curriculum is embedded in a web of relationships, using a Likert scale–type survey. The purpose of this series of scales is to identify and share with one's students several aspects of relationships as they affect curriculum and to allow any class to take a reading, from time to time, on how people are feeling about the material they are investigating.

I designed it as an easy instrument for students to complete, taking a minute or so per item, and offering the possibility of instant tabulation as a prelude to conversation and reflection by teacher and students on ways to make their work together more satisfying.

Having presented here the instrument in its current (still unfinished) form, in the next chapter I will examine each of these relationships in more detail, with examples from the literature and from the field.

CHAPTER EIGHT

Curriculum? Who Cares?

I remember a complaint from the director of an experimental "Renaissance Program" created for not-quite-honors-but-still-pretty-good ninth and tenth grade students in a suburban high school. He was frustrated because students were working on self-designed projects, as part of the program's emphasis on student motivation and independent achievement. But too many of the projects were poorly designed and sloppily executed, done out of a desire to "get it over with and hand it in," rather than from any deeper interest. He was particularly miffed at one girl who was at work on a model of the Eiffel Tower, made of Lego blocks. "The damn thing isn't even remotely to scale!" he complained.

I asked (rather cautiously) whether he had set, as a condition for beginning work on a project, that the student convince him that he or she really *cared* about it. It had never crossed his mind, he admitted, but he added that it might be a good idea for next time. Too many of his students were doing work because he had assigned it, not necessarily because they saw it as something worth doing. *Caring* wasn't in the curriculum. But it just might be the key variable.

If we were to visit a typical classroom and had the power to listen to students' thoughts as their teacher introduced a new topic, here is a sampling of what they might be thinking. From a student who is angry and defiant: "This stuff is *stupid!* There's no way I'm gonna bother trying to learn this crap!" Another, resigned to the inevitable boredom of the daily grind, shakes his head and murmurs, "Hey, this is school, and you gotta do what they tell you. Whatever."

A third student seems amiably neutral but willing to see what happens: "I'm not sure what this is about, but I'll give it a try. Maybe I'll learn something." Still another has a sense that there is something in the lesson for her and realizes that she must put some effort into it: "This is sort of interesting stuff. If I get into it and work hard, I could learn a lot." And our final representative just loves this topic and thinks, "*Wow!* This is pretty cool. I want to get so I really understand this and can work with it."

From defiance, at one end, to genuine excitement at the other, students react in a range of ways to the material to be learned, the "stuff" of knowledge. We can tell something from their facial expressions, their relative attentiveness, the questions they ask. But for most busy teachers, with too much to "cover" and a diverse group of students to instruct, the proof of the pudding, as far as curriculum goes, comes only when the test is given or the papers or projects are handed in. Then they can tell whether or not their students really bothered to learn the material. That's when they will know whether a student *cares.* But by then, it's too late to do much.

If the essence of a successful curriculum, as I argue in the previous chapter, lies in the *attitudes* that develop within the learner's mind and in the *relationships* that develop around learning, in the classroom and at home, there should be some way for learners and teachers to get a sense of how well things are going before the time for testing and grading. But attitudes are hard to measure, and relationships are ever-changing. It's so much less risky for busy teachers to focus on delivering the material and grading the test.

But as passionate learners, children need more—more than quiz grades or lists of "things they ought to know in second grade." They need to care about what they learn, to develop a positive disposition toward learning.

Caring is at the heart of learning. The care a student takes —in approaching a task, in checking an answer to a problem, in explaining to others how she arrived at a solution—is a measure of her thoughtfulness and self-respect as a learner. A teacher who cares about the quality of attention students bring to a task is a teacher who can help make passionate learning happen. A parent who cares about his child's feelings about learning is a parent who can help that child grow as a learner.

Let's investigate the phenomenon of caring using a series of scales that allows students, teachers, and parents to gauge their own and one another's attitudes toward what they are learning, and to measure the vitality of their relationships with respect to the skills and knowledge of the curriculum. These scales can be used for informal classroom surveys to allow students, teachers, and—when appropriate—parents to see how things stand and what changes might increase the effectiveness of a curriculum in any subject to make a lasting impression on a young learner.

The first, scale A, looks at the relationship between the students and the material in the curriculum. It asks, in effect, "How do the students feel about what they're learning?" Students would circle the number that best reflects their view. If we assign numbers to the students' thoughts that were listed earlier, they would correspond with the scale as follows:

Scale A: Relationship of Student to the Material or Academic Task

1	2	3	4	5
Anger, hostility	Indifference, boredom	Mild interest, openness	Active interest, desire to engage	Love of learning, pursuit of mastery

1. "This stuff is *stupid!* There's no way I'm gonna bother trying to learn this crap!"

2. "Hey, this is school, and you gotta do what they tell you. Whatever."

3. "I'm not sure what this is about, but I'll give it a try. Maybe I'll learn something."

4. This is sort of interesting stuff. If I get into it and work hard, I could learn a lot."

5. *Wow!* This is pretty cool. I want to get so I really understand this and can work with it."

I don't presume to read children's minds, and I offer these hypothetical statements only to help us differentiate as we move up the scale from anger or hostility to love of learning and a desire for mastery. When using this scale in a classroom, teacher and students can come up with their own translations of kids' attitudes toward the material to be learned, depending on their age and maturity. The purpose is not for students to rank one another or criticize their teacher, but for them to use such feedback (gathered anonymously) as a diagnostic tool to improve the quality of learning via the curriculum.

I trust that a teacher's willingness to employ this scale, diagnostically, will be viewed by students as a measure of their teacher's respect for them, and will open the way for more positive and engaging interactions. It shows students that we see them all as potentially passionate learners, capable of deep engagement in the material. It's the most respectful stance a teacher can take toward learners. And it leads naturally to the question of what it would take to make it possible for more students to care more deeply about their learning.

An Experiment in Process

I have tried a variation of this idea, this year, with a middle school in Boston. One of the humanities teachers with whom I'm working, Jim Heffron, told me how disappointed he was with the drafts of student responses to the book they had just read. The papers were not good—unfinished, minimal, slapdash, or perfunctory. Jim and I began by discussing, in front of the class, how important it is to have students care about what they are writing, that good writing requires caring. At the same time, we agreed that it's impossible for us to *make* anybody care. So, we told them we were going to try something new, with no idea how it would turn out.

We then listed on the board several possible descriptions of student attitudes toward this assignment (it was a list that I had composed in the minutes before class):

5. "I am excited and proud of the paper I'm working on."

4. "I'm confident that my paper will be worthwhile."

3. "I know I will complete the paper, and I'm aiming for a good grade."

2. "I'm doing it just to get it done, but I really don't care much about it."

1. "I care very little about this paper and don't know if I'll even finish it."

We asked the students whether they understood each of the listed statements (they did). We told them that we were exploring an area that neither of us knew much about, namely, how their level of caring affected the writing they did. It was something we would have to learn from them.

We invited the students to select the statement that most closely reflected their own attitude toward the book report. We put each student's name on the board and asked each of them to state, by number, how he or she was feeling—at this stage —about the assignment. The kids were brutally honest, with most assigning themselves a 2. Doubtless, there was some posturing here—letting us grown-ups know how far this assignment was from where their interests were. But we had their attention. They were very curious about what would happen next.

Jim Heffron was now able to say to them, in effect, "Look, I realize that the kind of book report I assigned you wasn't very interesting. So let's figure out, together, how to make the writing you do make more sense, so that you will want to put more effort into it and do a better job." This led to a brainstorming session, in which students proposed a variety of ideas to enhance their commitment to writing: giving them writing assignments that are more fun, that give students more choices; allowing students to help one another in writing; having kids read their written work to the class—ideas that are typically part of any well-designed approach to teaching writing.

Nothing revolutionary in the suggestions themselves. But what was new for Jim was the notion that good writing requires a genuine partnership with his students—one in which nothing is guaranteed but everyone has some responsibility for making things work better. The other point we made to the kids was that the effort to improve the writing program in this class was a true experiment and that caring was essential to the success of anything we tried.

The initial results seem promising. Students help develop the writing topics and read their work to the class. For one assignment—a scary story for Halloween—we invited a school administrator to come hear the stories, and students from another class swapped "best stories" with this class. Jim has asked students to select several of the papers they have been working on for publication in a class booklet. But he is requiring that they confer with him first and convince him they *care* about the piece they have chosen, before they get the go-ahead to proceed.

Again—none of this is groundbreaking stuff. It's what good teachers of writing routinely do. Jim Heffron is in his first year of regular teaching and, a history major, has not had much training in teaching writing. But his rapport with the kids is excellent, and he's willing to discuss the question of attitude with the class.

Caring as a Threshold

The true challenge for any teacher is to make caring the *threshold* for student work in any subject where thoughtfulness, imagination, analysis, reflection are important aspects of the knowledge and skills. When teachers focus solely on performance or compliance (e.g., has the student completed the assignment? Is it up to par?), we get the typical range of responses listed above. But if we first ask, "Does the student *care* about what she is doing?" we open the door to a more engaging dialogue, leading (we hope) to a more satisfying and productive teaching/learning relationship.

I am of course aware that we often have to apply ourselves conscientiously to a task before we develop a sense of caring, of ownership, in the task itself. But in our work with children it pays to examine—at the start of any task—conditions that help students develop a stake in what they are doing, things that help them care.

In assessing student work, I imagine a teacher saying, "Look, guys. I have only so much time and energy. I don't want to waste any of it grading work that you didn't care about when you did it. If an assignment seems dumb or boring at the start, let's figure out how to make it *mean* something to you, so that you *care*. That's not just *my* job—it's *yours*, too—figuring out how an assignment makes sense to you."

For children whose family and/or personal experience with success in education has been rare, reaching the "caring threshold" is a crucial step. Kids with low levels of confidence in themselves or little trust in their teacher's commitment to their success often choose not to put in their best efforts for fear that if they do so and still come up short they will merely confirm their already low self-estimation and prove how really "dumb" they are. So they do a halfhearted job and accept a low grade rather than risk such confirmation. Any teacher who accepts such work (out of a desire to appear "positive" toward the child) may only confirm the child's worst fears.

I am guessing that many teachers above fifth grade working with "low-achievers" or even with "average" kids would feel lucky to get 3s and 4s on the Scale A classroom survey, with only an occasional 5. And yet love of learning and pursuit of mastery is what teaching is all about! It's what people become teachers for.

There may always be required courses that some students will not have much interest in, and there will be periods when students are so wrapped up in their own emotional and social lives that their studies take a backseat. But how strange that classroom conversations are so rarely concerned with "love of learning" or with kids "really getting good at" something, in contrast to talk about grades, exams, or deadlines. Could it be that by *not* mentioning love of learning and pursuit of mastery, by *not* inviting our students to see how they relate to those aspirations, we contribute to an atmosphere of "indifference," "boredom," or "mild interest"?

How Teachers Relate to "the Stuff"

It is rare for teachers to poll students on their attitudes toward the material they are teaching. It is even rarer for teachers to pose such questions, openly, to themselves. These are considered private thoughts, to be shared (if at all) with trusted colleagues, not with students. Hence my second scale. I challenge teachers not only to complete it but to invite students to fill it out according to *their* perceptions of how they see us connecting to what we are teaching.

Scale B: Relationship of Teacher to the Material or Academic Task

1	2	3	4	5
Boredom, resentment	Perfunctory transmittal	Getting material across, teaching to the test	Teacher-as-learner, role model for students	Passionate teaching

If we were privy to a teacher's thoughts about the material, we might hear the following:

1. "Why do they make me I teach this garbage? I'd hate to learn it, if I were a kid."

2. "I'm getting paid to try to get this stuff across to the kids. So let's get on with it."

3. "It's my professional responsibility to teach this effectively, and it'll be on The Test."

4. "This material is quite interesting. I want to learn more about it so I can teach it well."

5. "I *love* this stuff and will do whatever I can to share my excitement with my students."

This scale raises the image of teacher-as-learner to what I think is its proper stature in the realm of pedagogy. "You can

only teach well what you, too, are learning" is the aphorism.[1]
Again, we might find, depending on the school, that a survey of
teachers' attitudes would disclose a concentration around the
middle, 3, with a modest array of 4s and some 2s and 5s. But
what would happen if teachers in a school (or within a department or grade level) regularly surveyed themselves in regard to
this question? And if they then set aside time to discuss the obstacles to their moving from point 3 to 4 or from 4 to 5? Would
not that very act of analysis, reflection, and conversation lead to
more individual and collaborative efforts toward intense and
satisfying teaching?

Pressing the issue further, what would be the effect of a
teacher asking his students to share their impressions of his engagement with the material? Would he be pleasantly surprised
to discover how many students felt that he was "really excited
about this stuff"?[2] Might not that discovery lead to yet more
fruitful interchanges?

Scales C and D explore how students and teachers relate to
each other with respect to the material to be learned.

Scale C: Relationship of Students to the Teacher Regarding Academic Work

1	2	3	4	5
Animosity, indifference	Grudging or minimal compliance	Respectful compliance	Working to make the grade or to please the teacher	True learning partnership

And, once more, as students might say it (to themselves or to
each other):

1. "I've no idea *why* he's making us learn this stuff—he's not
   doing it for *my* benefit."

2. "I'll do what I have to so she won't hassle me about getting it done."

3. "You're the teacher—you must think this stuff is worth-while, or else you wouldn't make us learn it. So I'll give it a shot."

4. "I'm an A (or B) student and I'm ready to do whatever my teacher thinks is right."

5. "*Wow!* Our teacher thinks this is really cool stuff—and it probably is!"

Scale D: Relationship of Teacher to the Students Regarding Academic Work

1	2	3	4	5
Burnout, indifference, "waste of my time"	Defensive monitoring	Hoping for decent results	Interactive coaching, optimism, eagerness	True learning partnership

1. "These kids don't deserve me. I'm wasting my time try-ing to teach this stuff to them." *Or* "Hey, no big deal. We get along just fine—I leave them alone; they leave me alone."

2. "My job is to expose students to the material, keep order, and get my grades in on time."

3. "*Some* kids are getting it. Maybe, years from now, the oth-ers will remember something."

4. "I'm going to help these kids really know this stuff; I think I can get everyone involved."

5. "We're doing amazing stuff together. They're learning from me, and I from them."

A Learner-Centered Cosmology

Most of those of us who grew up and went to school in the last half-century attended teacher-centered classrooms. Students of the twenty-first century will, increasingly, be attending learner-centered classrooms. The difference is roughly comparable to that between the Ptolemaic and Copernican views of the solar system. Long after most people were intellectually convinced that the sun was the center of our solar system and that the earth and other planets revolved around the sun, people's natural reasoning—what Howard Gardner calls our "unschooled minds"—kept telling us that the sun rises in the east, makes its way across our skies, and sets in the west in its journey around the earth.

Thus with the cosmology of the classroom. We are convinced—intellectually—that learners today have a vast network of information sources at their disposal: from the library to the Internet, from television to computers, and that we, as teachers, are but one source of information (however vital). We think the learner is central, and we teachers can best serve that center by coaching learners in their acquisition of skills and knowledge needed to access the many informational resources available. So we think.

But our emotional roots lie in the teacher-centered classrooms of our youth, memories both happy and sad. And our unschooled minds cling to the image of a teacher as the fixed source of knowledge, radiating it out to the students who orbit around us.

The problem with this Ptolemaic view of the classroom is that it reinforces the idea of the teacher as authority figure, dispenser of information, controller or manager of all behaviors and activities. Adults (administrators, teachers, parents) often find such a view comforting in its lack of ambiguity of who is "in charge" and who is "accountable" for effectively "deliver-ing the curriculum." Most kids accept it, too, for it reduces their responsibility for motivating themselves and allows them to play at the game of "kids versus grown-ups" whenever they detect a lapse of authority (e.g., when a substitute teacher takes over).

But both adults and children are ultimately losers in a game played for control of the classroom, where the responsibility of learners for their own success—so evident in infants and pre-school children—is too often viewed in terms of compliance rather than initiative, engagement, and pride. In maintaining the teacher-centered classroom, we retard the development of children as passionate learners, even as we confine ourselves within a "command and control" paradigm of instruction.

Note that in the first two scales, A and B, our focus was on the relationship of students and teachers to the academic mate-rial and tasks set forth by the teacher. In scales C and D we ask the more typical question of how are the teacher and students getting along with one another in the instructional/learning process. And in both I offer the concept of a dynamic learning partnership as the ideal to shoot for.

A caution: this learning partnership requires a level of shared responsiveness among students and teacher that goes against the traditional hierarchy of school. Such mutuality is critical to the emergence of a learner-centered school of the fu-ture. There is something powerful in the idea of a partnership across the age-and-experience span of teacher and students. In a learning partnership, the implied assumption is that "We'd be doing this, even if we didn't have to," or that "We are each re-ceiving something special from working together in this way, on this (project, concept, skill, etc.)."

Many of us raised in conventional schools experienced shared ownership of our learning only in extracurricular activities, like sports, the arts, summer camp, scouting, or church groups, and we had to wait until graduate school (if then) to feel that we were respected as "junior partners" academically. I'm not sure where it ought to begin, but elementary school doesn't seem too early for such a learning partnership to take place.

Another way to look at the learning partnership is in contrast to the other definitions on the scale. Working backward, on scale C, from a 5 ("True learning partnership"), a 4 ("Working for grade or to please the teacher") represents the norm in a good school, with well-disciplined and motivated learners. Most teachers are quite content if students do their work well, out of respect for the teacher or to earn a high grade. Mary Montle Bacon, a noted psychologist and advocate for African-American children and divergent learners from all cultures, once pointed out that "kids will do the work—even in a subject they don't like—for a teacher whom they really like. And they won't work—even in a subject they're good at—for a teacher they don't like." She paused while the assembled school educators nodded complacently. "So—when was the last time you signed up for a workshop on the topic 'How to Be *Liked* by *More* of My Students'?" she demanded, provoking a general look of embarrassment in the crowd.

Why that reaction? Why does it seem so strange to suggest that we owe it to ourselves (not only to our students) to figure out how we can make it easier for students to "like" us? What keeps so many academics from acknowledging that likability is a worthy goal to strive for? I won't gainsay a teacher who is proud of the large percentage of his or her students working hard to earn an A or a B, or out of a fearsome respect for the teacher's authority. But what happens after the grading stops or the threat subsides? How quickly the motivation fades. Yes, there may be more important things than being liked by one's students, but over the long run, esteem (rather than fear) may well produce better learning.

Still on scale C, a 3 ("Respectful compliance") reflects a goal of many teachers. It's a lot more pleasant than disrespect or *non-*compliance. But there's little assurance that students find any value in the subject being learned—aside from the fact that a teacher, whom they have been taught to respect, has assigned such work and expects them to complete it.

As for a 2 ("Grudging or minimal compliance") or a 1 ("Animosity/indifference"), nobody believes that such attitudes lead to academic success. The 1s and 2s allow disaffected students to identify where they stand, as individuals and as a class, in relation to their teacher. By discussing each category of responses, teacher and students can think about how to improve their relationship. That, in turn, may lead to improvements on scale A, how students relate to the material they've been asked to learn. The two are closely linked.

On scale D we are chiefly concerned with the teacher's "stance," how the teacher positions herself in relation to the students and the work she wants them to accomplish.[3] The scale goes from a 1, our nightmare of an exhausted, embittered practitioner, to a 5, representing a passionate teacher in an authentic learning partnership with students.

A common but problematic score is a 2, where the teacher basically sees himself as the guardian of knowledge against the attempts of undeserving students to get away with not learning it well or at all.[4] Such a teacher is preoccupied with compliance, with possible cheating, with defending her grades against any challenge by students or parents. Typically a teacher with this stance will keep a rank book filled with minute records of student behavior (academic or otherwise) in which the quality of the work being performed is less important than punctuality and compliance.

In between are scores 3 and 4. The 3s ("Hopeful of decent results") believe that satisfactory performance is likely from only a minority of students, and they feel they are "there" mainly for those students they view as "promising." But 3s, like 2s, are preoccupied with instructing, monitoring, and grading. Teachers who rate themselves as 4s, by contrast, exude optimism regarding student performance and, like good coaches, want to see success happen for all or most students. They represent the "good teachers" most of us have experienced, those who do all they can to help students learn.

But "good teachers" are held back from becoming "passionate teachers" by a school and classroom culture that makes genuine student/teacher partnership a rarity. We won't see more than a few teachers reaching a 5 ("True learning partnership") without deep and substantive changes in the ways schools and classrooms are organized.

CHAPTER NINE

Parents and Curriculum

A Partnership with Students and Teachers

Among all the players in the education of children, parents are most likely to be found sitting on the bench when it comes to curriculum. I think it's a huge mistake—and we educators shoulder the blame. We've generally kept curriculum to ourselves. For parents, gaining access to the curriculum, and to their children's feelings about their teachers in relation to academic work, helps answer the question, What can I do to help my child and her teacher establish a respectful and productive relationship? And it leads to other questions:

- What can I tell my child's teacher that will help her anticipate and respond appropriately to whatever learning difficulties or inhibitions my child possesses?

- What can I learn about the teacher's personality and style that can help me work with my child at home so that she will get the most out of her experience with that teacher?

- How open is the teacher to my sharing with her the evidences of my child's past successes (or frustrations, or both) in various skills areas, as part of our ability to work together for my child's academic success?

&. What will alert me to a potentially serious breakdown in communication and trust between my child and her teacher that might warrant intervention at another level (administrator or guidance counselor)?

Pattie Knight, whom I have known for several years, is the director of an after-school literacy program in Roxbury, Massachusetts, with links to Northeastern University. She has been actively involved in communicating regularly with her daughters' teachers about their education, and she spreads the word to other parents. She told me:

It's one of the things I tell all my parents, here at the center, and it's something I have done each year, even when my daughters were in preschool. I send their teachers a letter of introduction: This is who I am. These are my standards; this is my background, both educationally and culturally. I give them our family history; I tell them about my kid's personality, her likes and dislikes; I tell them some of the things they can expect from me and what I expect from them.

And the real message, the bottom line, is to say "I'm working *with* you, but these are *still* my kids. You only have them for a year, but I have them for life." I want to establish a partnership with teachers, to say "as long as my kids are in your class, then you and I need to figure out a way for us to work things out."

With my daughters, I say to them, "You don't ever have to *like* your teachers. You *will* always have to respect them. You *will* have to do what they tell you to do. And when you have a problem with it, you bring it to me.

And there have been times when teachers have made bad decisions. And I say to my daughters, "Now, that's *my* problem.

I'll go and deal with that." I let the teachers know: "I'll show up when I *feel* like showing up. I won't be disruptive, and I won't be disrespectful. But I'll be there when I want to see what's happening. And I don't need your permission to go into class, to question something that you're doing. Those are *my* kids."

I think my kids are fine; they aren't going to get into a whole bunch of personality conflicts with their teachers. But I advise some other parents who do have kids with *issues.* And I say to them, "You know, you really should have told the teacher, up front, that these are some 'issues' your kid is likely to get into. So that they'll know."

Parents as Partners

Scale E focuses on the relationship of students, parents and teachers to the academic work:

Scale E: Relationship of Students, Parents, and Teacher Regarding Academic Work

1	2	3	4	5
Cynicism, anger, lack of trust	No genuine communication	Acceptance without understanding	Frequent, friendly communication	Cooperating for student progress

It isn't so easy to construct the mental impressions of how students, parents, and teachers come to view the relationship evolving among all three concerning academic work. But here's a possible set of corresponding thoughts:

1. *Student:* "Teachers make us do stupid stuff."
    Parent: "Those teachers don't care about kids from this neighborhood."
    Teacher: "Too many of these parents don't seem to care about education."

2. *Student:* "Mom, why do I have to learn this?"
   Parent: "I don't know; your teacher must have her reasons."
   Teacher: "Most parents are too busy to get involved with school."

3. *Student:* "I gotta get my homework done."
   Parent: "That's good; just do what they tell you."
   Teacher: "Most of the parents are pretty supportive of what we do here."

4. *Student:* "Here's what we're going to be learning next."
   Parent: "I know; it was on that info sheet you brought home last week. Can I help?"
   Teacher: "I send memos to parents to let them know how best to help their kids learn."

5. *Student:* "These are the things for school we're supposed to work on together at home."
   Parent: "Looks really interesting; I hope you'll remember what Mr. Rivera told you about how to improve your writing. Now, what do you need from me to get you started?"
   Teacher: "Parent/teacher/student conferences offer us a chance to discuss what each of us needs to do to increase student understanding and to raise the level of motivation."

As I write this, today's *New York Times* has an article headlined "Report Cards Are Due, Only This Time for Parents."[1] The article invites us to imagine how it would feel, as a parent, to have the school assess our diligence in supporting our child's learning at home. There is a range of parent reactions to the "Parental Involvement Report Card" spawned in the spring of 2000 by the superintendent of the Chicago public schools, and currently being used in thirty schools, with two hundred others opting for a nongraded checklist. Some parents feel "deeply insulted" by "a one-way communication," whereas others say, "It gave me a chance to check myself and analyze my priorities. I felt it was important that I could be graded like my children." Says Chicago elementary principal Kathleen Mayer, "We're not here to say, 'You did this wrong.' Our motto is, Whatever it takes."

It will take a lot more initiatives from our nation's schools to convince parents that they have a dynamic and purposeful role to play as partners with professional educators in their children's education. It's no sweat for schools to say, "Get your kids into school on time with their homework completed and their pencils sharpened." It is something else for teachers and parents to say to one another (as in Pattie Knight's example), "The work we must do to promote and sustain this child's learning is so vital that it cannot be left just to either of us, alone, to meet this challenge. We want the child to become a self-starter, someone who eagerly and confidently seeks new skills and knowledge. I, as teacher, must be a role model for all children as a lifelong learner and as a professional dedicated to academic success for every child. I, as parent, will be an active partner and communicator with my child and his teacher, helping us all work together toward a common goal. The child looks to both of us for guidance and positive examples of what learning can bring to one's life. We two must be on the same team."

Here are a few ways parents can be active players in promoting or sustaining their children's love of learning:

- Parents should balance their desire for their child to do well in school with a commitment to maintain a child's love of learning. Whenever a child proposes an alternative to an otherwise boring assignment, the parent should carefully consider supporting the child in her

quest to make that assignment meaningful, and to share
this with the teacher—as allies working on behalf of the
child's spirit of learning.

∽ Parents should speak honestly with their kids about
"learning" versus "make work" assignments. Even if
the decision is to comply with a "dumb assignment"
rather than protest it, the child should not be confused
about parents' belief that the child's perspectives on
schoolwork are valuable. As parents, we don't always
have to close ranks with teachers when we disagree
with what they are asking our child to do.

∽ Referring back to scale A, "Relationship of Student to
the Material or Academic Task," help your child strive
to be in categories 4 ("Active interest/desire to engage)
and 5 ("Love of learning/pursuit of mastery"). Talk
with your child about how important it is to remain enthusiastic about learning and to retain the desire to master certain skills—as a reflection of the child's own
pride.

The answer to the question raised in chapter 8, "Curriculum? Who *Cares?*" is, of course, that teachers and students and
parents all have to care, and care a lot, if the goals of any curriculum are to be realized. With that in mind, let's look at the area
of curriculum that I believe to be at the core of what school, and
learning, is about: literacy and the development of the power to
use words.

CHAPTER TEN

Words of Power

When literacy is well taught and joyfully learned, it's wonderful to see:

- ❧ teachers reading books to wide-eyed children, who beg them not to stop
- ❧ children picking out their favorite books to read to themselves and to each other
- ❧ older kids coming into the kindergarten to share books with their "little buddies"
- ❧ children-authored books and stories on display at libraries and neighborhood centers
- ❧ parents, teachers, and students meeting to talk and plan together as "literacy partners"
- ❧ students having rich conversations (and even arguing) about the books they are reading
- ❧ letters to the editor written by students who obviously care deeply about issues
- ❧ teachers assigning thought-provoking take-home or open-book essay questions in place of short-answer tests, and students rising to the challenge

 ▫ teachers' book clubs that become the topic of
  lunchroom conversations

 ▫ students working on their college essays and having a
  hard time choosing among a range of issues, ideas, and
  experiences that they feel passionately about

Literacy is power, in the most meaningful sense of the term.
Reading and writing pursued in the right atmosphere become
powerful tools for children and young adults. A library card is
your first driver's license, allowing you to go anywhere in the
world you want to go. It is a vehicle of freedom, a chariot of
liberation.

All the more reason why we should be outraged, as parents,
educators, citizens, by the fact that kids in school so often experience literacy instruction as drudgery—the repetitive motion
syndrome of worksheets and spelling tests and book reports,
of teachers grading papers that students never wanted to write
in the first place, of students picking up an assigned novel as
though it were a yoke or a shackle.

Of all the sins we adults unwittingly commit against children's passionate spirit of learning, those that affect reading and
writing have the most tragic effects. As educators we forget the
empowering role of literacy in the lives of children even as we
emphasize the tactical aspects of literacy: spelling drills, grammar lessons, reading comprehension exercises.

In his remarkable *Book of Learning and Forgetting,* Frank Smith
asks the crucial question "How do we become members of the
reading and writing club? How do children—or grown-ups—
identify themselves as participants in the literate world?" Here
is his response:

> We don't have to be skilled readers to join the literacy club nor
> need we know very much about writing. Quite the contrary.
> It is not until we are members of the literacy club that we can

learn to read and to write. Literacy doesn't come as the climax
of a sustained regime of reading and writing instruction to
which we and our teachers have diligently applied ourselves.
Reading and writing should come as effortless as the understanding and mastery of speech. Everything else—all the
more prominent exercises, drills, corrections, and tests—are
distractions and sometimes insuperable obstacles on the way to
literacy . . .

   Unfortunately, whether members of the club or not, many
children when they get to school are introduced for the first
time to written language that *doesn't* make sense. . . . They may
decide or be taught that the literacy club is not for them . . .
they may learn that these are areas of life beyond their interests
and reach.[1]

Paolo Freire speaks of people "naming their world"—giving voice to the ideas, questions, imaginative journeys, skepticism, and emotions of their lives. "Literacy cannot be reduced
to experiences that are only a little creative, that treat the foun-
dations of letters and words as a purely mechanical domain."[2]

   Here is what I think: Literacy is fundamentally about intellectual power—the power of the child to reach out into the
world to gain useful information, the power to express to the
world valued thoughts and feelings. From such power comes
freedom, responsible citizenship, and social change. We see on
the face of every child as she or he first learns to speak the radiance of that power projected into the world.

   Passionate learners need to evolve as passionate readers and
writers if the promise of their early years is to be realized. It's
not all they need—it must be part of a greater vision of how
children think and feel and express themselves as people. And
some wonderfully creative and successful people in the world
are not strong writers or avid readers. But the encouragement
and celebration of literacy is primarily what formal schooling
should be about.

By the time they are into the first few years of schooling, however, too many children experience literacy as a series of activities that are not only divorced from family and community culture, but sort and label the "good readers" and "competent writers" from the "poor readers" and those who cannot or will not write. In Frank Smith's terms, experiences in school lead children to either see themselves as "members of the literacy club"—or not. As they advance up the grades, too many students see writing as a punishment; too many stop reading for pleasure once they are given routinized homework assignments or are tested on whether or not they have memorized a novel's characters, plot aspects, or symbolic meanings.

Parents and teachers devoted to child development view reading and writing as tools of emancipation, of actualization, of relatedness of self to one's culture and one's future. To focus solely on mechanics is against the best interests of children; it circumscribes their imagination instead of stimulating it and contributes to their failure to emerge as adults who are ready to take their rightful place in a democratic society.

That failure can begin in the earliest grades. I remember one painful lesson I observed several years ago. A student teacher, working from the regular teacher's lesson plans, was introducing one of those inane topical themes that substitute for authentic conversation between teacher and students about how a lesson relates to their lives. This, from my notes:

> Today, early in the month of March, the theme is (can you guess it?) "March comes in like a lion and goes out like a lamb." Now, there might be some engaging way to take on even this shopworn theme, but that is not to be. Following the teacher's lesson plans, the student teacher summons the children toward the blackboard at the front of the room. She asks them if they know what a lion is. Several nod or raise their hands. She says, "What can you tell me about a lion?"
>
> The kids, who sense the true purpose of the question, offer

a few responses in a desultory manner. "Brown," says one
child. "Very good." The student teacher writes the word *brown*
on the board. "What else?" she asks. "Big," says another boy.
That goes on the board, too. Other responses prove harder to
come by, but she manages to collect several more: "strong,"
"angry," "scary." That's it. The kids know, from past experience, what comes next. The district curriculum requires that
these first graders write two complete sentences each and every
day. The children go back to their seats to begin.

In due course they hand in their work. It has to be completed before they can go to lunch and recess. The results are
predictable. *"The lion is big. The lion is brown."* Child after child
offers up variations of the same two complete sentences and
lines up for lunch. Another triumph of literacy training.
Another reason, at age six, to become inwardly skeptical
that academic work in school has much to do with anything
of real value.

The student teacher and I were equally dismayed. The lesson
had "succeeded," according to its design, but literacy had suf-
fered a defeat. She knew it as well as I. It didn't have to be that
way. It could have been different.

Surely, as we look at the status of literacy in our society, especially among the young in this era of 135-channel cable and
video games, we have reason to despair. American students, by
and large, read only some of what they are assigned to read,
read little on their own initiative, and most of what they write
is stuff they don't really care to communicate. Reading advocate
Jim Trelease declares, "Simply put, we have 100 percent [of the
nation's children wanting to learn how to read] in Kindergarten and lose 75 percent of our potential lifetime readers by senior year. Any business that lost 75 percent of its customer base
would be in Chapter 11 overnight. That, in a nutshell, is the crisis facing America today."[3]

If we need more proof, we need only look at the quality of

student reading and writing at most colleges. Undergraduates tell me that they have not picked up a book to read, on their own, since middle school, when they were required to write book reports. I have others who dread writing so much that they rush in panic to the university's "Writing Center" before they have even thought of a topic. College students are, after all, K–12 success stories, relatively speaking. Yet for a large percentage of them, literacy is a bane. It's like paying taxes or cleaning the bathroom—you gotta do it, but nobody pretends to like it. And we're not talking here about high school dropouts, or those who feel too alienated from literate culture even to apply to college, or those who opt for vocational or trade school so that they will never again have to read a novel or write a persuasive essay.

We have largely failed, as educators, to grasp the whole picture, to embrace a vision of what a literate society would be like and what we can do in our schools to foster it. *We must embrace such a vision!* As things stand, active, engaged readers and confident, competent writers get the best of what our education system has to offer. We can argue—as many of us do—that our education system must change in areas besides literacy. But literacy remains the coin of the realm.

Literacy must become a dynamic, empowering force in the developing lives of children. We must help them join "the club" of authors and readers as active members. Literacy is the single most powerful and important subject for all children. Even for those of us who grew up surrounded by books, the culture of schooling can easily make us forget the sheer pleasure of the reading experience and of writing to help us understand our experiences. But in our role as the educators of children, we as teachers and as parents need to begin by discovering, or rediscovering, the passionate reader and writer within us.

Michele Gabor, a student in my course on children's and adolescent literature, entitled her final paper "My Harry Potter Epiphany."

My approach to teaching Reading/Language Arts was based on the belief that it was my responsibility to make reading and writing fun for my students. We'd play games to learn the vocabulary in whatever book we were reading. To improve comprehension I'd have the students act out different scenes from the book. . . .

Last Sunday night, I had an epiphany. For the past year I have assumed it was my job to make literature fun for the kids. In doing so, I was already assuming that it wasn't fun, perpetuating the belief that reading and writing are chores. If *I* believed they weren't fun, of course my students believed they were just another thing that had to be done. In all the humdrum of reading dry textbooks and professional journals, I had myself forgotten how much I loved to read.

Reading *Harry Potter* brought back the joy of reading. I remembered the endless Saturday afternoons I spent curled up reading the *Sweet Valley Twins* series. I remembered all the late nights when my mother had to yell at me to put the book away and go to bed, and all the nights I pulled out my flashlight and continued reading under my covers. With this wave of memories rushing past me, I realized that READING AND WRITING ALREADY *ARE* FUN! I don't have to *make* them fun; they are fun in and of themselves. . . .

The truth is, even with no direct instruction, reading and writing of any sort expands my students' minds and makes them better students. My job is to cultivate the love my students already have for reading and writing. With the right amount of support, my students' love for literature will grow and flourish. . . .

The students should be able to see my own enjoyment in literature by seeing me reading, by seeing me get excited about lit-

erature. I should also let the kids see that I'm a writer, too, that
it is something I do in my spare time to relax or to help me
through a problem. Setting an example and showing the students the joy I find in literature will rub off on them.

As with most teachers, I still have some questions, some
uncertainties that will only get resolved through trial and
error. What do I do if I am forced to teach certain books or
genres that I don't particularly enjoy? The biggest question still
unresolved is how I lost my love for reading and writing and
what to do if it happens again. This time, *Harry Potter* brought
those wonderful memories back and gave me new life as a
reader-for-pleasure. How do I avoid getting bogged down in required reading again? And what if this happens to my students?
I don't yet have an answer to that question.

Michele Gabor has it exactly right. *K–12 education in literacy
should be about the joys of reading and writing.* But that requires
teachers, working with students and parents, to create an atmosphere and culture in which reading and writing are intensely engaging experiences, instead of injecting literacy instruction into students who, we assume, are incapable of
experiencing those joys on their own. But neither can we coun-
tenance the huge gaps between students who do—and do not
or cannot—read and write well.

Some argue for teaching literacy all day long to students
reading and writing "below level." Others hold for an approach
that incorporates literacy with art, music, and other subjects. I
find myself on both sides of the argument:

> "We must devote most of our time and resources in school to
> helping all students learn to read and write well. Literacy is our
> foremost educational responsibility. To do otherwise is to per-
> petuate inequality."
>
> "But what if, by doing so, we deprive these same children of

a rich and varied learning experience, one that appeals to all of their intelligences, and by our single-mindedness make them resent literacy because they have been browbeaten with endless drills, quizzes, worksheets, and grammar lessons?"

"Well, then, we must learn how to teach literacy in a more effective and more community-centered way, bringing parents and neighbors into the conversation, so that children come to see reading and writing as a natural extension of their cultural identity, rather than as a repudiation of it."

"Easier said than done—especially when literacy education takes place under the gun of high-stakes standardized tests that pressure teachers and kids to focus ever more narrowly on test-preparation techniques, to the detriment of child-centered and culture-friendly approaches. We ought rather to champion the right of children to an education centered around ideas, curiosity, conversation, real-life experiences."

"Look at the record of failure that surrounds us—the dysfunctional illiteracy! The tests may be flawed, but without the pressure for accountability that such tests provide, we would sink back into the inertia and inequity that has long characterized school systems that serve people in under-resourced neighborhoods."

"The affliction is real enough, but we cannot apply bad medicine as a cure. We will only be doing a further disservice to our most at-risk children by punishing them with a top-down, regimented, insensitive barrage of canned literacy instruction."

I hear such arguments and counterarguments as I work in Boston schools and at Northeastern University. My evolving stance, as an advocate for passionate learners, is this: Teaching literacy is the most important thing we do in school. But it cannot be taught as an isolated, classroom-by-classroom technique-dominated instructional activity. Literacy must be about power, about dignity, about freedom. Literacy instruction is about helping each student develop a curious and truth-seeking mind, along with the skills and habits needed to extend the reach and power of the intellect. It should be taught with the interests of passionate learners in mind—in full awareness of our moral responsibility to help all of our children build an academic, economic, aesthetic, civic, and interpersonal foundation for life.

I see literacy taking up maybe two-thirds of the time children spend in school. But, that said, children should spend less time being formally instructed and more time reading on their own and developing their minds and their personalities through exploring the natural environment, drawing and painting, discussing and debating ideas and issues that mean something to them. These, in turn, provide stimuli for meaningful exercises in reading, writing, and speaking. For older students, literacy should be combined with off-campus apprenticeships in areas of personal interest—things they are passionate about and can build a reflective record on.

How we teach literacy is more important than *how much* we teach it. Our goals should focus on children reflecting and building upon—in class—the reading and writing they do *outside* of class, on their own initiative, and on helping kids develop good writing habits, such as self- and peer-editing. As I will argue in the next chapter, literacy instruction should take place in a "literacy lab," where such talents and skills get developed and practiced.

I propose that literacy instruction be a structured group activity, a social and community enterprise, punctuated by free-reading periods when everyone (including the teacher, nurse, custodian) takes out a book—rather than view literacy as "schoolwork" done by children working alone at their desks or as homework exercises.

For kids of all ages, acceptance by peers is the measure of

their standing and self-respect. People do learn from the company they keep. If their friends are reading, they will read; if their friends are working on projects that involve researching, interviewing others, writing things up and presenting their findings or opinions to a worthwhile audience, then they will want to engage in these things.

By contrast, if the only kids who read and write conscientiously are the "honors" kids—the self-motivated or parent-directed individuals who are already wired for college and high-status careers—then for many other students, reading and writing will come to represent frustrating, futile, humiliating toil rather than adventurous self-discovery.

This point cannot be overstated. A school in which literacy has become, by design or by default, an elite club for the top students and a workhouse of remedial exercises for the rest is a school that endangers our democratic society.

Literacy as Power

I propose that teachers and parents should be explicit about why literacy achievement is so important. Here is my version of "talking points" that teachers and parents might use as part of a conversation with children about literacy. I have drafted this to be used in grades six through nine, but it could be adjusted for other grades as well. It goes like this:

> *Knowledge is power.* People with knowledge and skills are able to do more things than people who don't know the stuff, who don't have the skills, or who don't know how to learn what they need to know. Everybody agrees about this, right?

> *School is a place to become powerful through knowledge and skills.* It's not the *only* place (libraries, after-school activities, jobs, neighborhood activity centers, church groups, hobbies, friends, family members, the Internet, even some television

programs can help), but school can be one of the very best places to acquire the tools to make your mind powerful—*if the conditions are right*.

❧ *You've already learned the hardest skill: speaking!* Everybody comes to school able to speak the language they learned at home. If you're good at more than one language or dialect, this is an incredible gift that you should by all means hang onto. It's also important to speak the language of books, newspapers, businesses, and colleges. Your challenge is to add "standard English" to the language you come from home with. School should *never* make you ashamed of the language of your parents and your neighborhood—it should give you access to other languages and make you more powerful.

❧ *Reading and writing can be great fun.* They often require concentration and effort, and it usually takes everyone a long time to learn to do them well. Without good reading, writing, speaking, and listening skills, it's really hard to get where you want to go. Reading and writing should *never* be used as punishments (such as a five-hundred-word essay about "Why I should not talk back to my teacher").

❧ *Why should you learn to read well?* Reading is your ticket to the world of ideas and people who can help you become the person you want to be. Reading can save you lots of time in not having to discover everything by yourself. (I'd rather read about being bit by a shark than have to learn about it through experience.) It's a way to let your imagination take you on a trip to see and do things in your mind that can shape your life.

❧ *Why should you learn to write well?* This is a good question. Talking is so much easier than writing, for most people. But someday you will want to connect with people beyond your friends and your family. It may be for a job, or for college, or because you want to let some politician or newspaper know how you feel. *Writing is how you let the rest of the world know how well you think.* People may judge the quality of your mind on how you write, and they will open or close doors for you based on that judgment. Writing also helps you become aware of what you think. It gives you a way to develop your ideas.

 What should you rely on your teachers for? Think of your teachers as coaches—only, instead of basketball or soccer or cheerleading, they are trying to help you become really good at understanding what you read, putting your ideas on paper, and speaking your mind in a convincing way. Good coaches are friendly but tough; they expect you to do your best; they show you how to avoid mistakes and how to enhance your talents. They never do it *for* you, but they are always on your side.

 What must you do for yourself? You will never learn to read and write well if you do it only in school or for homework. Reading and writing are not things you do mostly for other people—like teachers. You do them for yourself, on your own time, in your own way. That may be hard, but it's the truth. The desire and energy must come from you. It's your future.[4]

One ought not impose such a series of arguments on a group of students—it would seem to them like a trick to get them to agree to what the teacher wants them to do. Better to begin with a shared inquiry into the nature of literacy and see where the conversation goes. For example, a teacher might turn these arguments into a series of questions: "What does 'Knowledge Is Power' mean?" "Do you see school as a place to become mentally 'powerful'?"

The questions "Why learn to read?" "Why learn to write?" are too important to be posed and then answered by the teacher (as I have done above). Teachers should try to rework these focus points and questions into topics for discussion.

Malcolm Mitchell, Teacher of Literacy

Let's hear from a teacher who is trying to "do the right thing" with regard to literacy instruction for a challenging group of kids. Malcolm Mitchell is in his first year of teaching sixth grade humanities (combined English and social studies) in the Josiah Quincy Upper School in Boston populated mostly by students who are of Asian and of African-American heritage:

> My elementary education was an interesting story. I grew up in Cambridge, which was very multicultural, lots of diversity. Some of the experiences I had in Cambridge really helped shape me. I had, at Peabody Elementary School, probably the first black principal in Cambridge, a man named Ronald Walker, whom I'm still good friends with. He was really a role model for me, someone I could identify with—just the way he interacted with me. School wasn't just a place where you came to "behave and do your work." It was a place where I felt I had somebody there who cared about me. Mr. Walker would put his arm around my shoulder and ask, "Did you eat your breakfast this morning?" walking me around the school, just talking with me. It wasn't that he treated me so special—it was that he just expected me to do well, that I was "a good kid—Hey! I know what you're capable of." Those kinds of things were really powerful.
>
> My approach to teaching is that you have some kids with tough issues, and some kids who excel, but the majority are in the middle, and they need attention, too. It's easier for many of them to turn their hats around backward and let their pants hang halfway down their butt than it is to go home, study, and go to the library. So you have to deal with kids who think it's more important to fit in.

I asked him to say more about those he sees as "kids in the middle." Does he see them as readers? Or as kids who have yet to be recruited to become part of the literate world?

> There's no doubt—they need to be recruited. So much of their life is what they see and hear on television or through their mu-

sic, which many kids listen to for forty minutes while they're walking or riding the bus to school in the morning. So to read is a stretch. And I tell them that in my college years, when I'd be walking down the street with a few of my friends, I'd often see white people cross the street so as not to have to pass by us. To avoid me!? I mean, I was raised the proper way; I used to help old ladies carry their groceries; my mom would make me hold a door open; I would never curse in front of adults. But these people on the street wouldn't know that about me.

So I say to my students, "This happens to people like us every day. But how do you know what people of another race are really thinking, if you never take an opportunity to speak with them and get to know them?" And I said, "I used to be like that, before I went to college, stereotyping people, you know, '*all* girls think this,' or '*all* white people think like that,' or 'all teachers . . . .' " And we broke it down, racially and everything. I wanted them to know that when I was a kid, I did what they did; I thought what they thought. And they said, "Mr. Mitchell—you *crazy*. You just like my father" or "My mother thinks like that."

I had their attention, and I wanted to stir them up. So I brought in all these books from my college years—sociology books, novels, poetry, books on how women think about things, books on people who have immigrated to this country—and in each book, I put a tab on a passage that was gripping or intense. Then I said, "So what happened to me that made a difference? I listened to some *voices*. And they weren't people who were speaking to me, face to face. But I found these voices. And I've brought them all in today. And now they are in my closet, here in the classroom."

And the kids were wondering, "Who's in the closet? You got people in there? Is it your wife? Is it your son? Is it a guest speaker?" They all wanted to be the first to go and see who was inside. So I chose a boy and a girl, and they opened the door, and they said, "What!!!?"

And I picked out the first book, a book called *Always Running,* about a Mexican family in southern California. Where I opened to, a boy was being chased by a gang, and I said to the girl, "Read that!" And she was just standing there, and then she took it back to her seat; and it just flowed from there.

One or two at a time, I let them go into the closet and see who those voices are that made such a difference for me. And they'd pick out something and bring it back and sit down and open it up. And at the end, it's like a wrestling match with me trying to get the books out of their hands. These kids will sit there, for twenty-five or thirty minutes at a time, and read. Or they will raise their hands to ask why this person was thinking like this, or to say, "You mean to tell me that . . ." and they will go on and discuss what they see on the page. And I say, "Well, write it down in your journal."

It was *out of control!* Kids would come in, every day, and head straight for the closet. "Mr. Mitchell, can I read this?" or "Mr. Mitchell, can we go to the closet, today?" You have a young African-American boy reading about the first Chinese immigrants to Boston and what they experienced. This is an intense experience for a sixth grader. It has value. Before, when I would give him one of the books we were supposed to be reading for school, it was like pulling teeth to get them to read for ten minutes.

Kids are imitators. And when they identify with you and with what makes you think and act, they want a piece of that. They want to know how I can remember passages from all these books. Because they don't remember the book they read last week. And it meant something that I could remember these passages in these books. It was an opportunity for them to connect with me and to experience what I was experiencing when I was in my twenties. And then—Wow! They want to go to college; they want to do this. And that's what a classroom should do. It should help children visualize their goals, to say to themselves, "One day, I'm gonna become . . ." whatever it is they want to be.

I asked Malcolm about writing: Our kids don't see a lot of adults reading, and they see even fewer writing. And what about the way kids write, the grammar they use?

> I teach the grammar as it applies to the lesson. It's a question of awareness. I circle something on their page and then give them the opportunity to go back and edit what they write. It goes back to what we said about finding new voices. One Asian boy, reading a poem about an African-American that includes lots of dialect, said, "Mr. Mitchell, I can't read this stuff. I'm not black." And that was a learning moment. That was a teaching moment. That was a time when we stopped and talked about "Why are we in this class? What are we trying to learn?" That's why I think we need to help kids understand that there is a power in language, and that there is a way we can all communicate and understand one another, using our language.

The Community Connection

For such a commitment as Malcolm Mitchell's to literacy to be successful, especially in schools that are populated by students from families with less formal education and economic power, the emphasis must extend beyond the school to include the community—its cultural agencies, places of worship, local leaders, and, most of all, parents. The importance of this inclusiveness is illustrated by the following story:

I recently spoke with an African-American colleague of mine at Northeastern University. He told me he visited a local neighborhood in Roxbury, Massachusetts, and met a high school student who told him, "I like to read, but I can't be seen at school with a book in my hand, because the other kids accuse me of 'acting white.'"

Hearing him, I feel, at first, completely paralyzed. I imagine myself to be that young man's English teacher. I see the spark in his eyes when I'm talking about Shakespeare, or Hemingway, or

Toni Morrison. And then I hear this about "acting white," and I look at myself in the mirror and say, "What am I going to do? Am I the wrong color to tell him, and the rest of the class, "No, you've got it wrong? Reading books is not 'acting *white*,' it's acting *smart!*" What credibility will I have?

I can image what the kids' response might be—silence, a few muttered phrases, or some variation of my own teenage sons' "*Whatever, Dad.*" And the realization comes: No matter how good a teacher I think I might be, *I can't win this battle alone.* I can't do it by myself. I have to find some allies, in the home and in the neighborhood, and especially here in the classroom among the students themselves. It is arrogance, on any teacher's part, to believe that one can, acting alone, meet the challenge of literacy for one's students. Malcolm Mitchell can't do it alone. Without support from colleagues, parents, leaders in the community who are respected by the kids, much of Malcolm Mitchell's good work will be undone, his lessons unlearned, as his students move on to other teachers.

We want to say to all our children, "Reading and writing is your ticket to the world. We want every one of you to have that opening—even (or especially!) if you use it to gain skills and experience at college that you can bring back to your neighborhood." But to make that message real, teachers must find allies in that neighborhood, and at school, who can reinforce that message with cultural authenticity.

So let us assume that when teaching a diverse group of schoolchildren coming from various family and cultural backgrounds, we will have a rich array of strengths and resources to connect to, as well as a number of obstacles to overcome and a partnership to forge. Here are my suggestions of some approaches to literacy that a broad spectrum of teachers might agree with:

∾ A greater emphasis on literacy education does not simply mean more "time on task." It is primarily a matter of the quality of the relationships and of the experience. But in attempting to bring children from nonliterate households to a point where their reading and writing skills afford them options for higher education and full citizenship, we must increase the time spent on the *right kinds* of literacy education.

∾ A renewed literacy emphasis is for all kids. Children all along the socioeconomic spectrum need literacy experiences that are richer, self-directed, and stimulating. Most affluent kids have sufficient family and peer support to access higher education regardless of whether or not they enjoy reading and writing. But such an endowment won't make them good readers or more thoughtful citizens.

∾ Teachers and students ought never have to choose between activities that promote literacy and those that stimulate children's intellect through conversational, artistic, physical, and scientific pursuits. They must be integrated, so that children read and write about what interests them, and so that teachers help expand the range and depth of children's inquiries into issues of meaning and value.

∾ Finally, even as we try to produce more teachers who celebrate with children what Eleanor Duckworth calls "the having of wonderful ideas" as the highest priority of schooling, we must give our best guidance and inspiration to all teachers currently in the classroom who seek to do the right thing in regard to literacy but who work under tough conditions and with less-than-exemplary training and skills.[5] They need guidance, and they need to feel that doing the right thing is within their grasp.

Parents and Kids: Literacy on the Home Front

There are at least two basic issues of reading that most parents encounter. The first is with a child who has difficulty decoding words and is struggling in school, a child for whom regular homework assignments that involve reading are often very frustrating.

The second concerns the capable but nonperforming reader, the child who can read but chooses to spend her or his time doing everything but.

The symptoms may look the same: children who would rather talk on the phone to their friends, play video games, listen to their music, watch television, or engage in sports or musical activity—any or all of these things—rather than pick up a book and read it.

I was, for a time, in the first category. Classes in our elementary school were ranked in order of "smartness," 4–1 being supposedly made up of more capable kids than 4–5. It was fourth grade, and I was in 4–4. It seemed fine with me—I liked my teacher okay—but my mom was worried. She talked to the school and found out that I had been deemed a "slow reader." A friend warned her not to interfere with the school's decisions, but my mom sat me down with books, for a half-hour a day, and read with me. It seemed to work—actually I don't remember much about it—but I ended up in 5–2 and then 6–1.

Lily, a friend of our family, has intervened in a much more structured way with her son. She was told that the school wanted to "code" him for special education help in reading, but she knew that he hated being pulled out of his classes and sent somewhere else for another dose of what wasn't working in his own classroom. "They were good teachers, but they didn't believe in teaching phonics—and he needed the keys to open that door." So Lily asked the special education teacher what kind of intervention he would recommend (in this case, a phonics-based approach) and wrote away for the booklets. "I came to school and watched a special ed aide working with these materials," she said.

For about forty minutes a day over a period of three years, from fourth through sixth grades, she worked on phonics with her son at home. "It was never his favorite thing to do, but he did it," she told me. "He tends to look at the middle of a page and start guessing. This works great for him on the soccer field, but it's not a great way to read text. I had to remind him, 'Start over *here*—on the *left*—and move *this* way.' Although he still has some difficulties with text, the work certainly has paid off. We never allowed them to 'code' him, and now he's in honors English and history in high school and doing well."

What these two stories have in common is a mother able to be at home with her children when they return from school. Not many parents are in a position to do that these days, and most will have to rely on the school to carry the burden of teaching literacy. But along with having the time, both my mother and our friend Lily insisted on their right to be an educational partner with the school.

The second issue around reading is one I suspect even more parents are familiar with—the kid who *can* read but chooses *not* to. Even back in the days before radio, when reading was one of the few indoor pastimes available, not very many people chose to do any serious reading. Now, with every imaginable sort of media accessible to most children, the competition is stiff for time that might be spent in free reading. Parents who want to encourage their children to read on their own (as opposed to just reading what's assigned for homework) have their work cut out for them. Some try to control the television set or video games—no television/video games until homework is done; no television during the weekdays; one hour of television permitted for every hour of reading.

We faced this with our two boys with, initially, little success. The desire to spend time with friends (in person or on the phone), or playing guitar, or listening to music, or exploring the intricacies of the computer was a lot stronger than the pull of a book. In more sports-oriented families, practice and game schedules, combined with homework, militate against free reading. And then, of course, there are the after-school jobs for older students. Where will kids find time to read?

The truth, I suspect, is that given all the competing interests and activities of today's youth, kids who "just don't like to read that much" are probably not going to do much of it. I was tearing my hair out for a few years, as I watched my kids do almost anything but pick up a book in their spare time. I even considered bribing them—five bucks to complete a serious novel. Nothing worked until they went off to college—and then (out of eyesight of their overeager father), they began reading.

The most useful role for parents to play, I believe, is to read to your children when they are young (and even when they get older—my sons allowed me to read *Watership Down* to them in their early teens), and *let them see you reading* and talking about stuff you're reading. Something will get implanted. Kids will associate reading with things that grown-ups just naturally do. As long as you don't make too much of an issue about it (a real danger, in my case), most kids will come into their own, as readers, as they mature. As Frank Smith might put it, keep good company with books and authors, and your children will want to "join the club," too.

Knowledge is power. Literacy is about discovering and amplifying and refining and celebrating the power of one's imagination, one's aspirations, one's ability to connect with the world. Now let's see more about how to make this happen in the classroom.

CHAPTER ELEVEN

A "Good Enough"

Literacy Program

As I write this chapter, I am spending time each week working with sixth and seventh grade students, mostly Asian- and African-American, at the Josiah Quincy Upper School, a middle school in Boston. Many are from low-income families, many from immigrant families. It is a new and fascinating but also frustrating experience for me. Nothing in my experience has quite prepared me for this. My favorite theories fly out the window even as I grasp at them to try to restore my confidence after a brash eleven-year-old has laid me flat with an offhand remark.

The kids I'm working with are in two non-honors humanities classes, and I am assisting their teachers to try to achieve better performance in writing and independent reading—the reading that kids do on their own. Reading and writing are not favorite subjects for many of these kids, and my work teaches me humility and appreciation of the skilled professionals who do this work year after year and do it well.

In the sixth grade class, David Crane (a former attorney in

his first year of classroom teaching) asked me to teach a unit on poetry, partly so he can observe his kids from the back of the room. In the seventh grade class, as mentioned previously, I'm working with Jim Heffron to change students' attitudes toward writing. For most of these students, literacy is just about the last thing on their minds.

Few of these sixth and seventh graders believe that reading, and writing especially, has much to offer them. Literacy is something that few have been "good at." More often than not, reading and writing have been exasperating and embarrassing. What's more, literacy is something they see few adults in their lives making much use of. "Why do we have to do this—it's *boring!*" is the refrain. It doesn't seem to matter that their teacher and I have allowed them to select the topics they write on, or to choose books from a closet full of popular middle school novels. Actually, such freedom has had *some* salutary effect, particularly when we have encouraged them to prepare their best piece of writing for a class publication.

But clearly, for most, problems with grammar and mechanics (run-on sentences, lack of subject-verb agreement, punctuation errors), plus a tendency to write the minimum number of words that will enable them to "get by," stand as obstacles and reminders of previous failure.

Changing kids' attitudes here doesn't come easy—at least (to quote an old Maine saying) "not to me, it don't!" I am approaching some kind of crisis point. I cannot bear to watch these kids roll along in their studies, glad enough to come to school to be with their friends but largely unwilling to take reading and writing seriously. I feel I'm in danger of losing faith that I can make a real contribution here, to these students or their teachers. I am anxious to find something that will *work*.

But I'm convinced that nothing will "work" in the long run unless it brings about a fundamental change in these kids' attitudes toward literacy. Unless we are able to engage these kids in a genuine dialogue—to reach them *where they are* in their young lives and convince them that reading and writing can unlock genuine opportunities for them—we will make little progress. I wonder to myself what it means to do a "good enough" job at this. The whole experience reminds me how hard a job it is to teach literacy to kids who apparently aren't interested in it.

In 1987, the eminent child psychologist Bruno Bettelheim wrote a book on child rearing entitled *A Good Enough Parent*. He begins by noting that "perfection is not within the grasp of ordinary human beings. Efforts to attain it typically interfere with that lenient response to the imperfections of others, including those of one's child, which alone make good human relations possible." Bettelheim continues:

> But it is quite possible to be a good enough parent—that is, a parent who raises his child well. To achieve this, the mistakes we make in rearing our child —errors often made just because of the intensity of our emotional involvement in and with our child—must be more than compensated for by the many instances in which we do right by our child.[1]

I want to suggest a similar stance for teachers and parents with regard to literacy for children and teenagers. The perfect literacy program is not an achievable goal; a "good enough" literacy strategy just might be—one in which the mistakes we make, while trying to have every child read and write to some desired standard, are more than balanced by the things we do correctly. Getting everything right is impossible. Getting the most important things right for all kids, most of the time, is a goal worth shooting for.

A "Good Enough" Literacy in a Small New England Town
Last week I interviewed Christine Teague, who is about my age and has four sons, three of whom are in college or have gradu-

ated and the other a junior in high school. Chris served with me
on the local school board and later was its chair. She has just
completed a master's in elementary education and has obtained
certification as a reading specialist, and she has been working
for the past three years in a nearby town, where she now heads
the reading program. When Chris and her husband first moved
to New Hampshire in 1975, they bought a home in this town
and lived there for seven years before moving to Concord. So
for Chris, who grew up in a "factory town" in Maine, coming
to work in this community was a kind of homecoming in more
ways that one.

This is a classic New England factory town. There are still
several factories here, and much of its self-reliant, neighborly,
downtown character remains. The town has a sizable group of
highly educated young professional families who want their
children to be able to compete in the global marketplace. And
like many towns its size, it is also home to young families struggling to meet the basic daily needs of their children.

Typically (as in many urban and suburban communities),
children from the two groups begin school at significantly different ability levels in literacy. And from then on, despite the
good intentions of teachers, the gap widens, as some children
experience high levels of academic success and others struggle
and become frustrated or disillusioned.

I asked Chris about her perception of literacy instruction at
the town's elementary school when she began her work there.

> It felt scattered. I was working in special ed, so I got to see six
> different classrooms, in third and fourth grades. It was clear to
> me right away that your child would get a very different experi-
> ence based on which teacher he or she had. There was some
> great teaching going on, but everyone was doing his or her own
> thing. There were some efforts at linking children to pen pals
> and to have them interview folks in town as an intergeneration

project. Some teachers also offered a "workshop model" where children made choices in their reading and writing. But for most, literacy meant homogeneous groups of children reading books selected for them by their teachers and writing instruction that was inconsistent, without focus, and often not based on student ideas.

I wondered what Chris had noticed among the kids from families that don't do a lot of reading:

> For me one of the signs—it was like being hit on the head— was that there were an awful lot of special ed referrals in third grade. Why all of a sudden? I would try to piece together a picture of what kind of instruction each child had received, in order to see where the problem was. But I had a hard time doing that. No one could tell me, for example, whether these children had had a consistent approach to phonics or writing skills in grades one and two.
>
> And I said, "Well, that makes it very difficult to know what we're dealing with. Is this a reading disability? A learning disability? An environmental deprivation that's never been addressed in school?" That was my clue that perhaps what I was seeing here in third and fourth grade was being duplicated throughout the school. I didn't know for sure, but I sure did wonder about it.

"And what did the kids themselves say about reading?" I inquired.

> The ones who were struggling would say that they really didn't know why they *should* read. The connection between print and personal purpose had never been made. By the time I saw them in third grade, the attitude was "Why are you making me do this? There's nothing here for me." There was no draw—nothing to make them want to work harder to figure things out, as far as reading. And writing was even worse.
>
> What I saw was kids who didn't know where to go—they

were picking out books that either were too easy for them, that presented no challenge, or were much too hard for them and produced even more frustration. They didn't know how to select books, to find pleasure in books. They would roam the room during time set aside for "self-selected" reading.

It felt as though there were two distinct groups in town— those for whom literacy was part of their worldview and those who saw nobody they admired reading or writing. It's a white community; so the distinctions here are ones of income and education. There are many families who are struggling to provide the mere basics. Literacy isn't high on their list. It's often difficult to get such parents to come into the school, or to value their children having options different from theirs. They want what's best for their children—I really believe all parents do— but we haven't figured out a way to pull them in, to be partners with us.

The following year, Chris was hired as a third grade Title I literacy teacher, with school staff and school board support for her to improve instruction in reading and writing. Chris told me that when she began work with the third grade she had no set strategy. She pulled some ideas from a newly published literacy framework and incorporated her own instincts and training about how to engage and support struggling readers.

We worked together to change some of their instructional practices. Each teacher wanted specific focus areas. One sought to implement a "writing workshop" approach, with children setting purposes for their own writing; another sought a more heterogeneous way to teach guided reading. Because I knew there were many third graders who were significantly below grade level in reading—still figuring out *how* to read—I made phonics a daily feature.

There was another constant: Chris led shared reading activities in each third grade classroom at least three times a week:

Most days, I would go into the classrooms and require that everyone come together. I brought in poetry and songs on flip charts that I thought would be fun for everyone. These third graders would come and sit around the easel and as we sang the songs, we would follow the print. They had support from their peers and from me, so gradually they could do it on their own. We did Maurice Sendak's *Chicken Soup with Rice* and *Pierre: A Cautionary Tale*—and they loved those. And we did some classics like Poe and Stevenson and sang some rounds, some that were easy, some that had more difficult words.

We did "author studies"—Arnold Lobel's Frog and Toad books and the *Mister Men series* and *The School Bus Driver from the Black Lagoon* and some of the less familiar Dr. Seuss books, such as *The 500 Hats of Bartholomew Cubbins*. These were books that they at first saw as "baby books," but because I embraced them and we had fun with them, and because I left a box of these books in each classroom that they could go to when it was time for self-selected reading, there were some children who felt that this was their route to recapturing literacy. They had a place to go. It was already a story that had been read to them.

I told Chris that this sounded to me as though, faced with third graders who were already embarrassed and a little bit ashamed—and likely to be defiant about their inability to read fluently—she had decided to make reading a *social experience,* to make it fun and something everyone could succeed at. But, I pointed out, she had also introduced them to more complex language and more grown-up themes. She didn't segregate these kids along an "ability" spectrum or measure them against some external scale that many were likely to fail at. Chris agreed.

Sometimes, I also connected the poems with themes that they were working with in the class—if they were studying spiders for science, I found poems that dealt with spiders. We found

some playful ways to get kids reading and rereading, to help
them build fluency. I had noticed that some teachers avoid
poetry like the plague, and I love poetry, so it was my entrée to
them. One teacher even had a "Poetry Day" every Friday. She
would beg, borrow, and steal poetry books, and the kids knew
that on Fridays they would come in and find a poem, and they
would read it, and read it, and read it. They'd have a sort of
"beatnik" poetry reading.

"It seems to me that the "nonnegotiable" part was that every
kid had to *play,* to *get involved,* regardless of reading level," I responded. "But I wonder how this affected the kids who were already good readers."

They *loved* it! Even those who were more advanced were in on
all the fun of the conversation. When we did William Steig's
books, that was something they could relate to. Those who
were stronger readers still enjoyed the social interaction. I provided enough open-endedness in the conversation so that they
stayed involved. And they were great role models for the children who were struggling to find the words and who were sitting side-by-side with them. And I didn't hear anyone say,
"This is boring."

Chris then told me how the strategies she and the other third
grade teacher had developed have since evolved so that the
entire staff can embrace these approaches, teacher by teacher
and grade by grade. This whole-school focus, she said, helps
less confident or less experienced teachers feel comfortable
learning from their colleagues. Without a schoolwide approach
to literacy, it's "catch as catch can" for parents hoping to find a
teacher who will help their child become an eager, competent
reader.

Our elementary staff had been trying for years to figure out
how, together, to approach teaching literacy. The teachers

knew what they were doing wasn't enough, but they didn't
know where to go from there. A new principal was hired who
understood the importance of a schoolwide approach to literacy. So we began exploring options for a schoolwide K–6
approach, with the intent to decide on one. Teachers went out
to visit programs at other schools. We had people come in to
talk about literacy. Meanwhile, the third grade teacher and I
were busy with our pilot, talking and reflecting, trying out
writing rubrics, discussing what was working and what wasn't.
By the time we had to decide, our staff voted overwhelmingly
to adopt the framework we had been using as our guide for literacy instruction in third grade.

I believe that in making their choice, the staff recognized
that in this town we have a range of children in relation to family literacy background and preschool preparation. Our K–3
teachers wanted a structure to allow all children to be successful, to develop an appetite for reading and writing. And there
was a consensus in the upper grades that what was needed was
consistency of approach, so that they wouldn't be faced—in
fifth and sixth grade—with so many children reading below
grade level.

The approach we selected allows us to group children heter-
ogeneously for activities, with teachers preparing mini-lessons
that set a comprehension purpose for reading during one part
of the day. With writing, teachers provide some direct instruction and also time for students to share their writing. The
whole-class phonics work helps kids learn high-frequency
words and analyze words they don't know, to give them strategies they can apply during the reading they do. There's also
time set aside daily for "want to" kinds of reading, during
which time teachers confer individually with children on their
reading. Put together, this provides some continuity within and
between grade levels.

Teachers are free to select reading materials: basals, fiction, nonfiction (which allows teachers in the upper grades to

include readings in science and history) for comprehension reading lessons. Such integration is encouraged, along with balancing fiction and nonfiction. Children are building connections all day long—using what they are reading to write a report during writing time.

I asked Chris to compare the school district's approach to literacy—and its real impact at the elementary school—before and after adopting the new system

Before, they had an hour per day devoted to writing, reading, and punctuation (with other literacy instruction at the teachers' discretion). I believe it had been, more or less, imposed top-down, but it looked different in each classroom. At times, the focus was too much on the teacher "teaching" the curriculum—rather than children *engaged* with their teacher.

Now, by contrast, teachers spend about two and a half hours a day explicitly on literacy: about forty minutes of writing; forty minutes in guided reading; a half hour each in the phonics segment; and a half hour of self-selected reading. And it's happening consistently in grades one through six, with the fifth and sixth grades often using larger blocks of time for reading and writing, depending on the curriculum.

At all grade levels, teachers are integrating reading and writing with units in science, social studies, and even math. Strong community support has allowed us to create a guided reading library that offers many levels of books for science and social studies—teachers can have *all* kids reading about, let's say, magnets. What a difference this has made!

The remedial reading program has shifted emphasis, with tutors working almost exclusively in classrooms, rather than pulling students out for separate instruction. This is also true for special education. My overall sense is that there's a whole lot more time consciously being spent around literacy. And it's not just the minutes; the focus is a whole lot clearer.

I asked, "You are not one of those who see a dichotomy between 'phonics' and 'whole language'?"

> Researchers are finding that in classrooms where two or more approaches are used—such as independent reading and a phonics approach—children are stronger than if they had just one approach. My belief is that whole language, done correctly, embeds phonics. I'm a strong proponent of "shared reading" because it offers opportunities to move back and forth between a work of literature—be it a poem, story, or song—and the individual words, phonic patterns, chunks of words, punctuation, and so on.

I speculated, to Chris, that maybe it's the warm, social interaction she has modeled that took the regimentation out of phonics lessons: the conviviality among the kids, the choices kids have in free reading. In such an atmosphere, kids may be happy to sit still for some direct instruction in phonics, particularly when, for many of them, they're discovering missing pieces in their ability to read fluently.

> I do think that underlying all of this is creating a risk-free environment—an environment with standards and high expectations—but one in which you are instructing in a multilevel model so that every child can be successful. Nobody falls off the train. The classroom community supports everyone.
>
> It's print-rich, this approach; it's rich in consistency and expectations; it's language-rich; it has choice and focus and purpose. For example, in one of the reading blocks you set a purpose for reading, for example. "In the next part of the book, find out the three ways that Joe knew that Sally was skipping school," or "Everyone read to find out the parts of the plant necessary for reproduction." So, beforehand, the teacher gives students ways to approach their reading, as individual readers; then you support children in different ways during their read-

ing. Then you come back as a group and have a discussion to see
if our predictions were right about the text—and then the kids
go back at it. There's a pace and purpose to the instruction.

I commented that it seems that this approach, for all its structure, doesn't limit the more creative teacher from expanding
on the process. But it does offer scaffolding to the less experienced or less confident teacher who might otherwise not be
able to pursue a reading plan that is so ambitious and inclusive.

> Exactly. If you already come wired to teach reading comprehen-
> sion, and you have the background, you can innovate and inte-
> grate like crazy. If you come as a new teacher, you have a way of
> structuring the day to ensure that children are experiencing all
> of the ways that kids learn how to read.
>
> And kids in the upper grades are able to fill in the pieces that
> they missed out on earlier, such as "there, their, they're," learn-
> ing about suffixes and prefixes, looking at language in a deeper
> way. It allows children to shine who might otherwise fall fur-
> ther and further behind. Our approach is incredibly multilevel.
>
> What I hope is that we will begin to build a community of
> teachers, of children, and of parents around literacy, such that
> you can feel the pulse throughout the community that "This is
> a great place to be a learner." I want us to feel that we're going
> down the right path, and that kids from whatever background
> can join in the fun and the excitement.
>
> The school board has been at the forefront of this reform,
> too. They want to see something different and have embraced
> this effort. The community has supported us with the purchase
> of new books. And our principal is truly an instructional
> leader, participating in all the staff training in literacy, spending
> time in the classrooms, and helping us by writing grants that
> allow us to continue our work.
>
> Parents, too, have been very cooperative. We've made a
> major shift in homework. We're no longer sending home a list
> of spelling words, but rather asking parents to work with their

children on the much smaller list of weekly words we want them to really know and use. Some classrooms send home lists of activities similar to ones practiced in the classrooms. We're trying new ways to connect home and school, to build a partnership.

Our view of assessment has shifted, too. Teachers are doing more "kid watching" and less worksheet correction. The conversation is turning on how to make assessment more of an integral part of what we do, rather than saying "I need a minimum of nine grades in each area for my report card." We are using informal reading inventories and talking about looking at writing samples, to help us develop schoolwide portfolios.

It feels as of the whole community is on board: students, teachers, administrators, school board, and parents. We are embarking on a fascinating journey.

The Literacy Lab

What impresses me about Chris Teague's work with her colleagues is that it highlights the effectiveness of quiet, small scale (but *comprehensive*) reforms, which might begin with one teacher's pioneering efforts but don't stop there. The hardest part, often, happens *after* an initiative is successful, when one faces the challenge of bringing in one's colleagues. It takes tact and sensitivity and patience to help an entire school develop a "good enough" literacy approach—that's more than "good enough."

My conversations with Chris inspired me to design a good-enough program at the secondary level, one based—first and foremost—upon a change of attitude. I choose for this illustration a high school class that lasts for a full double period (about an hour and a half) each day, five days a week. I call it the Literacy Lab:

> The Literacy Lab class resembles a good art room or a newspaper office: lots of clutter, students moving around from their

chairs to the word processors located at the back, kids working on their own pieces and looking at those of their classmates to see what's being produced. The teacher, with an eye on everyone, sometimes waits to have work brought over by the student for review, sometimes wanders around and is permitted (usually) to read over someone's shoulder and to offer suggestions.

Student work is kept in a large portfolio that may include earlier sketches and drafts, from which the observer can see how the finished work has developed. The use of media—sound recording, video, musical accompaniment—may be added, at the student's discretion. But they are not substitutes for writing. And it's not just about "creative writing." Students ask permission to work on papers for other classes, and it is usually granted (although when handed in, it carries the acknowledgment "with assistance from the Literacy Lab." This may also offer a more even playing field to students who don't have highly literate parents at home to supervise their homework).

Grammar and usage are taught in the context of student work. When a particular kind of error (e.g., run-on sentences) or a general weakness (e.g., vagueness, lack of detail) seems to crop up, the Literacy Lab teacher announces a short grammar coaching session, with students taking part in diagnosing problems and explaining options. Every student keeps a list of his or her own "grammar bugs" and attaches a copy of it to the draft being reviewed by the teacher. Students are expected to make progress on eliminating their grammar bugs. Twice a year, students take mock diagnostic "exams" that reflect the state competency tests. The class then corrects their tests and discusses the areas of weakness and strength.

With regard to reading, a shelf of "favorite books" is prominently displayed, with teacher and students contributing books from their own collections, which classmates may borrow. Each student's chosen "favorite author" is displayed on one wall, including a photo, list of works read, and space for comments. The class library houses a diverse selection of works written in various styles and dialects of English, as well as student-friendly "handbooks" of proper usage.

All native English-speakers in the class are very much encouraged to try to become bilingual. This is the occasion for a great deal of fun, as kids learn words and phrases (lots of "cool" expressions and acceptable slang) from their classmates as a way of enriching their understanding of the role of language and culture in literature (and vice versa).

In addition, all students serve as tutors ("big buddies") to younger kids who are bilingual or whose home language is not standard English, or kids who have difficulty with reading and writing. The older students talk often and in depth about their responsibility to the younger ones, the fact that these kids will pattern themselves on their older buddies. Each high school student keeps a careful file on his or her buddy, to mark progress made and strategies attempted.

One day a week is devoted to high school students delivering speeches they have memorized or that they read from notes and extemporize upon (this will be expanded upon in chapter 12). It is a semiformal occasion, with students sitting as an audience and the speaker working from a lectern. Students from the middle school are sometimes invited in to hear such speeches (which they are also preparing). The topics are the student's choice but must be approved by the teacher. The students practice their speeches with a team of three or four (they use small practice rooms or work in the corridors to do this).

At the end of the Literacy Lab course, the students all present their portfolios to the public at an evening gathering at the school. The portfolios are on display in the school library or lunchroom. For their teacher, the students write up a detailed self-evaluation on reading, writing, speaking, and listening (which goes into their portfolio to be reviewed by the next teacher). The "course grade" is a blend of "progress made" and "skill mastery achieved." When this Literacy Lab is taken at the eleventh or twelfth grade level, students are offered the

chance to submit three pieces of their best writing to a panel
of college freshman English teachers, to be "graded" as they
would be in college.

Teachers from disciplines other than English are very
strongly encouraged to take on a "literacy lab" assignment, at
least for one semester a year, so that they can infuse the lessons
learned there in their own courses. Such teachers bring with
them something from their own disciplines: ethical issues in science, examinations of possible bias in history texts, even appli-
cations of music and art. The normal course load for an English
teacher is to teach two such "Literacy Labs" a day, plus one
forty-five-minute "literature" elective seminar in an area of his
or her choosing. The labs have an average of twenty to twenty-
two students each, which means that an English teacher normally has about forty-four students whose portfolios he or she
supervises, plus whatever writing is assigned to students in the
seminar.

Extra funding for lower class sizes and the hiring of more English teachers might have to come, initially, from grants. After a
few years, the results in terms of student writing performance
should have improved to the extent that a district will adopt
the Literacy Lab concept and begin to add permanent positions
in the humanities in place of teachers in various other disciplines who retire, leaving only a small permanent increase in
the district's budget to account for smaller class sizes in the literacy labs. Although there may be somewhat fewer electives in
some areas of the humanities, most in the faculty will accept
the trade-off.

Small Victories: Poetry Can Keep You Out of Trouble

Until I am in a position to organize such Literacy Labs in the
middle school where I am now assisting, I'll continue to learn
from the students I encounter. With the sixth graders, I've
been focusing on poetry, trying to follow Kenneth Koch's approach in his inspiring book *Rose, Where Did You Get That Red?* in

an effort to get kids to recognize that the written word is a powerful and useful tool for self-expression with dignity.

Just the other day, while we were exploring Walt Whitman's "Song of Myself," I invited the students to compose a "song of myself" to share with their grandparents, or other relatives, as a holiday gift. While most of the class was gearing up and beginning to put some phrases on paper, one girl, Tiffany, announced defiantly, that "I got no song of myself, today. I'm depressed. I'm mad at the world." I suggested that Tiffany write down her thoughts, angry as they might be. A few minutes later, she read her poem to the class. I can't remember her exact words, but they were something like this:

> I am depressed. Angry at everything.
> I just want to jump up, run around, and cause trouble.
> Nothing working right. I want to tear things up
> And scream at everybody!

She looked up, a scowl on her face, expecting to be criticized for her "negative" thoughts (I had urged the children to create a reflective poem about themselves to share). I said, "Tiffany, what do you think would happen if you *did* these things you talk about in your poem?" She answered, "I'd get in lots of trouble." I then asked her teacher, who was watching the whole scene unfold, "How do you feel about Tiffany's poem?" He said, "I like it. With a little more work, it could be worth an A."

"There you go!" I crowed to the class, happy to be handed one of those all-too-rare teachable moments. "If Tiffany *does* this—she gets in trouble, agreed? But if she *writes a poem about it,* she can earn an A—and she *still* gets to keep her feelings. Nobody's going to punish her for having them."

CHAPTER TWELVE

Lift Every Voice

Yan Li Xu is shy, a shy girl from a Chinese-American family. During the poetry sessions I conduct in her sixth grade class, with teacher David Crane, Yan Li never volunteers to read aloud. But today, I have brought a tape recorder and everyone, shy or not, is gently encouraged to recite their first poem, based on William Blake's "Tyger." I have followed the poet Kenneth Koch's advice and have invited the kids to address an animal, who may also speak to them.[1]

The class, normally plagued by lots of goofing off, watches more attentively than I've yet seen as their classmates take the microphone, in turn, to read their poems. When it's Yan Li's turn, they give her the polite but casual attention due a shy person who is by no means a class leader. She reads:

> Horse, horse, why do you have to work for humans?
> Because my cousin, the Unicorn, stole my wings.
> Why do you jump this high?
> Because I can try to be free, by jumping.
> Why can't you fly?
> Because, as I told you, my cousin stole my wings—DUH!

It is this final "DUH" that grabs the class. They beg to hear all the poems over again, on tape, and when Yan Li's voice begins, there is a hushing sound of kids trying to get everyone quiet so they will hear every word. When the tape comes again to Yan Li saying "DUH," the class erupts with laughter and appreciation. Yan Li smiles. She savors, at least for a moment, the power of her voice.

Children—as passionate learners—are meant to be heard. Classrooms should be places where children learn to talk (not to just sit quietly and listen). This goes beyond the popular practice of group work or "cooperative learning." For some kids, talking up in class is no big challenge—their problem is learning when not to talk. But even for these ever-ready talkers, school should be a place where they learn to shape, hone, and deliver their viewpoints with style and thoughtfulness.

For a people with a lot to say, we Americans often have a hard time getting it out, in public situations. For many students, the classroom is the last place on earth they want their voice to be heard publicly. Many kids are verbal powerhouses, nonstop talkers—except in class. Only rarely is it fear of a teacher's criticism that holds them back; more likely it is fear of put-downs by one's classmates. How do we counter that?

An incident I witnessed years ago in a first grade classroom in an African-American neighborhood in Hartford illustrates the power of children lifting their voices:

> The student teacher is pulling out some materials to use in a reading lesson. Among the "big books" she is considering reading with them is "Five Little Monkeys Jumping on the Bed." While she thinks about which books to use, one little girl notices the book about the monkeys and begins chanting it out loud. A friend joins her, and both begin singing in a still-louder voice.

Five little monkeys, jumpin' on the bed
One fell off and bumped his head,
Momma called the doctor, and the doctor said,
"No more monkeys jumpin' on the bed!"

At each chorus, more and more children are drawn in. The student teacher attempts at one point to intervene, to get the class "in order" and begin the lesson, but the children ignore her, and she, with some ambivalence, decides not to stop the singing. Children reading aloud is, after all, part of the intended "lesson"—although that might seem beside the point if the student teacher feels that her first priority is to be in control of the class at all times.

As the chanting girls count down: four little monkeys, then three, then two, more and more students join in. By the end of the last chorus, most of the class is on its feet, raising the rafters with their voices, shouting in unison: *"NO MORE MON-KEYS JUMPIN' ON THE BED!!"* The children then go back to their seats, and the girl who started it all hands the book back to the student teacher with a smile on her face. Both the student teacher and the regular teacher seem somewhat confused and, finally, they call the class to order. There is no mention of what has just happened.

As I observe all this, I am overwhelmed by the dynamism and radiance of the spontaneous performance. It is as if the girls sense the power of their command of the word, and of the fellowship of the other students, and are reveling in it. It reminds me of a church service, where the full-throated participation of the parishioners is welcomed. This was the only time, during my observation of the student teacher, that I saw the whole class attentive and engaged. That I still remember it so vividly tells me that it holds an essential key to the issue of children and learning—the primacy of a sense of ownership and power as a condition for literacy development.

Children, of course, experience the power of speech long before they go to school. Malcolm Mitchell relates how he and his wife were alerted to the power of speech while observing his mother play with their infant son. I asked Malcolm, during our interview, "You've used the word *perspective* a lot to describe what you try to get across to your sixth graders. What does that word mean, in that context?"

I started the year by calling attention to a series of words: *Voice, validation,* and *perspective*—words that come from my personal narrative. I told my students that when my son was an infant, my mother came by for a visit. Pretty soon, she's changing his diaper, and she's just talking into this boy's face. My son starts making sounds, looking back at her face. My mother's having a conversation with him. And my wife and I are saying, like, *"What's going on? . . ."*

And my mom says, "Please be quiet. He's *talking*."

Now this is an infant who's four or five weeks old, and he's going "Blah, blah, blah." But he's obviously responding to my mother's voice.

As I said to my class, "Then my mom told me that *that's how you validate him as a person*. You have to let him know that he's a human being, and that when he *says* something, there's somebody *listening*. That's how he feels validated and knows that his voice is significant."

That concept of *voice* and *validation* led us to the idea of *perspective*. Just because people look different, and speak different—even if they're a four-week-old infant—they have a voice and deserve to be validated for who they are. That's how we got to the idea of *perspective*—looking respectfully at what's going on for someone, looking through the eyes of the other, even it it's a baby.

The philosopher Alfred North Whitehead, writing in 1929, speaks of the miracle of children's speech in arguing that educa-

tors should not hold back challenging mental activities for fear
that young students are not ready to engage with them:

> It is not true that the easier subjects should precede the harder.
> On the contrary, some of the hardest must come first because
> nature so dictates, and because they are essential to life. The
> first intellectual task which confronts an infant is the acquire-
> ment of spoken language. What an appalling task, the correla-
> tion of meanings with sounds! It requires an analysis of ideas
> and an analysis of sounds. We all know that the infant does it,
> and that the miracle of his achievement is explicable. But so are
> all miracles, and yet to the wise they remain miracles. All I ask
> is that with this example staring us in the face we should cease
> talking nonsense about postponing the harder subjects.[2]

Four Kinds of "Talking Problems"

Before exploring in more detail some of the advantages of emphasizing children's oral speech as an essential element in their
evolution as passionate learners, I'd like to look at four typical
situations that teachers experience as problematic. These four
do not include neurological or physiological speech impediments, such as might be diagnosed by a specialist. They are the
kinds of obstacles teachers routinely encounter. In each case, I
will suggest a few ways that teachers, students, and parents can
act to overcome the difficulty:

1. *Shyness:* kids who don't appear to have the confidence or
    courage to speak up;

2. *Aggressiveness:* kids who regularly speak out of turn and
    who interrupt others;

3. *Cultural—and other—differences:* kids who speak a form of
    English not normally approved of in school, and related
    issues

4. *Resistance/peer influence:* kids, quite capable of contributing to a class discussion, who choose not to, often to avoid appearing to be "brown-nosing" the teacher.

Shyness

For shy kids, an unwillingness to speak up publicly may, of course, be a factor of personality—some people are more reticent than others. But part of their shyness may be the result of how rarely we practice public speaking in school. Another factor is a child's fear of ridicule by other kids. Each is preventable or curable.

We normally don't permit students to plead "shyness" about their assignments in math or writing; instead, we work with them to overcome obstacles to their performance. But we allow shy speakers to remain silent in normal class discussion, often out of a misguided concern for their esteem. Yet we bemoan the lack of public debate, of people who can get up in front of a crowd to speak their mind without stuttering, mumbling, or having to read from notes every word they say.

I think many educators are quite ambivalent about the sound of children's voices. With a quiet child, there's one less obvious problem to contend with. With a shy child, there's the worry of our causing acute embarrassment or tears. There are time pressures, too: a teacher poses a question and looks to a normally shy child in hopes of a response. That response may, indeed, be forthcoming, but by the time the child feels ready to speak, the teacher has moved on to an eagerly waving hand elsewhere in the room.

Personal shyness cannot be overcome by a few suggested techniques. But any teacher can take the lead in working to create a classroom environment in which the following regularly occur:

ᑫ Anyone who mocks or makes fun of a classmate's attempt to express ideas or feelings is quickly challenged,

often by stopping the class and having "a little talk" together about respect and manners and people's feelings.

- ❧ A teacher approaches shy children, one by one, to help
  them gain confidence in her and to attempt to find out
  under what conditions each child might be willing to
  open up.

- ❧ A group of the shy students meets with the teacher,
  during lunchtime, or study time, or after school, to talk
  about "finding their voices"—helping them to support
  each other in class.

- ❧ Oral reports are regularly scheduled, in teams, so that
  students can present their ideas as part of a supportive
  group.

For parents, a blend of support and encouragement might
help a shy child find self-respecting and low-risk venues to practice public speaking, such as by reading aloud to younger children or joining a chorus or cheerleading group. This is one of
those things best addressed naturally, without pressure. Since
shy children often have shy parents, overcoming shyness can be
something that child and parent agree to work on together.

Aggressiveness

As every teacher knows, there are the shy kids and then there
are the kids who just won't shut up—kids who speak out of
turn, blurting out answers or comments (appropriate and otherwise)—the bane of every inexperienced teacher. This includes children who crave attention so much that they will accept public disapproval from the teacher if that's the only way to
remain in the spotlight.

For too many kids, school is the place where they learn that
"talking is bad," that what they have to say is welcome only
when it fits into the grown-ups' plans. Speaking is the one

thing, in the area of communications skills, that many kids can really do well, yet as their formal schooling proceeds, many children feel that they mostly get chastised for doing it. In my brief stints in front of the sixth and seventh grade classes I work with, I too try to keep kids from "talking out of turn." And I often don't succeed.

The problem, of course, is that some children don't play by our rules. In the conventional classroom, the rules may well include such injunctions as no talking unless the teacher permits it, no talking unless you raise your hand and are called upon, only one person permitted to talk at any one time, no talking while students are working at their desks, and so on. Not bad rules. Except that they don't seem to work unless all the "shushing" is accompanied by threats of sanctions. And from what I can see, the impact of well-intentioned rules about talking is often to silence the obedient children while stigmatizing the most avid talkers as disruptive, or defiant.

How do we help kids learn the rules of good listening and good speaking, while supporting them in celebrating their verbal gifts? Does the spontaneous desire of children to speak in the normal performance of their learning activities challenge our desire for control? Does it make us uncomfortable? What is the right balance, in a classroom, between our desire for orderliness and good manners and the benefit to kids of participating in "the marketplace of ideas" through speaking? And what can we learn from "disorderliness" about the way our students respond to the material or skills we are trying to teach them? Are they "acting up" because they lack internal control, or because they see no purpose to the lesson? Or both?

Experienced teachers often use the first week of the school year to set forth class procedures, rules, and guidelines that help students know what to expect and how to behave. But I've found it very difficult, in my part-time work in a middle school this year, to stick by my own rules in a class where more than a few emotionally needy students clamor for my attention. This is especially true when I am challenging the students with a difficult question and am desperate for someone to offer a thoughtful response. One kid yells out an interesting thought, and I can't help but acknowledge it, raised hand or no. I've seen other teachers act this way, too. Anyway you look at it, verbal assertiveness by students, of any age, is tough to handle.

Nor is the much-acclaimed "consistency" always the right approach. With kids, nothing works the same all the time. Whatever the in-class rules about talking, there should be time for spontaneous conversation, especially during a brainstorming session where students are generating ideas at a rapid rate. In answer to the question, Which do you prefer, an orderly classroom without intellectual spontaneity or an often disorderly classroom where ideas from lots of student are flying around, igniting more thinking and responding? I must prefer the latter. Of course, most any teacher would want the best of both worlds, but that isn't easily obtainable with kids.

Rather than list all the ways effective teachers keep aggressive talkers in line, I'll just paraphrase what Deborah Meier's elementary school in the Roxbury neighborhood of Boston uses as its "school rules":

> ୶ No one may say or do anything that hurts other people.
> ୶ No one may say or do anything that interferes with another person's right to learn or teach.

Such rules are especially relevant to teachers who face verbally aggressive students. When one child is yelling out an answer, or interrupting the lesson to grab personal attention, or teasing and putting down another student, that child is violating one or both of these rules. I like these rules because they are only two and are easily understood, and because they apply to everyone in the room (adults included). But it's a lot easier to enunciate these rules on paper than to put them into practice in the classroom.

Cultural and Other Differences

" 'Spoken soul' was the name that Claude Brown, author of *Manchild in the Promised Land,* coined for black talk." Thus begins a book by John Russell Rickford and his son, Russell John Rickford, that celebrates the language of African Americans at a time when the conscious attempt to incorporate that language—styled Ebonics—into the Oakland public schools' curriculum had provoked a furious national debate. Although the Oakland action was specifically aimed at "facilitating the acquisition and mastery of English language skills, while respecting and embracing the legitimacy and richness of the language patterns" of the students' own cultural heritage, the effort to legitimize "black talk" drew a firestorm of criticism, much of it overtly racist in character.[3]

Scholars such as Lisa Delpit and Theresa Perry have explicated what they call "the real ebonics debate" and argue persuasively for reframing the way this debate is usually cast.[4] I would like here to mark the phenomenon of non-standard English-speaking as a significant challenge to teachers across the country and to connect it to issues of engagement and alienation with school, that is, with issues of passionate learning.

I am reminded of John Dewey's thoughts on the vitality of children's language and its tragic misdirection in much of conventional schooling:

> Language is primarily a social thing, a means by which we give our experiences to others and get theirs again in return. When it is taken away from its natural purpose, it is no wonder that it becomes a complex and difficult problem to teach language. Think of the absurdity of having to teach language as a thing by

itself. If there is anything the child will do before he goes to
school, it is to talk of the things that interest him. But when
there are no vital interests appealed to in the school, when language is used simply for the repetition of lessons, it is not sur-
prising that one of the chief difficulties of school work has come
to be instruction in the mother-tongue. Since the language
taught is unnatural, not growing out of the real desire to communicate vital impressions and convictions, the freedom of children in its use gradually disappears, until finally the high-school
teacher has to invent all kinds of devices to assist in getting any
spontaneous and full use of speech. Moreover, when the language instinct is appealed to in a social way, there is continual
contact with reality.[5]

My "contact with reality" is to watch Asian-American and
African-American students conversing in sixth and seventh
grade classrooms in dialects that are often quite expressive and
just as often clearly "incorrect" from a standard English viewpoint. Their written work mirrors this confusion. My question
is, Do we stop them from speaking and writing in nonstandard
code until they learn to "do it right"? Do we ignore their non-
standard speech patterns as a sign of cultural respect? Do we
allow them to have their say, and then gently correct them? Or
do we refrain from interfering with their verbal expression in
the hope that once they develop a zest for speaking and writing
about school matters, they will naturally seek to adopt the conventions of standard English when the occasion calls for that?

The most eloquent argument for acknowledging the vitality
of, in this case, black English, comes from Toni Morrison, who,
in an interview, said that the distinctive ingredient of her fiction was

> the language, only the language. . . . It is the thing that black
> people love so much—the saying of words, holding them on
> the tongue, experimenting with them, playing with them. It's

a love, a passion. Its function is like a preacher's: to make you stand up out of your seat, make you lose yourself and hear yourself. The worst of all possible things that could happen would be to lose that language. There are certain things I cannot say without recourse to my language. It's terrible to think that a child with five different present tenses comes to school to be faced with books that are less than his own language. And then to be told things about his language, which is him, that are sometimes permanently damaging. He may never know the etymology of Africanisms in his language, not even know that "hip" is a real word or that "the dozens" means something. This is a really cruel fallout of racism. I know the standard English. I want to use it to help restore the other language, the lingua franca.[6]

Lisa Delpit argues for viewing a child's family language as a distinctive and valuable part of one's culture. She clearly states, however, that schools have a responsibility to provide all children with access to the language of the wider society. In her book *Other People's Children,* Delpit asks, "What should teachers do about helping students acquire an additional oral form?" She argues:

First, they should recognize that the linguistic form a student brings to school is intimately connected with loved ones, community, and personal identity. To suggest that this form is "wrong" or, even worse, ignorant, is to suggest that something is wrong with the student and his or her family. On the other hand, it is equally important to understand that students who do not have access to the politically popular dialect form in this country, that is, Standard English, are less likely to succeed economically than their peers who do. How can both realities be embraced?

Teachers need to support the language that students bring to school, provide them input from an additional code, and give them the opportunity to use the new code in a nonthreatening, real communicative context. . . . For example, memorizing parts for drama productions will allow students to "get the feel" of speaking Standard English while not under the threat of correction. Young students can create puppet shows or role-play cartoon characters. (Many "superheroes" speak almost hypercorrect Standard English!) Playing a role eliminates the possibility of implying that the *child's* language is inadequate, and suggests, instead, that different language forms are appropriate in different contexts.[7]

Delpit goes on to suggest that teachers should become active learners and participants in the cultural diversity of the communities their students come from, and that teachers should invite their students to become their "teachers" in this regard:

> I am suggesting that we begin with a perspective that demands finding means to celebrate, not merely tolerate, diversity in our classrooms. Not only should teachers and students who share group membership delight in their own cultural and linguistic history, but all teachers must revel in the diversity of their students and that of the world outside the classroom community. . . . Teachers who do not share the language and culture of their students, or teachers whose students represent a variety of cultural backgrounds, can also celebrate diversity by making language diversity a part of the curriculum. Students can be asked to "teach" the teacher and other students aspects of their language variety. They can "translate" songs, poems, and stories into their own dialect or into "book language" and compare the differences across the cultural groups represented in the classroom.[8]

Theresa Perry has commented that one of the casualties of the desegregation of southern public schools was that no longer were African-American children surrounded in school by men and women who celebrated the cultural importance of oral speech, including school educators who required children to memorize and recite the words of famous black orators.[9]

And, indeed, memorizing and reciting speeches, along with reading stories aloud, is becoming a lost art. Forums, debates, speeches, and Socratic dialogues are training grounds for personhood and citizenship. Again, culture is of great significance—especially for African-American, Hispanic, and immigrant children.

Finally, there are other societal factors that affect student speech. There are gender differences—settings where we find girls being afraid to speak intelligently out of fear of being thought "too smart" by boys. There are studies that suggest that girls become much more intellectually reticent as they approach puberty. Sometimes, the gender factor works in reverse. I once visited a high school class in California that had mostly children from Mexican-American families. I noticed that a few of the girls spoke up in class, but never any boys. When I asked the teacher about it, after class, she said, in matter-of-fact tone, "Oh, with *these* children, the boys like to show what they can do on the ball field. They leave it to the girls to do the talking in class."

And then there are class differences. Do poor kids feel okay about speaking up in the presence of more affluent kids? A *New York Times* article of a few years ago highlighted one fairly affluent Midwest community in which the few kids from the mobile home park lived in fear of being dismissed as "trailer trash" whenever they were too visible or spoke up.

The issue of allowing and encouraging every child to "find his or her voice" is complex, but that only means we should give more thought to its ramifications, for they are many and they significantly affect how children learn. Sensitivity to cultural diversity should accompany training for all in speaking articulately and in listening respectfully.

Resistance / Peer Influence

A seemingly intractable feature of classroom life is the nonre-
sponsiveness of students, especially in their middle and high
school years, to inquiries and prompts from teachers. Typically,
the teacher asks a question and looks around for a response. The
students, aware of the dynamics of the classroom culture (i.e.,
the teacher has all the power; kids' options are to offer or withhold participation), look around to see who's going to raise a
hand. Predictably, a hand goes up, attached to the body of a student who seeks to curry favor with the teacher, or one wishing
to test his or her intellect on the issue.

Whatever the reason, unless this is an honors class where academic competition is encouraged or a class where the teacher
has managed to overcome normal student resistance by creating conditions for a genuine, nonthreatening dialogue, most
teachers simply get used to the notion that relatively few students will really participate.

It's a set-piece confrontation. Students—particularly if they
feel undervalued or not well respected as members of the
school community—withhold their voice out of solidarity
with their peers. By the time they've reached high school, the
habit of not talking during class discussions has become in-
grained, such that students often don't know why they de-
mur—it just seems a lot easier to remain silent.

I find this is also true in college. I regularly see in my classes a
preponderance of students—future teachers—who wait until
somebody else speaks up rather than do so themselves, even
when they realize that their verbal skills (especially an ability to
respond spontaneously to verbal prompts of one sort or another) are a critical aspect of being a teacher. Many are self-
critical: "Somebody else always manages to say what I thought
of first, but I never seem to want to raise my hand." Others are
baffled by their own reticence, as though they had never really

come to grips with the problem. The response I often get is "I dunno —I'm fine when I'm talking with my friends. Just not in class, in front of—you know—kids I don't know so well— and, of course—teachers."

If we eliminate coercion (fear of getting a bad grade in class participation) and bribery (offer of extra credit for participating), we're left with that notion, oft repeated in these pages, that *discourse in the classroom is a function of attitudes and relationships.* Kids will participate in classes where they feel respected, where there is mutuality of discourse (i.e., teacher and students feel they will learn something from one another—it's not a one-way street), and where they perceive a connection between the topic under discussion and what's important in their lives.

So, if we want more kids to "talk" in class, and to do so thoughtfully, and be listened to with respect by peers, we need to treat them like people who have ideas worth sharing, people whose interpretations of ideas, based on their life situations, are interesting to us. We return to John Dewey for the last word:

> There is all the difference in the world between having something to say and having to say something. The child who has a variety of materials and facts wants to talk about them, and his language becomes more refined and full, because it is controlled and informed by realities.[10]

Strategies to Promote Oral Literacy and Self-Confidence among All Students

If we truly wish for our children to develop the power of their spoken voice, as individuals, in groups, and in public performance as citizens contributing to the common good, we will have to devote some time to teaching them how to do that. The practice of oratory should be revived as part of a twenty-first-century media consciousness. What we need are not more of the speech courses, as some of us remember them, led by teachers who taught only Speech or English, but exercises that are part of the enhanced Literacy Labs described in chapter 11. Oral literacy should be emphasized and integrated into all subjects. Students, for example, should be regularly expected to take their turn presenting math problems, explaining the results of science labs, and so forth, to the class. Here are some other suggestions and examples:

❧ *Emphasize storytelling and read-aloud skills, up through the grades.* Build a school tradition of storytelling, tall tales, rapping. All middle school and high school kids—the boys especially—learn to read books, with expression, to younger children. An African-American teacher in New Jersey makes this a requirement of her high school English class. She told me, "This way, when a boy visits his girlfriend's house, he has a way of relating to the younger kids who might be there. It helps teenage boys connect to children."

❧ *Bring back some forms of memorization.* People remember the poems or speeches they memorize for school. Parents, teachers, and community leaders might develop a list of poems reflecting the diversity of the community from which students can select some to memorize. Such a list helps unite school and community through respect for oral traditions in literature.

❧ *Create a ritual of classroom "conversation" as a prelude to other academic tasks.* Break into groups to discuss the lesson at hand: (1) "How much do we already know about this topic?" (2) "What do we *want* to know about this topic?" (3) "What is a good question to get everybody started?" so that the teacher can stimulate curiosity and build upon the awareness, biases, areas of ignorance that students have identified. Help kids learn to brainstorm.

❦ *Have students work in small groups for speech making.* Teams go up front together, stand together, and support one another while they're presenting, to reduce stage fright.

❦ *Create a classroom culture that shuns teasing or put-downs,* which are so common in many school settings. Nothing inhibits shy or vulnerable students as much as the threat of being made fun of by classmates.

❦ *Celebrate oral tradition.* Every student, up through the grades, researches and recites a piece of folklore, long poem, or children's story from that student's culture and heritage. These are recorded on cassette as a part of every student's portfolio.

❦ *Base graduation speeches on merit, not just on grades.* Salem High School, in Conyers, Georgia, has a committee of graduating students who invite all seniors to submit short speeches they wish to make at graduation, and they choose the best five or six. The salutatorian and valedictorian also make speeches, but it's not just the two kids with the highest grades who have something worthwhile to say to the graduates and their families.

We have only begun to explore the range and depth of potential experiences for students of all ages that build on their capacities to speak—that most difficult literacy skill which they have, in a sense, already mastered before coming to school. In the next two chapters, I want to reflect on what makes for excellent performance from passionate learners (and from young people we hope will re-emerge as passionate learners). But also, what are the ways we unknowingly undermine excellence, even while trying to promote it? And when we do see evidence of true excellence in student learning (as distinguished from an obsession to "please the teacher" or to "get everything *right*"), how can we assess it and help kids demonstrate it?

PART FOUR

Passionate Teaching

and Learning

in an

Era of Standardization

A Passion for Excellence—

and How We Undermine It

Quality and *excellence*—these words are part of every ad for au-
tomobiles, mail-order foodstuffs, Internet clothing retailers,
or retirement communities. It's what we want out of life, in the
things we buy, but also in our relationships and life situations.
We want quality and excellence in our children's education,
too, but we're not sure what it looks like—how to assess the
quality of a school our child is planning to attend, or how to
tease it of our child's report card.

As parents, we want to know that the learning experiences
our children will get from a school will be high-quality experiences. But what we hear from the school, about itself, has
mostly to do with the school's "proud tradition," its "talented
faculty," its facilities, and how many of its students get accepted
at which colleges. Proof of quality in our children's learning achievement is what we yearn for, but grade-point aver-
ages, honor roll listings, and awards certificates are what most
schools offer. And confusion is too often what we settle for.

As teachers, we want to know not only that our students are

excited about and engaged in their learning, but that they've learned *well*. We want evidence that the instruction we offer them results in excellent student performance. But again, all too often, we settle for something else: tests, grades, rates of attendance, or homework completion.

The Quality of Excellence and Young Learners: A Quandary

Part of the problem is that we often confuse "excellence" or "high quality" in student work with "perfection" or "completion" of assigned tasks, exams, and papers. A student who grapples with a fascinating problem may evince excellent thinking even if she does not solve that problem. And one who explains some scientific phenomenon in a way that makes his classmates understand it may display a higher level of knowledge than it takes to hand in an error-free lab report. Excellence may have more to do with a student's *quality of engagement over time*—intensive and purposeful involvement in things that matter, working thoughtfully in the right vein (even one that hasn't as yet produced a lot of ore)—than it has to do with the more common measurements we use in school.

I argue that "quality of engagement" is a useful way to represent excellence, since it reflects—in terms of a student's initiative and enterprise—much of what it means to be a passionate learner, namely, *the desire and capacity to keep on learning in the field*. For young or amateur scholars, excellence is often discerned not always in the *product* of the learning endeavor, but in the active pursuit of meaning or truth or acuity within the field.

There will always be students who produce products "of distinction" (essays, research reports, scientific studies, highly creative and well-designed artwork) that are, in themselves, wonderful and inspirational. We don't want to belittle such performances. But many more students have the potential for high-quality engagement in our fields of learning than may yet be able to execute polished pieces of work. We must recognize and nurture those longer-term impulses.

So what am I calling "excellence"? What about the kid who has great enthusiasm for a field of learning—poetry, math, science—but who's sloppy; doesn't seem to care about quality; rushes from topic to topic as his interests wax and wane? How far toward excellence can attitude *alone* carry him, absent demonstrated performance that meets some standard? Are we being asked to abandon high "standards" of performance in deference to nurturing a student's "self-esteem"? Or can we set forth and support high standards of approach, engagement, inquiry, speculation, estimation, hypothesis-forming, that have the effect of keeping the door of excellence open for those who need more time, a little coaching, or the maturity that comes with experience? These are important questions, for which quick or easy answers are unavailable.

If we seek to refine our notion of excellence so that it extends beyond mere obedience to teacher assignments, or a kind of surface competence or perfunctory completion, how as teachers can we structure our class work to best promote this kind of long-range passionate learning? And how can we avoid getting in our own way?

Getting Caught in Our Own Trap

I believe that most of us, as teachers, commit a form of self-sabotage. We lock ourselves into a pattern of stating objectives for our students and then assessing student performance that denies us our most cherished goals for students. I call this *structural disharmony,* and it goes largely unnoticed in schools and colleges everywhere.

We are rarely successful in linking our desire for student excellence to a viable assessment process. We sacrifice quality in student work for precise grading. We try to be "fair" at the expense of our wishes for student growth. We tie ourselves in knots around grading while our students subvert their own learning in trying to comply.

There is a way out of this assessment morass. It requires the courage to set forth goals that cannot be easily or "objectively" assessed, and it offers a way for teachers to help students to document progress on learning objectives that we think are truly important. But first I may need to convince you that we have a problem.

At a workshop I often conduct for teachers from middle school, high school, or college, I invite participants to pick a course they are now teaching—a favorite course, if possible. If you, the reader, have not yet done this exercise, please try it now. Take it one step at a time. It goes like this:

1. List on a sheet of paper your five top goals for student learning—the five things you most want your students to retain and apply a year and more after the course is over. This list represents the quality of results that you want them to get from this course.

2. Put a percentage next to each of the five items, corresponding to its relative importance to you, so that the total adds up to 100.

3. Draw a big circle, a pie chart, and give each of the five items its proper slice of the pie. If each is worth 20 percent, all the slices are the same; if one is really worth 50 percent, it gets half the pie.

I will use, as an example, a twentieth-century U.S. history course in high school:

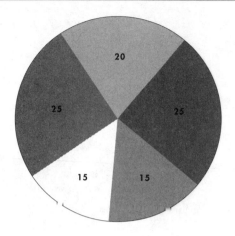

1. Understand struggle between allure of isolationism and growing sense of U.S. responsibility as a global power: 20 percent.
2. Link struggles of workers, African Americans, other minorities, women, and other groups for social justice: 25 percent.
3. Understand concept of "liberalism" and "conservatism" as it pertains to economic and social issues of our times: 15 percent.
4. Develop issues and questions that students hope to remain interested in as they become citizens of the twenty-first century: 15 percent.
5. Relate students' life situations and choices to the challenge of being an active citizen, locally and nationally: 25 percent.

Allow me to suggest that this page represents the "passionate teacher" in you; it's the heart of why you are a teacher of this subject for these students. Even as you might want to adjust or amend this list, it represents the quality you seek from your work with them. It defines the goals that, if achieved by your students, constitute excellence in your course.

Now, put this page aside. Take out another page and draw a similar pie chart that will explain how you currently grade students in this course. On this new page, list the five most important things students are graded on (e.g., quizzes, final exam, class participation, homework assignments, research paper or project). Again, give each of these a percentage, adding up to 100 percent and place them on the second pie chart.

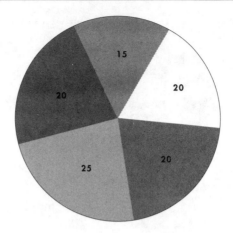

1. Class participation in discussions about issues raised by the course topics: 15 percent.
2. Quizzes, chapter tests: 20 percent.
3. Homework assignments: 20 percent.
4. Individual project on issue of choice: 25 percent.
5. Final exam (given by the history department): 20 percent.

This page represents, roughly, your grading structure for the course. It reflects the grading objectives that guide your students as they pursue their learning tasks. It's what students usually want to know most about any course they enroll in.

The next step is often anticipated (and may be accompanied by a few groans), as I say, "Now, place both pie charts side by side, and tell me what you see."

The looks I get run the gamut: bemused, awkward, skeptical, angry.

The first thing we should acknowledge about the two pie charts is that they are talking about quite different things. They speak to our students in different languages.

On your first pie chart, you have very likely listed things that are highly prized by amateurs and professionals alike who work in this field of knowledge. You've talked about knowledge and skills and ways of relating to ideas; you've mentioned attitudes such as attention to detail, looking below the surface, being reflective in examining one's biases.

On the second pie chart you have displayed the nitty-gritty language of numbers and scores and other quantifiable stuff. It's what people in school view as "the bottom line." But the bottom line is that if you offered both pie charts to your students on the first day of class and told them they could keep only one of them, you know they'd pick the second pie chart. "If I told them they could keep *both* of them," a teacher often interjects at this point, "I'd find the first one on the floor or stuffed in the back of their desks. It doesn't mean anything to them."

Here's where we get trapped. It's a bigger problem than just coping with a traditional grading process. It stems from two factors: (1) as teachers we must be ready to defend the grades we give; and (2) we naturally emphasize what we can more easily measure.

By doing this exercise, we underscore our own predicament regarding quality and excellence. In fashioning a grading structure that we and our students can live with, we abandon our deeply held goals for teaching and learning excellence.

Some teachers tell me that this exercise has taught them to be more conscious about how they relate the first pie chart to the second. We focus too heavily on calculations drawn from the second without articulating—to our students (and ourselves)—the assumptions of the first. Thus, our goals become the victim of our grades.

This exercise often gets me into trouble with my audience. They think they've been tricked. They're right. I have tricked them into revealing, on paper, the fundamental contradictions between their quality goals as educators and the nasty reality of what they have been led to believe it takes to get their students to do the work.

With a college faculty audience, I get grumbles of "Well, there are lots of damned important things we all try to do that just can't get measured. There's no use trying, either. It's part of life in the Academy; the students just have to get used to it." In a less sophisticated gathering, I might hear, "Well, after all, the students need to know that we're going to grade their homework; otherwise they just won't do it."

I understand and sympathize with all such complaints, but I accept none of them, for myself or for other teachers.

The truth is that few of us, as teachers, make a practice of articulating the linkage between (1) the qualities that we ourselves strive for as scholars and teachers; (2) how we share these values with students who may (at this stage) be merely "sampling" the things we have devoted our lives to; and (3) how—given our awesome power in grading our students—we can increase the chances that our students will understand, begin to assimilate, and *hold on* to these essential aspects of what we teach. How can we hold on to the quality we seek while being fair to our students?

Our desire for excellence in learning comes smack up against the notion that students will "do the work" only if they are motivated by the threat or promise of a grade, and moreover that it's our duty to guarantee that those grades will be based on criteria that are clear, objective, and in general conformity with school norms.

These contradictions have become second nature to the teaching profession, and their impact on passionate learning is devastating. Put bluntly, we find we are unable to accurately assess what we most value in student learning, so we assess what we can measure with a fair degree of objectivity. The result is that our students have little choice but to value only what we measure. And, over time, most students lose their ability to hear what we really want to inspire them with. Their receptivity to "quality" atrophies. And, in time, so does ours.

Finding Our Way out of the Trap

I suggest to the workshop participants that they take another look at their second pie chart and try to come up with language that reflects their true purposes. The aim is to rework our goal statements for student learning so they can be more readily assessed—without losing their vitality as representations of what we care most about as teachers. When we do so, our second pie chart (on grading) looks something like this:

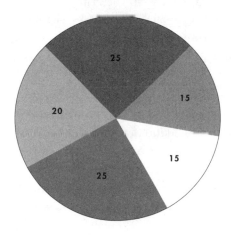

1. Evidence, via journals and class discussions, that the student can relate themes of the course to her own life situation and has thought through and discussed with family and friends what it means to be a "liberal" or a "conservative" and an "isolationist" or a "globalist" in the times we live in: 25 percent.

2. Short-answer test on major terms, people, and events of twentieth-century America. Test may be taken up to three times, with highest score counting: 15 percent.

3. Student essay on twentieth-century struggle for social justice by one of the following: workers, women, minorities, showing how their struggle compares with two other groups: 15 percent.

4. Self-designed individual or group project researching major person or event (e.g., Vietnam, the Depression, FDR) based on a preapproved question that student seeks to answer: 25 percent.

5. Final exam (given by the history department): 20 percent.

In comparing the original grading pie chart with our new one, we discover that things we assumed were essential parts of the grading process—quizzes, tests, homework, attendance—may be the result of a need to come up with numbers to put in our grade book. Such traditional grading criteria poorly represent the long-range impact we hope our teaching will have on our students.

By now the exercise has become more interesting, and even more revealing. The first two pie charts reveal an apparent *conceptual and linguistic contradiction:* the goals and language of the first don't match up with the criteria of the second. In attempting to bridge the gap, we grapple with a deeper *structural* contradiction. Almost always there is an initial mismatch between the percentage of the grade accorded to mastery of specific skills and knowledge and the relative weight of those same skills and knowledge and capacities in our stated goals. We say, for example, that we value students "relating" concepts, events, struggles for equity, to their own life situations and, in effect, *acting as amateur historians* in the way they deal with events and people of the twentieth century. This makes up about 75 percent of our "desired goals" wish list (with the remaining 25 percent keyed to students viewing themselves as "active citizens").

And yet, in our initial grading pie chart, we place upwards of 60 percent of the course grade on something different: testing the absorption of facts and information, plus completing homework assignments. The grading tools and mechanisms we regularly rely on leave out important components of desired excellence. We systematically skew our assessment tools to assess things we must confess that we don't value nearly as much.

Our students aren't fooled for a minute. They take the second pie chart seriously. As they should. And then we wonder why many of the students we regularly give an A or a B to seem little inclined to continue to act as amateur historians or active citizens.

What we want most of all, as Seymour Sarason keeps reminding us, is that our students should develop a desire to keep learning in this area or subject after they have finished the course. But we are so hobbled by an inability to convey this hope—in a manner that places it at least on a par with our students' anxieties about the grade we will be giving them—that we relegate our pursuit of quality to the status of fantasy. "Maybe one or two of these students will take inspiration from their experience with me in this course of study and pursue it on their own—someday."

And, in fact, some do. They tend to be the students who did best within the grading criteria we've established, the ones who not only feel favorably disposed toward our subject area but have been given confidence, in part by receiving high grades from us, that "this is a field I may be good at." That is fine. But don't we want other students, also, to feel motivated to keep alive an interest in what we teach—even if they are "not so good at it"?[1] And what do we do for *them,* save to lay out a banquet of sorts and invite them to partake (knowing, as they do, that they are going to be evaluated on their level of current consumption and their ability to, as it were, repeat what they have eaten back to us—with no apparent regard for the future of their appetite)?

As mathematicians, scientists, historians, artists, philosophers, lovers of literature, and champions of clear and concise writing, we hold strong beliefs about how we want students to investigate and begin to work with certain ideas (number sets, experimental data, original source material, moral dilemmas, epic poetry, essay topics).

Nothing is as disheartening as seeing students reacting cavalierly or superficially to things we care deeply about, or finding ourselves continually making compromises between what *we* value in our field of knowledge and what we think students will be willing to put up with, however grudgingly.

But what can we do? The semester is nearly over. We decide that the best thing is to grade the student on our rough estimation of the quality of work, but in a manner that is not likely to cause us further argument. We call it "being generous." It happens all the time. Whatever has remained of our desire for quality has vanished in the rush-to-judgment before the deadline for posting grades.

We must try to keep from sabotaging ourselves around issues of quality.

Building Quality into the Teaching Plan

Let's go back to the exercise we began with. Take a second look at the first pie chart, "the five things you most want your students to retain and apply a year and more after the course is over." Spend some time working over and refining that list, if you like, *but do not alter or eliminate any item just because you think it will prove difficult or impossible to assess or to grade.* If anything, strengthen the list with your dreams of what it would be like to be a teacher with a class of passionate learners. But try to write it in a language that your students can more easily relate to. Set your standards high, but make your language clear and inviting. Then, put this list aside while we investigate other traps we set for ourselves along the route to advocating and promoting the excellence in student work that mirrors passionate learning.

In outlining a course syllabus, we tend to focus on the "material to be covered," rather than to envision our course as "journeys of exploration and discovery" into areas that we hope will lead our students to become more powerful and to forge connections with important things in the world. I have discussed the preparation of units and courses in some detail in *The Passionate Teacher,* particularly in chapters 4, 15, and 16. The gist of the argument is as follows:

1. A course syllabus or unit plan should be an inviting communication to your students (rather than something designed for the head of curriculum). Talk directly to your students as junior partners in the exploration ahead.

2. A course syllabus or unit plan should clearly outline the *performance expectations* you have for students by the end of the course or unit—*the knowledge, skills, and attitudes* that successful students will have gained by the time the course or unit is over and that includes some items—especially skills and attitudes—that students already have at least some grasp of. (See, below, the "performance expectations" I've set for my course in children's literature). Begin with a discussion of why anyone should care about this area of knowledge, and include some catchy open-ended "hook" questions about the topic, questions that invite students to enter as *active players* rather than passive spectators—even if they don't know much about the material that's in the course itself.

3. A course syllabus or unit plan should offer students several ways of approaching or organizing their work in the subject area, based on the fact that not everybody learns in the same way or is attracted to the same aspects of the course. The availability of choices about the work is particularly important in promoting self-motivation and a sense of ownership by students.

4. A course syllabus or unit plan should focus on the really important and lasting ideas and issues, rather than having students memorize all the details (unless, of course, it is in the details that the true importance lies). Keep emphasizing how the areas under study connect with things important to your students now and in the not-too-distant future.

5. A course syllabus or unit plan should try to find ways for students to work in small groups on projects or presentations (but make sure they accept the responsibility to make their presentations interesting to their classmates).

6. In all of this, position yourself as a "coach" for your students—on *their* side in the effort to make sure they "get something valuable" from the course—rather than as the "judge" whose role comes principally when the learning is over and it's time to tell them "what they got."

I have seen in classroom after classroom (my own, my students', and other teachers') that this approach to developing a unit or a course can focus students' attention on excellence, on their own passionate interest in the material. Here is an example of how I am currently using this model, especially in regard to number 2 on the above list:

Performance Expectations for ED 1405:
Children's and Adolescent Literature

Let's begin by imagining what you will *know, be like, and be able to do* once you have successfully completed this course—it's a bit different from listing the topics we will be "covering." What follows is a list of performance expectations for ED 1405. It's what I want you to end this class knowing and being able to do (realizing that most of you have experience and skills in some or many of these areas).

A. *I will have successfully completed ED 1405*
   once I know
   1. at least fifty children's books that might be interesting to a wide range of kids
   2. what the state frameworks in literacy are and how children's literature relates to them

3. what types of children's and adolescent literature are likely to find favor with the diverse kids who live in the communities where I expect to be teaching

4. how and why traditional nursery rhymes and fairytales have had such durability down through the ages (and why they might be in danger of losing their appeal)

5. how to help my students find access to their own and other cultures through books and oral storytelling traditions

6. how to increase access to literature by students and parents outside of school

B. *I will have successfully completed ED 1405*
once I have the skills to

1. read aloud, expressively, to children of different ages, so that they ask me for more

2. encourage children to read to me and enjoy the experience of being read to

3. create a children's book on my own, perhaps with help from a young person

4. organize a classroom to promote interest in reading by a wide diversity of students

5. teach children how to enjoy reading on their own and with each other

6. help my students' parents play a larger role in their child's enjoyment of reading

C. *I will have successfully completed ED 1405*
once I have an attitude that

1. appreciates the power of children's and adolescent literature to help students become independent and self-motivated readers and learners

2. understands why for some children books are strangers, and how to help them make friends with books in the homes and neighborhoods where they live

3. seeks out and involves me in the experiences of other cultures and their literature

4. allows me to get in touch with my own early experiences with literature so that I can use my own memories (good or not so good) as ways of connecting to my students

5. encourages students to express their individuality in the stories they read and create

6. understands and supports parents in doing the best they can to help their child become a happy reader, regardless of the parents' level of formal education

These eighteen items, from the three categories of *knowledge, skills, and attitudes*, represent my view of what it takes to be able to bring the power and wonder of literature to children and young adults of all cultures and backgrounds. I invite your comments and suggestions on ways to improve and enrich this list.

This page is the heart of the syllabus. But most students have never seen anything like it, and it takes some getting used to. They want to know what they're getting graded on.

The Trap: Precision and Fairness in Assessment
as the Enemy of Excellence

In reviewing our second and third pie charts, we haven't fully dealt with the reality and necessity of assessment and the ways that traditional grading structures undermine the approach to unit or course planning that we've just now walked through.

I believe that we too often fall into a trap with regard to assessing student work and assigning grades, and that the trap leads us away from excellence and passionate learning. I'm convinced there is also a way out.

There are few teachers, of any subject or grade level, who

would not want to be thought of as "fair" by their students when it comes to assessment. To have as much power as we have in the grading process may mean to all teachers of conscience that they dare not be anything *but* fair when it comes to giving grades. But such an emphasis on fairness, especially if fairness becomes associated in teachers' minds with "precision," may lead to a trap.

The trap is that we become dependent on assessing student achievement by using measures that offer the illusion of precision. Here's a hypothetical example:

You are teaching a diverse group of fifth graders, and your unit topic is "Discovering Our Heritage." A big part of this assignment is for students to interview the oldest living relative they have ready access to and to ask that person about what life was like when he or she was growing up. The kids are excited. Together, in class, they have been practicing interviewing techniques, devising questions, writing down responses. It's a big deal, and the students are supposed to write a summary of their interview and make an oral report to the whole class on their findings.

What will you tell your students about how you will be assessing their efforts? How much of their grade for this unit will depend on (1) the skill and style of their oral presentations, (2) the grammatical correctness of their written report, and (3) the range and depth of topics covered in that report? Let's say you've worked this out for yourself: 30 percent for oral presentation, 30 percent for grammar and spelling, and 40 percent for range and depth (or some variation of these percentages).

But then there's Luisa, who was born in Puerto Rico but has lived in the United States since she was five years old. Luisa is rather shy, and she has some problems with written English, although she's been working hard at it and showing steady, if slow, improvement. Her oral report is halting, not very polished (she's very afraid of being teased by some of the boys, so she tends to speak almost in a whisper). Her written report, likewise, has more than a few errors, and it looks as though she has been constrained by her insecurity about writing to limit herself mostly to simple words and phrases. At best, a mediocre job.

Two of Luisa's friends in class, who attend church with her, come up to you and tell you that Luisa is a celebrity now, because she was able to get her grandfather to talk about his life as a peasant boy in Puerto Rico. Provoked by Luisa's questions, the old man has opened up his history to his family. It turns out that it was her questions that broke through his silence, during a family meal. And Luisa was invited by her youth group at church to talk about it, which she did, bringing her grandfather along. Everybody has been congratulating her since.

You ask Luisa about the story and, shyly, she confirms it, smiling broadly. So what are you going to put down in your grade book for this unit? The grades you have already recorded for Luisa, based on her performance in class and on her written report, amount to a C at best.

But now you have new information. How can you give Luisa credit for doing something that is apart from the criteria you announced in class? How can you *not* give her credit for achieving such an apparently wonderful result? But if you do, aren't you being unfair to all the other kids who may have had very good interviews at home that you don't know about? And if you don't, won't you be sending Luisa a message that her triumph on the assignment is irrelevant to your assessment? What a mess! Perhaps you'd better not use this unit again. It's just too much of a hassle to grade it fairly.

That's the trap. And teachers tell me they get caught in traps like this all the time. Most of us find some way out, and we each can think of how Luisa's teacher might do right by the girl without disregarding the carefully established grading criteria. She can quietly give Luisa extra credit in the grade book, or add points to her final average when it comes to the report card—using the discretion that all teachers value, to shade a grade one way or another based on "other" evidence or the student's "attitude." But I am worried that Luisa's teacher may seek, in the future, to avoid potential hassles by opting not to teach creative units because they present such problems with assessment.

My point is that the *"trap" is inescapably linked to a teacher's justifiable desire to make grading as precise as possible.* "Fairness" in grading demands reliance on numerical grading criteria that have been selected *precisely* because they can be more easily measured. When we equate fairness with precision, the trap closes. Since we don't want to have to make judgments that we or others might view as subjective, we grade what we can easily measure, not what we truly value. Our students ignore high-quality learning and focus, single-mindedly, on grading criteria. We then feel we must protect ourselves from kids who might "cheat" in order to get an undeserved grade.

What worries me is not only that kids like Luisa will often fail to get the recognition they deserve because their best learning has taken place outside the teacher's angle of vision (or in another context that isn't acknowledged by the criteria used to generate a grade), as serious a problem as this is. I worry most that teachers will find it "just doesn't pay" to put their energies into creative projects for fear that they will be vulnerable to a student or a parent who doesn't like a particular grade and complains about it. Far better to have, for one's defense, that grade book, with its long line, next to each name, of homework checks, quiz grades in small numbers, chapter tests in bigger numbers, an assortment of plusses and zeroes for daily participation, lateness notations, extra credit marks given or not given. I fear that that will in the end define assessment and the learning that precedes it. For teachers who want to encourage true excellence in our students, valuing only what we can easily measure comes at an unacceptable cost.

CHAPTER FOURTEEN

Celebrating

"Inconsistent Excellence"

It is a too-often-used analogy to say that we pay millions of dollars a year to a baseball player who, as a batter, fails to do what he's supposed to do seven out of ten times. If he maintains an average of .300 (actually, in school grade terms, a 30 percent), he's a star. But if a student makes more than one mistake in ten (i.e., bats less than .900), she risks losing her A. Agreed, the analogy is flawed. You don't get to the majors unless you can hit a ball with great consistency against average pitching.

In reality, there are relatively few endeavors in which consistency of *results* is a necessary attribute of excellence (e.g., performing surgery, canning vegetables, piloting an airplane, filling prescriptions). Certainly not in the arts, or politics, or the stock market, or parenting. Consistency of *effort*, perhaps (i.e., consistent, concentrated effort may be the only way to generate truly excellent moments). But excellence in a profession rarely if ever means absolute consistency of product. It is great when a writer produces a string of masterpieces or when an honest politician wins every election or when a broker picks one winner after another. But it's not expected. Talented adults in many walks of life—people with years of experience behind them—do *wonderful* things *some* of the time.

Why cannot we be similarly generous toward young learners? Why must they perform well on every quiz, get every report in on time, accomplish every task flawlessly in order to be an A student? Why create a structure of assessment in which the learner must perform as the teacher wishes 90 percent or more of the time in order to be considered excellent?

I want to make a distinction here that I feel is vital. I am not proposing that we lower standards or define as "excellent" student work that achieves 85 percent or 80 percent, much less 70 percent. I am not talking about "dumbing down." I am talking about *consistent standards of high performance* (including opportunities for learners to make mistakes in getting there) as opposed to *high expectations of consistent performance*. This is not complicated

> Maria is the kind of student who works very hard and does
> quite well on tests, papers, homework, and class participation.
> She is very steady, nearly always on time, and very willing to
> help others. Antonio is the kind of student who is a bit erratic
> at times but who produces really thoughtful and well-executed
> work. He is sometimes late; he does only a mediocre job on as
> signments in which he has little interest; but when he's excited
> about a topic, he goes well beyond what's required and gives it
> his all, regardless of how much the assignment "counts."

I submit that Maria and Antonio are *both* "excellent" students, although each demonstrates excellence in significantly different ways. If we were writing letters of recommendation for employment or for college, our letters for Maria and for Antonio would highlight different qualities—one college might grab Antonio because of his brilliance; another would be impressed with Maria's maturity and consistency. But if they were receiving grades in a typical high school class, Maria would probably be an A student and Antonio might have to settle for a B.

In my classes, I regularly meet students who have been hobbled by their "straight-A" image. They have learned "what it takes to come out on top" in their classes, and when I ask them about it, they admit to me that what it usually takes is "single-minded focus on what the teacher wants." They rarely even question it—that's how the game is played. Many of these students get quite anxious whenever I change "the game" to require inventiveness and risk taking. They plead, "What do I have to do to get an A?"

The same holds for two other students I might describe, John and Michelle, who are somewhat less proficient than Maria and Antonio, but who possess similarly differing ways of exhibiting their achievements—John is the more consistently B-type student; Michelle, more erratic but capable of episodes of higher quality work, might struggle for a C. It may seem like a small distinction, one letter grade, more or less. But to the inconsistently excellent (or inconsistently "good") student, the message may be harsher: "If you want to succeed in school, you must submit to your teacher's will in all things and not follow your own interests or timetable, *even when your agenda more closely touches the essence of the subject you are studying.*" And for teenagers in the process of redefining themselves in relation to adult authority, that message is deadly. It leads either to a subjugation of the learning process in deference to adult authority, or to rebellion, to a temporary or more lasting break with school.

It does not have to be thus. As teachers, we can uphold standards—raise them, even—without demanding from children and adolescents that they subvert their passion for learning. We can find common ground. We need not, as teachers or parents, become subservient to the whims of our teenage students or children.

What we must strive to do is to separate, in our minds, those "standards" that merely uphold the conventions or regularities of school culture from those that highlight and promote ongoing intellectual or artistic engagement for young learners. Let's look at a few practical ways to do this:

1. *Require fewer—but more engaged, complex, and thoughtful—performances from students.* (More focus on big projects than on everyday homework completion; more options for students in choosing essays or research papers).

2. *Place more emphasis on student self-evaluation than on teacher monitoring.* (When students have to propose and defend their request for a grade, based on their own work, they can help us cope with the uncertainties of grading.)

3. *Use quizzes primarily as diagnostic—rather than evaluative—tools.* (Allowing students to grade their own quizzes and then report back on their strengths and weaknesses emphasizes individual accountability and responsibility.)

4. *Base the grade on a scale of 120 or 125 points, rather than 100, with any grade over 90 being equal to A.* (By using a basis larger than 100, students are allowed to excel in one or several areas of high-quality performance, even if they remain less proficient in other areas. For example, a student who puts a lot of extra work into a project—"more than it's worth" in terms of a percentage of the total grade—is able to offset a low score on a test she wasn't able to study for. The idea is to encourage students to take risks by engaging in high-challenge learning activities, since points lost to mistakes can be made up elsewhere.)

This last point, attacking as it does one of the most universally relied on teaching tools in education—the numerical sense of what an A is—is bound to raise eyebrows and hackles. But hold your fire, and let us take a closer look at grades and grading.

A Closer Look at Grading

The main reason we teachers have for using grades is to have some leverage with which to make reluctant students do the work they're supposed to. "And a very good reason it is!" many will say, "Can you imagine how little work most of these kids would do if all we did was to give them a little pat on the head if they had done well, or a disapproving frown if they had not?" But as an advocate of passionate teaching and learning, I don't accept this rationale *in and of itself.* Grading can sap motivation as well as spur it; there are better ways to make students want to learn well.

There seem to me to be only two valid rationales for giving grades to students. (I surmise that the "motivating power" teachers seek actually comes as a function of these two other rationales.) The first is that *it gives an occasion for a teacher and a learner to have a conversation about the quality of the learner's efforts to date.* The second reason is that *a grade is an expression of a teacher's judgment as to how a learner's current performance is likely to affect the future course of that learner's formal education.* In other words, a grade on a report card is a message to a current student, ar.d to future teachers of this student, about what to expect from him or her.

At first glance, these two purposes appear unrelated. The first provides the context for a conversation, whereas the second makes a prediction. We may in fact be amiss in using the same instrument for such divergent objectives. Of course, most teachers will cite a third reason, namely, that it is their *duty*—a part of their job—to evaluate student learning. But one can assess performance without assigning grades.

Since preoccupation with grades dominates the thinking of students and their teachers (and parents!), from elementary school to graduate school, and since I believe that issuing grades is in most ways detrimental to the pursuit of quality in learning, we are obliged to take the process very seriously and to look at its effects on the learner.[1]

Many have written about the long-term negative effects upon students of receiving grades of F or D or of not getting that much-sought-after A. I have written in *The Passionate Teacher* that grades of F and D are counterproductive and should be eliminated, with the "passing grade" at C or B indicating the *minimal acceptable level of genuine competence* in the subject or skill being learned.[2] A student who has not yet achieved that competence level should be so informed, with no other penalty than that he or she must complete the work or not receive credit for the course.[3]

But let's go back to the first rationale for grades, that they focus the teacher's and the learner's attention on assessing the learner's performance. This is a very important objective, one that should take the form of a friendly but structured conversation. This seems to me to be so vital a purpose that *we should not consider abandoning traditional letter or number grades—for all their flaws—unless we can be fairly sure that whatever we replace it with will guarantee that such a serious conversation takes place.*

Experienced teachers may argue that one cannot have a serious conversation with a student who's performing poorly without the threatening pressure of a grade, but this speaks to the broader goal of establishing a climate of mutual respect between teacher and learner, something that grading (with its inherent power differential) often subverts. In any case, in such a conversation, the learner and teacher ought to talk about some or all of the following:

ᔖ How much quality is reflected in what the learner has thus far demonstrated?

ᔖ What strengths and weaknesses are evident, and how might the learner build on the strengths and overcome the weaknesses?

ᔖ How has the range and depth of the learner's interest in this subject evolved, and what connection has been made to the learner's life?

ᔖ What can the learner do to try to reach a level of proficiency and interest that is both satisfying now and enabling of future learning?

Notice that intermingled with these questions is an emphasis on words like *interest, quality,* and *proficiency,* rather than words that describe levels of compliance. And in these respects we use grading too little, rather than too much. We need more conversations about interest, quality, and proficiency, not fewer. But like any interaction between people, there must be mutual respect for the conversation to be worthwhile. And that condition is by no means assumed in the processes by which teachers grade students' work.

The idea here is that we want our students to focus on the depth and quality of their work, not on the hurried completion within an arbitrary time frame of something that has a veneer of being finished even though we sense that it has little meaning to either the student or ourselves. In fact, we teachers hope for nothing so much as that, for a number of our students at least, our work in class will be "incomplete"—that they will remain actively engaged in pursuing the themes, concepts, ideas, values of our subject after the course of study is over. Imagine! To have students (more than one or two of them) dropping by a year or so after a course is over just to fill us in on the learning begun in our course that they have continued to pursue! We can promote this desired result by nurturing and celebrating their incomplete forays, their inquiries, speculations, imaginative projections into our field of knowledge.

Few teachers feel free to radically revise how they grade, though in most cases, we probably have more freedom than we think. But I believe there are ways to help all teachers and learners, from third or fourth grade through graduate school, to derive most benefit (and least angst) from the grading process.

Consider another example from the course in children's literature that I am now teaching. Here is what I say about grading in my syllabus:

About Your Grade . . .

The conventional way to inform students about grading is by telling you how much each aspect of the course "counts" (e.g., 20 percent for class participation, 25 percent for final exam, etc.). But although many students prefer this, since it seems to simplify the process of getting the grade you want ("I'd better raise my hand and say *something* during each class"; "I'd better not turn my paper in late or I'll lose points"), it really doesn't say much about what you actually *know* and *can do* in the subject area being studied.

Instead, I will try to describe what differentiates students in the A range, the B range, and the C range. You can then approach this course bearing in mind the kind of student you are (or would like to become), rather than to count up the percentages and hope for the best. So here is a rough idea of what each of these categories means. Note, for every grade there is a range (+/ −) to allow for differences in the quality of student work produced:

Students in the A range (A+, A, A-)
🥃 Are self-starters who take the initiative—they don't wait for the professor to tell them what to do; approach

the subject with an independent and conscientious viewpoint; take some risks, such as expressing opinions that may be "unpopular" or that may differ from the professor's; read articles and commentaries with a critical eye—looking for authors' biases that may color the meaning

~ Come to class consistently and interact with other students and the professor about books and ideas; really try to "get into" children's literature by reflecting on what books meant to them as a child—and also what kind of reader they have become; read to children and talk to them about what they like and don't like about reading; spend time in children's libraries and bookstores looking at books; say to themselves, "This is something I want to learn for myself and for kids—not just because it's required"

~ Spend time putting their thoughts and experiences on paper—don't wait until a week before the final essay is due to get started; end up with lots of thoughts, experiences, examples to choose from in writing, rather than having to scramble to find something to say; proofread and edit their papers so that they best reflect what they really want to say; ask for feedback from others to improve early drafts of their papers

~ Develop and improve their skills by practicing reading aloud to children with drama and with exuberance; put lots of creativity into the children's book they create; bring their own original perspective and critical ideas to books for children and teenagers; conscientiously build their own libraries of children's books

Students in the B range (B+, B, B-)

~ Are very conscientious about their work; strive to do what's expected of them in a competent and timely man-

ner; listen carefully to instructions and try to follow
them; are honest about what they think and write

❧ Come to class regularly and take part in class discussions; try to discover the most important aspects of children's literature through their readings; reflect on their
own childhood experiences with books; read to children and talk with them about what they like and don't
like about reading; spend time in children's libraries and
bookstores looking at books

❧ Care about the quality of their written work—don't
wait until a week before the Big Paper is due before
getting started; write competently and expressively;
proofread and edit their papers with care. Essays may
not be as in-depth or reflective as papers in the A range
but are clearly expressed

❧ Do a very good job of creating a children's book of their
own; improve their ability to read aloud expressively to
children. Themes and illustrations in their own books
may show less originality and creativity than those in
the A range

Students in the C range (C+, C, C-)

❧ Tend to "do the minimum" to get by; focus on what the
professor is emphasizing (rather than on how they react
to or interpret those issues in terms of their own experiences); tend to wait to be told what to do, or not to do
much of anything unless it is clearly "required"

❧ Come to class most of the time but tend to let other
students carry the conversation; summarize the main
points of a book or article, rather than trying to discern
what they believe is really valuable; tend to avoid focusing on their own childhood experiences with books;
spend little time browsing in bookstores or libraries

    ❧ Write in a manner that does not display much originality or reflection on experience; tend not to proofread their writing but rely on the spell-checker to find errors; generally avoid taking risks with expressing ideas or experiences that are meaningful to them but instead try to write what they think will allow them to "get through" the assignment

    ❧ Show little creativity in the children's book they write; read aloud without a lot of expression or evidence of interest

------

When I showed a draft of this to a former student who was considering taking the course, she remarked, "God! That's my worst nightmare—telling me what an 'A-student' *looks like!* I'm the kind of student who needs to know *just what I have to do to get that A,* you know, how long the term paper needs to be, what's going to be on the final exam, how much 'class participation' counts for. It's what I've always been used to. It's what got me this far." We talked some more. I told her that I had already seen lots of creativity and spontaneity on her part and hoped to see more of it as she immerses herself in children's literature.

    I hope I lowered her anxiety a bit. But I take her words to heart, and it is on her behalf that I want to urge my colleagues at all grade levels to help students avoid that "grade-grubbing" mentality. It's not just that D and F students begin to feel like failures as learners, or that B or C students go through school with a second-rate status and a feeling of inadequacy as learners. It's also that our most energetic and capable students find their initiative stifled by a knee-jerk obsession with teacher-pleasing and the fear that one false step, one blown exam question, one project idea that didn't work out as planned might mean loss of that much-desired A.

Thus, in reframing grading, as illustrated in the preceding syllabus excerpt, I hope to help my students think differently about what it takes to "please" *this* teacher—it takes being willing to fall in love with kids' books, to take initiative (such as by handing me a draft of their final essay before it's due so I can offer suggestions), to take risks, to say "unpopular" things, to go "whole hog" about reading aloud to kids, and to put one's thoughts and reflections on paper without being overly concerned with "getting it right." Time will tell whether this approach can at least partially undo years of standard grade-conditioning (or if, sadly, I have merely substituted my own teacher-pleasing criteria for the traditional type). I hope other teachers will experiment as well and that we can learn from one another's attempts.

Parents and Children: Thinking about
Quality Learning Before the School Year Begins

Any change in grading procedures needs the understanding and support of parents. Grade-consciousness by children often begins at home, where the report card assumes a power wholly beyond its intended purpose. If teachers and students are to make headway in reforging their relationship around excellence in learning, there must be communication of such a new vision to parents as well.

For every parent, as for every child, the beginning of a new school year is full of hopes and fears: *"Who will my child's new teacher(s) be?"* "Will my teacher be nice or mean?" *"Will my child be appropriately challenged?"* "Will I make friends with other kids?" *"Will my child do as well as or better than last year?"* and so on.

This is the perfect time for parent and child to have a good talk about their expectations for the quality of the learning they anticipate for the year ahead. The parent should set the scene—

a nice lunch, maybe in the child's favorite fast-food restaurant—with the clear expectation that parent and child will be talking about something important that neither is fully able to control but that both can work toward together.

It's not just a conversation about "doing better in school." That may, indeed, be something worth talking about, but that is another conversation. It's not just about "better study habits" or "getting higher grades," though, again, these may be important topics for another day. Rather, this conversation is about planning the year around the notion of *quality learning*. The first task is to describe what it is and what it isn't:

- Quality learning is something that only a student can achieve—it can't be done to you.

- Quality learning is how you *feel* about a learning experience that makes it special, that gives you a feeling of being connected to wonderful things, skills, ideas.

- Quality learning is likely (at some point) to result in higher grades, but that's not the primary goal. In fact, it's quite possible that a particular teacher may not fully recognize it as valuable learning, because it doesn't conform to his or her expectations—but it's what *you* think makes sense.

- Quality learning has a lot to do with making sure you see the connection between what you are learning and what's important in your life.

- Quality learning means separating the "busy work" from the aspects that have real meaning, and devoting energy to activities that are rich in meaning (even if parents and child agree that doing what's expected by the teacher is also very important). The child should know that the parent respects the difference between true learning and busy work.

ஃ Quality learning requires the parent to be both patient and supportive, holding in check the voices that want to push the child toward short-term, less-authentic rewards, and keeping in one's mind a vision of the child as a lifelong learner.

ஃ Quality learning has a lot to do with taking what's given—an assignment from the teacher—and figuring out how to make it correspond to the child's idea of a quality experience, how to find an angle on the assignment that the child can be enthusiastic about (or at least help the child not feel insulted or overwhelmed by the assignment).

In the best of circumstances, teacher, parent, and student will share the vision of the child as a self-initiating seeker of truth and power through knowledge and skills development. The teacher will, in most cases, take the lead in creating such a vision, but the student and parent must understand and interpret "excellence" in ways that make sense to them.

In closing, I'd like to bring some words from Alfred North Whitehead to help me illuminate this notion of "excellence" in a child's learning:

> Let the main ideas which are introduced into a child's education be few and important, and let them be thrown into every combination possible. The child should make them his own, and should understand their application here and now in the circumstances of his actual life. From the very beginning of his education, the child should experience the joy of discovery. The discovery which he has to make, is that general ideas give an understanding of that stream of events which pours through his life, which is his life.[4]

The parent is a crucial part of such an experience, for it is the parent who can become the child's first and best audience for assessing what happens in school and for developing a strategy for substituting meaning for meaninglessness in schoolwork. The parent, with more experience in life, is also better able to help the child gain perspective on the kinds of learning that help maintain a healthy, confident, creative attitude toward the work of the mind. As Whitehead says,

> What education has to impart is an intimate sense for the power of ideas, for the beauty of ideas, and for the structure of ideas, together with a particular body of knowledge which has peculiar reference to the life of the being possessing it.[5]

These ideas must ultimately belong to the learner; they must be owned by the learner. They cannot be imposed upon the learner by others, not if "the power of ideas" is to become an internal part of the meaning system within the developing person.

If we want children to love learning, to love reading, working with numbers, discovering scientific or historical truths, creating art, and so forth, we as parents must do our part to help our children empower themselves to find the value and joy in such activities—*not to see learning, primarily, as act of obedience or submission to a teacher's authority.*

Now, all this may sound a bit conspiratorial: brave mother and renegade child fighting to save the one, true vision of learning from the polluting regularities of school culture. This is not a film script. But it can be a crucial drama in the educational life of a child, a moment at which a wise adult's intervention, coupled with a child's willingness to risk disfavor with authorities or peers, can engender a passionate learner.

For most families, the scenarios will be a lot less dramatic. Most kids actually like school and strive to do well. Most teachers do their best to relate their lessons to their students' interests. Most parents and teachers are eager to see the spark of learning in children's eyes and are very proud of their achievements.

But even here, the confusion of goals between "doing well in school" and "developing as an engaged and passionate learner" is too common a phenomenon to avoid notice. For too many kids (and their parents), a good report card is the alpha and omega of learning in school. And far too many fail to sustain that bright-eyed, adventurous, risk-taking love of learning that all children possess. The suggestions in this chapter for teachers and parents are meant to give us tools for changing this dynamic and creating passionate, excellent learners.

CHAPTER FIFTEEN

Education

at the Millennium

The Bad and the Good

For new parents and parents of teenagers, for aspiring teachers and teachers with many years of practice to their credit, for learners of every age and life situation, these may be at once the best of times and worst of times. As to the worst, it's not hard to find images that make for a bleak picture of "Education in the New Millennium":

- An economy that promises rich rewards to those who devote themselves single-mindedly to their careers (at the expense of spending time with their families), which leaves many kids growing up having little daily involvement with their parents

- Media and technology overwhelming children's imaginations and luring them into passive consumerism

- A persistent and growing "achievement gap" between

children of privilege and those from low-income and minority households

⁞ The continued segregation of most secondary students "by ability"—which easily becomes a self-fulfilling prophecy, as "high-achievers" succeed and "low-achievers" drop out

⁞ Political forces pushing "accountability" and "high standards" onto children, teachers, and schools— with severe consequences for those who don't pass "The Test"

⁞ A corresponding narrowing of academic freedom and professional respect for teachers, who must now "teach to The Test" or face sanctions in many school systems

But the case can also be made that never before has the educational picture looked so promising:

⁞ Increased recognition of the vital role of parents as active, continuing partners in the education of their children

⁞ Near-universal acceptance of the value of learning as a lifelong pursuit, with community colleges and postsecondary training much more widely available

⁞ A growing consensus that young people all need an academic (rather than purely vocational) preparation for life in a complex economy

⁞ A new emphasis on "high standards" for students, along with measures at every level to help teachers work together to meet those standards

⁞ Advances in technology that allow teachers and small schools access to intellectual resources once reserved for elite institutions

&. A concerted effort to attract people to careers in education and to reform teacher training

&. The creation of new options for schooling: charter schools, pilot schools, magnet schools, homeschooling—allowing choices in public education where few existed previously

So there it is—the bad news and the good news. Good arguments are being made for both viewpoints, as well for the individual points within each. We may agree or disagree with any of this, but no one can claim that education is being ignored in America these days. And while some education professionals are dismayed at the chutzpah of ordinary citizens declaiming on issues that they would prefer be left to the "experts," there is also a sense of democratic participation in an issue of such tremendous consequence for our society.

I tell my college students that there has never been a more exciting time to be entering teaching, never a time when so many options were open and so many issues were "on the table." To say, as many initially do, "I want to be a teacher because, well, I just love little kids," is a necessary but increasingly insufficient basis for making that career choice. We have to not only love them, but love them wisely. And to do that, we must understand ourselves better—as parents and as teachers—so that within this confluence of visions, ideologies, goals, and strategies we can keep our eye on what it takes to nurture passionate learners.

I feel for those who struggle to make sense of their lives as educators and as parents: of teachers "under the gun" to produce higher test results, even when such single-mindedness tears at the soul of passionate learning; for parents who worry that their child is losing a sense of wonder and delight in learning or isn't adjusting well to the regimen of schooling (and wondering whose fault that is).

As if the responsibility and vulnerability of teachers and parents wasn't heavy enough, we are surrounded by a chorus of skeptics, advocates of quick-fix solutions, and one-right-answer idealogues who focus on immediate "measurable" results while ignoring a longer view of children's empowerment as curious questioners and eager, motivated learners.

Facing the Crisis Together

As we look for ways to sustain passionate teaching and learning during these tumultuous times, I want to invite individual teachers, individual parents, and teachers and parents *working together* across school/community boundaries to try to *influence student attitudes toward learning.*

By "attitudes" I mean more than just how kids *feel* about what they're doing in school. We must influence the disposition of learners toward learning itself—raise their confidence, zest, curiosity, and energy with respect to learning within school and without.

I think of towns along the Mississippi River with schools threatened by flooding, where students, teachers, townspeople work together filling sandbags to protect their school against the threat of rising waters. A clear enemy or a common goal that requires teamwork and mutual respect among stakeholders can bring out the best in people.

Here is one such crisis and its impact on teaching and learning. It comes from Lea Johnson, who recently completed my graduate seminar in curriculum. Her story is called "Thank Goodness for Head Lice."

> I will never forget my first experience teaching poor and minority children. I'd landed the job because mine was the only sci-

ence teaching resume received by the school. I signed my contract on Friday to begin the following Monday. As the only science teacher at Rockdale School, I was responsible for teaching all 125 students in the junior high division.

At my previous school, the children came from a middle-class farming community. Every day had been a new adventure. It was fun to teach these students. They wanted to learn. But in my new school I quickly realized that I was in over my head. At Rockdale School it was not possible to use the methods I'd used in the past. After two weeks of trying to build a curriculum around the existing textbooks, I knew it was hopeless. I was attempting to teach in a culture that I knew nothing about.

Rockdale was a poor factory town. Parents were often absent from home because of work constraints. The children were left to fend for themselves. I found my students uninterested in anything related to academics. Many seemed depressed, tired, and hungry. Over 50 percent of my students were reading at a second to third grade level. Several displayed serious acting out behaviors that frightened other students and faculty. The more vocal students seemed angry at the world. Every statement I made was taken as a challenge. I was certain they despised me. I was probably correct. And I was clueless as to how to make them want to learn. How could I interest them in science?

I soon realized that until I understood my students better, I had little hope of actually teaching them science. I felt I had to push my way into their thoughts, into their lives. I was desperate to understand the students, thus I took the chance.

We started talking about life in general. I learned that a lot of my kids really were hungry and tired. More than a few kids did not own bicycles and lived in corrugated metal shacks. They aspired to join the ranks of the blue-collar worker or the unemployed. They only wanted me to pass them on. School was the least of their problems and low on their list of priorities. I sensed that unless I could make the study of earth sci-

ence, chemistry, and biology relevant to their lives, I could
write off science for the year.

Then the entire school contracted head lice. What started
as six cases in kindergarten spread to over three hundred cases
within two weeks. There was widespread panic among students, teachers, and parents. There was talk of closing the
school until the lice somehow disappeared.

As the science teacher, I was asked to coordinate the daily
head checks. Checking 450 students and faculty daily took
almost two hours, even with a team of four faculty assistants.
The students were humiliated—I didn't know how humiliated
until the day a co-worker found two lice in my hair. I understood my students' feelings and decided that we should address
the issue.

My plan was simple. We studied lice. We learned all about
them. The students were fascinated. We decided as a group
that there was nothing to be ashamed of. Several students do-
nated their lice to our "lab," and we tried to raise them in cap-
tivity. We borrowed microscopes and studied them, then made
drawings of what we saw. We mounted dead lice and nits on
slides. Students led question-and-answer periods on lice.

We became the in-house school experts on head lice. Soon
students stopped being embarrassed by the problem. We were
amateur scientists. We were also becoming united as a group,
engaged in solving a problem. How could we stop their spread?
What did they eat? How long did they live? My faculty colleagues made up louse poems and a song in support of our
scientific effort.

This was my first real success in teaching science. Once the
students were engaged, it opened doors to other areas. Soon
the students were studying the biology, chemistry, and earth
science I'd originally hoped for. But this time it was on their
terms. Perhaps the most important lesson learned was to listen
to the students. One student decided to adopt the louse study
and make it a science project. His enthusiasm became conta-

gious, and soon other students decided they wanted to study problems of interest to them. Two of the most disruptive seventh graders proposed a study of a polluted creek.

Class by class we tackled problems and discussed issues. The students became excited about coming to class. We grew alum crystals, mounted leaves, dissected preserved animals, built models of the atom, learned about earthquakes, and developed new recipes for toothpaste. No area of science was off limits.

I wish I could end this paper by telling you that three of my students became Nobel Laureates or received their Ph.D. in a scientific area, but in truth, I don't know what became of my students. Nevertheless, this I believe to be true: by stepping down off my teacher's pedestal, learning about my students, listening to their ideas, and finding areas of relevance to their lives, we all learned a lot of science in the winter and spring of 1974.

So it wasn't *just* head lice that saved Lea Johnson's career—as critical as the lice were. It began with her realization that *unless she really knew her students,* they would continue to distrust and ignore her. She had to abandon the conventional stance that it's her job to convey the information and the students' job to acquire it, and adopt the role of learner—of one who was truly curious and eager to learn about their lives. The integrity of her new role put her in a position so that when a "common enemy" appeared on the scene, she could rally her reluctant scholars to meet the challenge.

Lea Johnson's story is a wonderful example of passionate teaching, of what it means to create passionate learners out of the kinds of kids one finds in a typical classroom. But it is more. It is also, I would argue, a model for how to engage students at a time when standardized, high-stakes testing and the machinery of bureaucratic "accountability" dominates life in school.

The Great Debate: "Resources versus Responsibility,"
"Progressivism versus Tradition"

Educational inequity among people of different ethnic, cultural, and economic backgrounds—inequity of opportunity, as well as the oft-cited "achievement gap" for minority children—is perhaps the dominant political issue in education today. It hits everybody where they live, be it in relation to the property taxes they pay on their house, the candidates they support for local and national election, the choice (if they have one) of what school to send their child to, or whom their children should be grouped with for instruction (i.e., by "ability," by age, or in a multiage, heterogeneous setting).

Many parents who consider themselves "liberal" or "progressive" on other social issues, and who support providing more money for under-resourced schools and funding programs for underperforming children, regularly opt to place their own children either in private schools or in "honors" or "gifted" programs where they will, in effect, be separated from "low achievers."[1] A number of politicians who consider themselves "conservative" and who have, in the past, decried "throwing more money at a failing education system" have recently taken a public stance on behalf of government intervention to significantly improve the results of public schooling for low-income and minority children. Proponents and opponents of standardized testing often find themselves in strange company, politically, on issues of high-stakes tests and teacher accountability.

It is understandable that parents and teachers might feel bewildered by the dimensions of the equity issue, about which so much has already been written and spoken. I am constrained here by two conflicting impulses: (1) a desire not to open up the topic of educational inequity if I do not have the space to do it justice, and (2) my own belief that passionate learning belongs to all children, not just to those whom circumstances have favored with highly educated parents and well-funded schools. For me, the issue of equity is at the heart of the matter. My belief that passionate teaching and passionate learning can contribute to the debate about equity outweighs my reticence.

Let us examine the divisions between social liberals and their conservative counterparts, on the one hand, and educational progressives and traditionalists, on the other, on the politically volatile question of why poor and minority children, particularly African-American and Hispanic children, have such high failure rates in schools.

Spread out on one axis we have those I'll label as "liberals" and "conservatives." In brief, liberals point to inequities in spending and to the enduring legacies of poverty, racism, and disenfranchisement. Conservatives blame a lack of discipline, self-motivation, and/or deficiencies in family and cultural "values" on the part of many disadvantaged students and their parents. Liberals argue that equal resources will produce, in time, comparable results. Conservatives argue that if more failing students would only do what those who *do* succeed do— namely, resist the pressures of their peers and commit their energies to "working hard and doing their homework"—they, too, would succeed. And so it goes.

I think "liberal" and "conservative" are not the most useful labels for these educational stances. What seems apparent to me is that one side is *"resource-focused"* (more funding, more school construction, better teacher/student ratios, more compensatory programs, and the like), whereas the other side is *"responsibility-focused"* (more discipline, self-reliance, accountability, rewards and sanctions, etc.).

But the issue of low achievement and inequity facing students from under-resourced low-income and minority communities is more complex than the argument between liberals and conservatives over resources and responsibility. There is also, especially within America's urban communities, another axis that pits advocates of "progressive/child-centered" educational reforms against those who take, for want of a better term, a more "traditional/authoritarian" stance. On this scale, *progressives* seek a more learner-centered, nongraded, opportunity-rich climate in which intellectual exploration, student self-expression, and focus on "habits of mind" abound, whereas *traditionalists* look for a more tightly structured, instruction-driven, core knowledge–based curriculum that encourages students to show respect and obedience to the adults who can impart to them skills, knowledge, and pride. I prefer the combined term "traditionalist/authoritarian," because neither alone fully encompasses a point of view that says, in effect, "Before we can embrace the kinds of 'individuality' and 'options' that progressives advocate, we must utilize traditions of respect for elders and emphasize skills of reading and writing so that our children can compete with suburban kids in schools, in college, and in the marketplace." I specifically do not include in this definition those "traditional" and "authoritarian" school practices that have led to sorting and labeling children and that have contributed to high levels of alienation and failure in conventional low-income urban and rural neighborhoods.

Indeed, we can find lots of examples of schools organized around very different principles that seem to be quite successful—even when they serve high percentages of students commonly considered to be at risk. There are urban schools, for example, allied with the progressive stance of Ted Sizer's Coalition of Essential Schools that have exemplary track records with regard to attendance, graduation, and college success rates. There are also a number of highly successful urban acade-

	Progressive/ child-centered	Traditionalist/ authoritarian
Resource-focused		
Responsibility-focused		

mies and parochial schools in poor neighborhoods that adhere to strict discipline and traditional teaching methods.

What they have in common are high levels of parent and community support for teachers' insistence on high standards, as well as a high degree of pride, esprit de corps, and sense of mission among staff and students alike. In fact, as my friend Evans Clinchy observes, "given the enormous diversity of interests, talents, home backgrounds, etc., among kids, no single kind of schooling, no single curriculum, no single pedagogical approach is going to be satisfactory for all of them." Clinchy advises me to "come out and say that kids are not going to become passionate learners unless there is a genuine *diversity* of schools . . . guaranteeing that every kid can feel comfortable, wanted, and successful."[2]

Thus, in my taxonomy, one can place oneself anywhere within the matrix formed by these two axes—and still be an advocate for passionate learning (see figure).

No matter where you stand, as a parent or a teacher, regarding "resource focused" versus "responsibility focused" or "progressive/child-centered" versus "traditionalist/authoritarian," the children's experience of passionate learning is necessary for real progress to occur—so that children can aspire to learning excellence that lasts a lifetime.

You can be an advocate for "whole language" or "phonics" instruction (or a combination of the two). You can be pro- or anti- on school uniforms, sex education, special programs for gifted kids, community service for all, even performance-based diplomas or graduation exams. But if you believe that adults can "make" children learn well—in the absence of or in defiance of a child's inner sense of confident engagement with the power of discovery and of mastery—then, in my view, *you are placing that child at great risk of failure as a learner.*

I, of course, have my own beliefs on most of these issues. I obviously favor progressive approaches to teaching over strictly traditional ones, and I'd urge advocates of traditional methods to experiment in new directions. But I realize that, for any teacher or parent, the "right philosophy" must be in tune with one's character and values, or else the child experiences confusion rather than advocacy.

Parents and teachers often have to require children to do stuff that kids would rather not do. As discussed earlier, "doing what you're supposed to" can be an important part of "getting in gear for success" as a learner. What's critical is not just the voluntary nature of learning, it's the connection the child makes (often with parental or teacher guidance) between *learning* and *personal power.* Adults often provide the perspective, drawn from experience, that can help a child see the rainbow through the storm.

To conservative critics who argue that nothing will change until the attitudes of young learners and their parents change—from antagonism toward schooling to respect for the hard work and persistence that leads, by slow degrees, to pride and confidence and mastery of essential skills and knowledge— I say, "I agree." But I don't believe that a noxious cocktail of sanctions, threats, and superficial rewards will move the soul of learners and teachers toward new and productive relationships half as well as will a generous dose of tolerance, respect, and recognition of the dignity that is due everyone who devotes their lives to children's learning achievement.

In the end, when all's said, we have either a young person who seeks learning as a useful, inspiring, and empowering activity, or else we have a child who may "do work" but only with close adult supervision and under threat of punishment or promise of reward—and whose commitment to the learning process remains shallow and temporary. If that "connection" evolves from a child's or a teenager's willing engagement with ideas, with questions about the world, with books or music or art, so much the better.

But if the spirit be unwilling in the child, we who teach and who parent—we who shepherd that child's spirit—ought to speak to that child, regarding homework, reading books, studying for tests, *in terms of* power, choice, freedom, success, individual happiness, and connection to the world. This is what every baby, as a passionate learner, seeks. We must devote ourselves to the recovery of that search by all the children to whom we are devoted, professionally and personally.

Regardless of our political or educational views, we had better acknowledge that standardized testing, with all the pressures and incentives that accompany it, is our government's key mechanism for trying to enhance the performance of students, teachers, and schools. This is where passionate learning confronts its greatest current challenge.

CHAPTER SIXTEEN

Passionate Teaching and Learning in an Era of Standardization

Teaching is a profession on probation. Legislators and state bureaucracies, acting with considerable public support, have placed the teaching profession under a cloud. Probation happens to college students with low grades, to rookie police officers, to citizens who commit minor offenses, or to employees who are no longer trusted to work without being closely supervised.

For teachers, the imposition of state-mandated standardized testing (to see whether students really have learned the stuff) is one manifestation of their probationary status, but it is not the only one. In many states, new teachers must pass proficiency exams in addition to all of the traditional requirements for certification. Entire schools may be put on "probationary status" if the performance of their students falls below official expectations.

The impact of such disapprobation on teachers is profound, as indicated in an e-mail I just received from a high school teacher who had wanted to bring me to her school to help her colleagues lift their morale. "If anyone needs to hear about passionate teaching, it's us," she had written earlier. Now, after finally getting approval for a summer workshop, she was writing to tell me that the district had canceled it for budgetary reasons related to Massachusetts's standardized tests, or "MCAS":

> It's true. Money has become extremely tight. We have to focus *all* our professional development efforts on getting kids to pass MCAS. You should see how much pressure we are now under to teach to the test. If the proposed workshop doesn't focus on implementing the standards that MCAS tests, it is rejected. I've given MCAS to sophomores every year it's been out. It's the most elitist, unfair, preposterous exam you can imagine. Inner-city kids at the low end of the curve don't stand a chance. It should be a test of basic skills, not a trivia game. Teachers are opting for early retirement like sailors deserting a sinking ship. There's no joy left in teaching; joy is a luxury we don't have time for.

Many teachers feel that being on probation is unfair and demoralizing, even though they agree that reforms are needed to improve student learning. We all know schools whose administrators do not effectively monitor the quality of instruction, schools that retain teachers who are not emotionally suited to working with children, or are not up to date in the subjects they teach, or are incapable of teaching competently. Parents "in the know" try to avoid having their children placed with these individuals, and when parents complain, these teachers are shuffled around the district rather than dismissed.

In response to such perceived lack of accountability or inadequate results, the heavy arm of the state comes down upon all teachers: "Since you educators evidently cannot vouch for the competence of your colleagues or the effectiveness of your teaching practices, we will evaluate your students for you!"

The emphasis on "accountability" may be the result of years of inadequate education offered in schools where poor and minority children predominate. But it also deprives teachers of creative freedom to teach as they know best based on their years of knowing well the students in their classes. However valid or invalid the accusations, the current climate has made many teachers feel anxious and vulnerable.

The critics say that we're not preparing our able students to compete in a world economy, that we're not educating poor and minority students so that their diplomas mean something. The proposed solution is to "raise academic standards" so that students, teachers, and schools will, under threat of sanctions, correct their flawed practices. I will deal with these charges later in this chapter. Other writers, particularly Alfie Kohn and Deborah Meier, have responded to these charges with detailed, data-filled refutations.[1] Virtually no one supports the status quo, but opinions differ widely on what needs to be changed, how it needs to be changed, and by whom.

There is no better way for individual teachers to overcome public skepticism about the effectiveness of what they do than to engage with one's students in passionate teaching and learning. Of course, getting students to that point is the real challenge. I do not discount the negative power of "the system" to undermine and dishearten many teachers. And I am not asking teachers to act alone in confronting the forces arrayed against them. But I do believe that passionate teaching and learning can help teachers and students overcome many obstacles.

The question for me is not "if," but rather "how." Creating passionate learners is the best defense against our critics—local, statewide, national. But first, I think we must look at the roots of the drive toward standardized tests, roots that tap into some of the most important social issues of our era.

The Emergence of "The Test"

It all began quite optimistically, from my recollection, and quite positively. About a dozen years ago, operating in a loose confederation, educators in a number of states began to formulate lists of desired knowledge, skills, and intellectual attributes that they believed all high school graduates should possess. These were published as a "Common Core of Learning," in states like Maine, New Hampshire, Connecticut, and Massachusetts. In most states, such documents were cosponsored by the state departments of education and forward-thinking business groups, who sought both to raise the level of knowledge of high school graduates and to give a sense of wholeness to K–12 education.

The implication of such "Common Cores" was that twelve or thirteen years of education ought to "mean something" for students—far more than the traditional adding up of "credits" in various categories that had come to define a diploma. When implemented, these Common Core goals would draw together teachers of various grade levels and disciplines to try together what, obviously, high school teachers could not hope to accomplish alone—help students build and reinforce such a foundation.

As an elected school board member in my hometown of Concord, New Hampshire, during the late 1980s and early 1990s, I helped articulate such a holistic vision for our system. Our "mission statement" was typical of the times:

> The mission of the Concord School District is to enable every student to acquire and demonstrate the skills, knowledge, and attitudes essential to be a responsible world citizen committed to personal, family, and community well-being.

But we then put forth seven "District Outcomes" that held that graduates of Concord High will be

- *Active self-directed learners* who inquire creatively about their world, take risks, and examine options as they initiate actions and complete tasks

- *Effective communicators* who write well, read widely and in depth, listen perceptively, share ideas orally, and use language, numbers, and symbols to convey and receive information

- *Effective collaborators* who assume various roles to accomplish group or community goals, using self-knowledge, compromise, cooperation, and respect

And so on, including such attributes as *"Informed decision makers," "Creative producers of art," "Life planners,"* and *"Community participants,"* all operating through a school environment "in which each student can retrieve, access, analyze, synthesize, evaluate, and apply information in realizing these outcomes."

But we in Concord and state-level thinkers and policy makers elsewhere made a huge mistake, or we were dissuaded by opposition from traditionalists from carrying such a vision to its logical conclusion. We failed to insist that such desired outcomes, over time, would become *the basis for graduation,* replacing the tradition of kids passing enough of the right courses and accumulating enough "credits" or "Carnegie units" to get a diploma. Credits are measured in units of time—you get a credit for spending forty-five minutes a day in a class for 180 days, regardless of how much or how little you actually learn and retain. If you "pass" that course, you get your credit. Nobody knows whether you can actually *do* anything with the knowledge you've obtained in the process.

Predictably, school systems praised the spirit of these Common Core of Learning documents and then filed them away. Since the Common Core was merely *appended to* the existing diploma process, it could be, and was, readily ignored. To teachers and administrators, it just meant "a lot more work." It's far more difficult to determine what knowledge and skills a student actually possesses than to require that student to pass the required courses and accrue the mandated number of credits. The Common Core of Learning died because it never became the basis for graduation.

Except that it didn't quite die. It became a zombie—a body without a soul. The idealistic movement toward *a diploma based on actual student learning* was translated, over time, into a more punitive demand for "accountability" in the educational process, spurred on by the charge (clearly exaggerated) that millions of students were graduating from high schools "unable to read the diplomas they had been awarded." And, in their rush to implement "accountability," politicians reached for the one weapon they could quickly and inexpensively wield—a *test*. Legislators who had for years championed "local control" of education (meaning, mostly, that local taxpayers should pay the lion's share of educational costs in their communities), now embraced a statewide standardized test that would inevitably oblige all towns and cities to teach the same curriculum and be judged by the same standard. So much for local control.

But what to base the new standard curriculum on? Why not start with something akin to the "Common Core of Learning," only now it could be called a "Curriculum Framework." And in a number of states, including Massachusetts and New Hampshire, teams of educators and curricular experts were brought together to fashion new or revised lists of what students should know—so that standardized tests could be written to test that knowledge. Other states have opted to buy or commission standardized tests without ever worrying about developing curriculum frameworks. In state after state, forty-nine out of fifty, the momentum for accountability became focused on *one test,* or series of tests, that would determine whether or not a student should be promoted or receive a diploma. These are known as "high-stakes" tests.

This, after all, was much the easiest way to force change upon a supposedly entrenched and stagnant cadre of public school educators. Instead of winning them to the idea that all teachers, K–12, will collaborate to help students prepare for life in key areas of skills, knowledge, and attitude, why not just slap a high-stakes test *on the kids* and leave the schools to sort it out as best they could?

A state's "curriculum frameworks" might be offered, free of charge, to all schools. They could use or ignore them at their peril. In the end, it would be the test scores that mattered, and since the test questions would be based on material included in the curriculum frameworks, the smart thing for schools to do would be to insist that teachers "cover" the information contained therein.

Thus, the impetus to help educators rethink K–12 education so that it would "mean something" to all kids led, disastrously, to a test that puts students, particularly those from disadvantaged families, at great risk of losing out on a diploma. And for millions of other students, students who would be able to "pass" such a test, it meant that all the lofty goals of education, all the dreams of teachers and parents for the enlightenment of children, would be superceded by one test.

The Educational Case against Standardized Testing

Our society's current obsession with standardized tests, which I refer to as the "War of Standardized Tests against All," will, I predict, fall of its own weight. Its political weaknesses are already apparent, as districts across the nation pull back from the rush to deny promotions or diplomas to children who have not

yet achieved the arbitrary levels of discrete information or unconnected skills established by test makers.

Most politicians will walk away from the tests as soon as it
becomes apparent that they don't work: that high school students *don't* learn more or better because they are afraid of failing a test; that younger kids *don't* become better readers and
writers or devotees of history or science because of multiple-
choice tests in those subjects; that teachers *don't* become better
teachers because agencies of government are holding a club
over their heads; that schools *don't* become more effective envi-
ronments for learning because their test scores are being compared in the newspapers with the scores of other schools or
other towns.

When politicians and newspapers begin to play the comparison game: this town's school scores versus that town's, this
school versus that school, last year's kids versus this year's—*in
the absence of serious and collaborative conversations among faculty,
students, and parents about the quality of teaching and learning*—the
system of standardized testing causes serious damage to the enterprise of learning. Comparisons lead to big headlines "Scores
go up!" "Scores go down!" "Podunk moves up three notches in
state ratings!" But it doesn't help any child learn. When scores
go up, we tend to forget about the significant percentage of test
takers who scored below the level of proficiency; if scores go
down, we tend to demand quick fixes and to ignore promising
but slower-developing teaching trends. Most tragically, such a
fixation on test scores discourages teachers who are often the
most creative and passionate about their subjects and their
students, turning them away from encouraging student initiative in learning projects, and turning themselves into test-
preparation functionaries. As Alfie Kohn relates,

> A few years ago, a middle-school teacher in Cambridge, Mass.,
> devised a remarkable unit. Every student picked an activity that

he or she cared about and became and expert in it. Each subject, from baking to ballet, was researched intensively, described in a detailed report and taught to other children. The
idea was to hone researching and writing skills while also
heightening children's appreciation for the craftsmanship involved in many different activities. It was the kind of experience that people look back on years later as a highlight of
school. But thanks to the new state standardized exam, that
unit has been struck from the curriculum. The teacher is too
busy helping students master prescribed material.[2]

In a recent op-ed piece in the *Boston Globe*, Deborah Meier
stated it thus:

No one test—even the best—can or should try to capture by
itself our definition of a well-educated person. Schools focused
on scores encourage a one-right-answer mentality at a time
when what life rewards are those who have been intellectually
prepared to respond flexibly to novelty and change—to tough
thinking about matters of substance, not tough memorization
about matters soon forgotten.

A test-driven environment may make some kids work
harder, but there's an adage worth remembering: harder may
not equal smarter. Tragically, such a focus prevents schools
from doing what's necessary to engage the young in ways that
produce real-life success. . .

I've lived through these test-driven reform eras. It hurts to
watch us cycle though panic-driven fads and put on hold the
kind of surer, slower, and even tougher reforms that we know
work. Good school accountability and high standards go hand
in hand; in contrast, poor systems of accountability drive standards down.[3]

I don't know if a single student, anywhere, has yet had her
learning enhanced by standardized tests. If anything, such tests
terrify many kids and demoralize yet others. What does it
mean, for students in a disadvantaged neighborhood to spend

weeks and weeks prepping for a series of exams that they know in advance most of them will not pass? Sometimes, students find a way to fight back. At one urban high school, where a state-devised tenth grade test was being piloted, a teacher told me that several of her students had said, "Sure we could've passed that test. We just didn't want to make this damn school look good."

But more often the result, I would surmise, is to open up yet another chasm between the spirit of learning and the child. For too many children "learning" has already been redefined by the school culture from "things you do to acquire knowledge and skills that can make you a more powerful and more capable person" into "work you do in school, or as homework for school, because the teacher tells you to." The learning they might pursue through a world of sights, sounds, experiences, feelings, and reflections has for some years been restricted to what the teacher says, what the teacher assigns, and what the teacher evaluates. But now somebody else—someone remote from the learner, from the classroom, from the school and community itself—is deciding what "learning" *is* and how you have to prove yourself in order to be allowed to continue your education.

Positive Aspects of Standardized Tests

The strongest argument in favor of standardized testing is that it focuses the minds of supposedly "complacent" or "burned-out" teachers on the results of their teaching efforts, positive or negative, as measured by a common public scale. A companion argument, voiced by a number of minority educators, is that such tests—provided they remain consistent and are not changed at the whim of bureaucrats—will at least provide students of color, their teachers, and their families with a more level "playing field," allowing the community to rally behind high achievement for its young people and to hold urban schools accountable for student achievement. Even many of those most strongly opposed to standardized testing agree that such arguments have some merit and must be taken into account in proposing alternatives to testing as a means of raising standards and achievement levels for our poorest-performing schools.

To the extent that within schools the faculty's discussion of and preparation for such tests actually focuses their conversation on "how to help kids become better able to understand and apply what they've learned in the particular areas of skill and knowledge covered by this test," this is a gain. Jolting otherwise isolated or demoralized people into thinking about results is better than allowing them to remain oblivious to the impact of their teaching, or worse, to continue to congratulate themselves for the little their students have gained by saying things like "We do a tremendous job in this school, considering what we have to work with."[4]

Yet all too often the results of such test-driven discussion among faculty and staff is to redefine teaching and learning even more narrowly, to focus more attention on a smaller area of the spectrum of learning. I have heard veteran teachers tell me that they were ordered by their principals "to forget about teaching anything but what's likely to be on the test—no science or social studies for the next six weeks!" I have heard other stories of teachers being advised by nervous principals to concentrate their attention primarily on those students who last tested close to the next higher proficiency level—to help boost them into the next category—even if that meant giving other students short shrift.

There is a valid role for standardized testing. We do, as a profession, suffer from a woeful lack of reliable data on how well our students are learning. High schools, for example, rarely if ever survey their graduates (and dropouts) two, five, and ten years later to learn from them what has been effective in the education they have received.

Each state, city, or school district could regularly select a statistically valid sample of children, K–1 2, and test them, anonymously, so as to generate diagnostic data on the strengths and weaknesses of the educational program in an area such as science or writing or math. Teachers could use such data to reflect upon how to teach more effectively.

Alfredo Fuentes, a former graduate student of mine whose approach to teaching math was highlighted in *The Passionate Teacher,* was for a time assistant principal in a suburban middle school with an ethnically and economically diverse student population. Fuentes used the results of a sixth grade statewide math test in just such a manner, and to good effect. Students in his middle school (there were two in town, one—where he served—in a lower-income section of town, the other in a mostly white, more affluent neighborhood) had scored about twenty points lower on the math test, on average, than those at the other middle school. Fuentes met with the math teachers at his school and proposed that they analyze the results to see what kinds of questions the kids were doing well or poorly on. He invited math teachers from the other middle school to join in the self-study, but they declined, pointing out that their students had performed twenty points higher.

"It was the conversations that the math teachers had together that were of most benefit," he told me. "The teacners and I discovered, by looking at how the kids had done, that we were doing okay teaching certain math skills, such as numerical calculations, but not well at all in helping the kids analyze word problems for their mathematical content. We began meeting fairly regularly, after school, and swapping ideas on what might work. Gradually, with lots of mutual support, we began to put those ideas into practice. As a result, when our students were next tested, as eighth graders, they had made up the twenty-point gap with the other middle school."[5]

The theoretical and ethical case against "high-stakes" standardized testing is strong and, I think, conclusive. But public schools in America are still "on probation," and standardized testing is here to stay for a while. There are organizations working hard to push back against an unwieldy and wrong-headed testing monster, but the weight of American political opinion is still demanding "accountability" from discredited school systems and using standardized tests to carry out that political objective.[6]

Teachers, parents, and students must cope with such pressures until the nation comes to its senses about standardized testing. I fear that it may not come to its senses soon, that teaching may become more restrictive rather than less so, and that, as usual, students who are already the most vulnerable will suffer most. Until the tide turns, teachers can explore ways, as did Fuentes, to try to make the testing process one that invites good conversation, among colleagues but also with parents and students, on how we all can more effectively assess the kinds of student learning we value.

What Teachers and Parents Can Do to Confront Standardized Tests and Other Obstacles to Passionate Learning for Children

How can teachers and parents collaborate on behalf of passionate learning despite the pressures of the standardized testing environment? Much of my advice here consists of techniques, approaches, and attitudes I've mentioned before, both in this book and elsewhere,[7] but I'd like to underscore several points as well as make a few new ones:

1. Teachers and parents should talk about the impact of standardized tests on the educational philosophy and practices

of the school. Children come home with lots of fears about testing, and parents are subject to media exposure on the subject. School forums, including small group discussions among parents and teachers, can help everyone pull together to support student learning. Working together, they can view test results diagnostically, as Fuentes did, rather than as a summation of the achievement or potential of any teacher or any student.

2. Schools may also use standardized tests to provide political "cover" for teams of teachers who opt to work for several years with a group of students around common themes or core objectives. Often such teachers are vulnerable to skepticism or antagonism from fellow teachers, administrators, or school board members. There's nothing like significantly higher test scores (yes, I realize I am sanctioning the "comparing" of scores in this case) to buttress an innovative program that may otherwise be politically vulnerable. The chances are quite good that if such a collaborative team has been able to create a sense of identity and esprit de corps among the students involved, students will enter the test wanting to validate their teachers' investment in them, to "make us look good."

3. Teachers should rededicate themselves to creating a positive, uplifting classroom atmosphere, where students are excited about learning. Parent and other adult volunteers are essential to this effort. Their presence in the classroom allows students to receive more personalized attention and reinforces in children's minds the idea that learning is for people of all ages. If such an atmosphere doesn't exist, ask the students how to bring it into being.

4. Celebrate young children's learning, their questionings, their playful explorations of the world around them, even

(or especially) when children present their learning in ways that upset the decorum of traditional school culture. This is not a plea for "permissiveness" (oh, how that word is misused!). It doesn't substitute for the often-painful process of helping children adjust to school rules like sharing, taking turns, talking things out instead of hitting. Some ways of celebrating include show-and-tells or song, story, and dance routines that are a regular part of the best early childhood programs.

5. The question of whether or not learning is perceived by kids as "cool" is also worth pursuing (despite the real risk that students will initially declare—quite definitively— that learning in school is *not at all "cool"*). If it is not, what would it take to make it so? And how can adults and kids come together around the notion of knowledge-as-power—that "what we learn can give us options and make us stronger"?

6. Teachers and parents should emphasize student initiative and motivation in the learning process. I see too many teachers and parents relying on their "right" to require students to do their assigned work, instead of appealing to the students' own sense of value and purpose. Again, this is a matter of one's own pedagogy and philosophy, but for most adults the roles of coach and guide and mentor are more effective, in the long run, than that of "boss."

7. Schools can celebrate learning done outside of school, under the heading of "Things I Learn Outside of School, on My Own or with Family and Friends." Two days a week (including weekends) can be reserved as "Homework in My Neighborhood and in My House" days, when students set their own goals for learning (including sports and sportsmanship, music listening and playing, helping the

family, hobbies, going to the library). This emphasis begins in kindergarten and could evolve through elementary and middle school (even high school).

8. Neighborhoods can celebrate the writing of children and young adults—about their lives, their heritage, their dreams, their frustrations—in schools, civic centers, local places of worship, and libraries. Students should find "writing partners" in the neighborhood, among area business and civic organizations, and via the Internet. They need to become confident that their "voice"—as expressed through writing—*matters* and connects them to the world. A rotating library of children's writing should become a neighborhood tradition.

9. School conferences should be opportunities for teachers, parents, and students to talk. The meetings should be "chaired" by the student, beginning in grade four or five. The focus should be on the accomplishments of the student, with respect to key areas of knowledge and skills (especially in literacy), *and* on the status of the student's learning spirit, motivation, and personal sense of growth. To focus the parent/teacher agenda solely on a student's behavior, grades, test scores, and homework completion denies both student and family an opportunity to acknowledge learning outside the schoolroom.

10. To foster such conversations, all parties should have copies of a "curriculum," written in family-friendly language (and translated, where needed, into the languages parents speak). Using such a guide, parents and student can talk about those skills that are regularly practiced outside of school (e.g., helping a younger sibling with reading, going to the library, reading and being read to before bed, writing letters to relatives, helping with family calculations

such as shopping and paying bills), as well as those practiced in the classroom.

11. Teachers and school staff must resolve to view parents as "learning partners." We must learn how to make parents feel comfortable and valued as partners in their child's education. This process may take some doing, especially when interacting with parents already overburdened with child care or work responsibilities or whose memories of "school" are replete with shame and humiliation. But there is no substitute for such active partnerships.

12. Underlying all of the previous points is the notion of a shared enterprise, of collaboration, of people who pursue their individual agendas in conjunction with colleagues. Learning is often seen as a lonely process—an individual trying to assimilate knowledge gleaned from books, notes, research, practice, and application. In fact, learning is usually a social enterprise, fostered within a supportive environment. People teach and learn together, and that is what makes individually motivated learning possible. It is the lack of such collegial support that leads to the frustrations and alienation that plague so many school cultures.

Unsung Heroes

The core ingredients that will allow us to fill our classrooms and schools with passionate learning are not hard to enumerate:

- Kids need aware, upbeat, good-natured, engaged, fairly knowledgeable but ever-learning grown-ups.

- Teachers need energetic, curious, spontaneous, talkative, fair-minded, playful students.

Fortunately, the supplies of both are potentially plentiful, in all neighborhoods.

Unfortunately, if the dominant mood of either teachers or students is one of frustration, anxiety, withdrawal, self-protectiveness, or distrust, they may never get to see each other as partners in passionate teaching and learning. What we will have, instead, is a loss, a failure, a tragedy of enormous proportions.

Fortunately, such a tragedy is usually preventable.

Unfortunately, too many potentially passionate teachers lack the confidence, conviction, or bravado to walk into a class and *assume* that the kind of kids described above will be waiting for them and that they can create such a partnership and unleash such learning energy among even those children who have been "turned off" to learning previously.

I ought to know. I am (or was) (or may still be) one of those people who lack the required confidence and experience—at least when it comes to working with the sixth and seventh graders I've met this year at Josiah Quincy Upper School. After six months of weekly visits to the school, the impact of my work there seemed dwarfed by the enormity of the needs of many of the students, especially those who lack strong literacy skills.

The experience has made me profoundly appreciative of the dedicated teachers I have worked closely with. Time after time, I would see them face a difficult situation—an angry, defiant student, or a posturing, taunting student, or a silent, withdrawn student—and I would wonder, what would *I* do if this really were my class? When it *has* been "my class," at those moments when I took over to teach poetry or help guide a writing assignment, I have felt the weight of my doubts and my inadequacy.

Fortunately, I found someone to show me how it can be done. You've already met him. His name is Malcolm Mitchell, a first-year teacher. Here's how we connected.

A few weeks ago, Malcolm (whom I had observed occasionally but had never co-taught with) approached me to help him with the design of a unit on the period in history when America was being settled by Europeans. This unit was coming up next, in the agreed-upon curriculum, and he wasn't sure how to make it mean something to his sixth grade humanities class.

Now—*this* is a situation I know I can do something with. We arranged to meet at a coffee shop one morning and hatch a plan. We began with Malcolm's overarching goals, which were as follows:

1. Students would gain a sense of the importance and relevance of history to their lives, here and now.

2. Students would develop their writing and researching skills, instead of copying stuff out of a textbook.

We also quickly agreed on some other objectives:

3. Students would place themselves in the shoes of would-be settlers who had to decide whether or not to come to this new land and to face the risks and rewards of doing so.

4. Students would involve their families, somehow, in their research.

5. Students would learn how to put together a high-quality research product and present it orally.

My main contribution was to adapt the structure of a unit I had long envisioned (and described briefly in *The Passionate Teacher*) but had never seen implemented, that involves asking students to discover an "unsung hero" in their family's history and to research that person's accomplishments and present that person (or a relative) with a specially designed award.

The application here seemed perfect: all of the children in his class (of mostly Asian-American and African-American heritage) would trace the history of their family's arrival in Boston. They would relate their histories to those of earlier settlers.

I proposed two other additions to my "unsung hero" theme:

1. We would plan an icebreaker activity around the idea that these kids might one day have to choose whether or not to be part of the colonization of the planet Mars. We would ask them, "What kinds of things might have happened to you that would make you want to seek a new life in a totally different environment (Mars)? And what kinds of promises, or incentives, might tempt you to take your family there, even if you were not trying to get away from your life here in Boston?"

2. We would focus the research for an "unsung hero"
   around the sacrifices and risks that a family member or
   relative had made in bringing their family to Boston.
   "I wouldn't be here, now, if it wasn't for _____."
   This would tie the unit in with American history, and
   allow students to compare the risks and conditions of
   people seeking a better life then and now.

The plan sounded good. We felt it would be equally perti-
nent to Asian American kids whose parents or grandparents
had emigrated here and to African-American kids whose relatives had moved up here from the south in search of a better
future.

But (I wondered to myself) would it fly? Would these kids—
who had not been selected for the school's advanced class in humanities—"buy in?" More important, would they stay in it for
the long haul, conduct original research on an unknown topic,
and produce and present a high-quality report before an invited
audience of family members? All these are attributes that are
sometime hard to come by in honors classes and conspicuously
missing in most others. I admit, I had my doubts. I knew I
couldn't make it happen on my own.

Malcolm Mitchell had come into class on my first day working with him with a simple family tree outline and asked the
kids to list as many of the people on their mother's and father's
side of the family as they could—their names and where they
were born. Few of the kids could go beyond one grandparent
(and many not even that far).

We asked them, "Who are the experts here? Who knows
this stuff? Do you think Mr. Mitchell and Mr. Fried can give you
this information?" Just about every hand went up—they assured us that we two were the *most ignorant* people in the class
on the subject of their family lineage. They were curious, ener-

gized by the idea that we—the teachers—were the ignorant ones, and they—the students—would be the "experts." Malcolm gave them as homework the task of asking their parents to tell them who was the keeper of their family's history? Who was the *source*?

When I came to his class the following week, the kids were brimming with questions. They had identified parents, grandparents, great-grandparents, aunts, uncles, nieces as "sources." But some of these people had been skeptical—why did we want to know? We asked the kids to list some of the differing reactions, and they came up with "surprised," "amazed," "shocked," "interested," "hopeful," "suspicious," "unbelieving," "wondering why," and "not telling." The kids knew they had more work to do. And when we asked, "Who should write a letter that will explain to parents what we're trying to discover?" the kids told us that it should be their letter, but that we could help.

We next had them sit in groups of three or four students and develop questions to ask the "source" person. They set to work and in ten minutes came up with the following questions; a student volunteered to put them on the board.

- Where did our family come from?
- Are you proud to know this information about our family?
- How do you know this information?
- Why did you bother to remember it?
- What was your response to the new land?
- Did war make a difference in your deciding to come here?
- Where did our last names come from?

❧ What was daily life like where you came from?

❧ What things were the same there as here, then as now?

❧ What were you most ignorant about when you came here?

❧ What were the sacrifices you had to make to come here?

❧ Did you really want to come, or were your forced to?

❧ Were people racists, or did they stereotype others?

❧ Was it hard to be able to go to school there?

We then asked them to speculate on what were some of the common experiences and differing experiences of the family members in this class who had moved from the "old place" to the "new place." Again, they responded with atypical energy. Among the things they speculated were common to families in coming here were "better life for children," "we all came for freedom," "start a new life," and "experience a new part of the world." What they thought might be different, was "some cherished the past, others wanted to forget the past," "some wanted to come, others were forced by a family member to come," "some had family here to support them, others had to be self-reliant," "some already had freedom where they came from, others were fighting to be free," "some had to deal with catastrophes and tragedies, others didn't have that," "some had to do military service (there or here), and others did not."

There's nothing special in these questions and speculations—not unless you recognize that *this is not the way most low-achieving sixth grade kids are supposed to behave in school.* These are abstract and complex issues we were raising. But the kids reacted to them as if their fluency in responding is something we should take for granted.

I had seen some of these kids, elsewhere in the building. Some had been in trouble, early in the year. Others still had

run-ins with authority figures. Some have great difficulty expressing themselves in English; still others are quite shy. But in
Malcolm Mitchell's class they act like scholars.

The atmosphere is electric with energy; the kids' hands
shoot up in response to every question. We discuss the unit, he
and I, in front of the class, talking about our hopes and worries
as if we are having a private conversation. They break in to our
discussion to raise questions, argue points, clarify things. I am
amazed at how ready the students are to take on an academic
challenge of this magnitude.

I realize that my initial surprise is a measure of how easily I,
too, fall into the pattern of "low expectations" for kids from
educationally disadvantaged situations. As concerned as I had
been about how the students were being segregated "by ability"
in some of their classes, my concern had been based mostly on
ideological grounds. Too many of my prior experiences this
year had confirmed the wide gap of expectations and results between certain classes. How to explain what I was seeing now?

My hypothesis has two parts. One part concerns Malcolm
Mitchell's personality, his being a black male teacher in a class
of students of color, his being also a coach, his youth and connection to popular culture and its idioms. He is, in a word,
"cool." Of course, we can't all be black, male, young, or cool.
But over the centuries, teachers of all ages, colors, and degrees
of "uncoolness" have inspired their students in much the same
ways that Malcolm Mitchell does. They do so through the force
of their ideals and their passions. Passion, too, is "cool."

The other part of my hypothesis—also applicable to each
one of us, parent and teacher alike—is that Malcolm Mitchell
has never made it a secret that his humanities class is all about
kids becoming *powerful*. He has, to my knowledge, never let up
on the theme that all kids—each and every one of his students—can become powerful through the use of their mind

and the development of their intellect. The kids reflect this vision, in the way they use words like *perspective* and *voice* and *stereotype* and *ignorance,* in the way they applaud respectfully when a student says something they think is especially intelligent, in the way they act so unself-consciously about using their minds in class.

We can, each in our own way, work to convince our students that we believe in their right and their ability to become powerful through learning, to become strong and articulate, to have and express opinions, to seek and synthesize knowledge. But first, we must believe it ourselves.

This "unit" is still in its early stages. Malcolm and I are working together to see just how deep the kids can delve as researchers. We have already warned them that some of what they find may not be pleasant, that there may be tears involved as relatives remember the hardships and the sacrifices, that family members may want to keep some things secret. We haven't told them, yet, that we want them to present their research before a large audience of parents.

But I have already learned much more than I bargained for. My "unit design" around unsung family heroes is much richer than I once thought. And the students, buoyed by Malcolm Mitchell's belief in the power of their minds, treat me as a useful resource. They let me know they want me to come back.

What can teachers and parents do to help learning remain a worthwhile, sometimes joyous, often challenging and rigorous, but ultimately successful and rewarding undertaking for all students? How can the young child's delight with discovering her world remain a moving force in her formal education?

Children need time and space and materials and loving guidance from adults to pursue the joys of learning in an atmosphere where their creative pressures come from within—free from prejudice, or mockery, or the intellectual and emotional disfigurement of labels. They require of us that we make—in our schools—a safe place for the mind and heart of a child or a teenager to grow, where each individual's efforts are joined in the execution of a task, a project, a performance by the work of classmates and mentors, where they can count on finding adults who will help them become powerful.

Children come to us as passionate learners. It's our charge to help them develop the disposition to sustain, over a lifetime, an openness to things worth knowing.

Notes

Prelude: Of Passionate Learning,
Food Fights, and Who Needs Soccer?

1. From Esther Kingston-Mann and R. Timothy Sieber, *Achieving against the Odds* (Philadelphia: Temple Univ. Press, 2001).

2. Evans Clinchy, in a forthcoming book about evolution and education, makes this point explicitly.

3. *The Book of Learning and Forgetting*, by Frank Smith (New York: Teachers College Press, 1998), is all about this.

4. See, especially, Seymour B. Sarason, *Parent Involvement and the Political Principle* (San Francisco: Jossey-Bass, 1995).

5. *Punished by Rewards*, by Alfie Kohn (Houghton Mifflin, 1999), has much that is excellent to say about this.

1. The Promise

1. From Marcia D'Arcangelo's interview with Meltzoff in the November 2000 *Educational Leadership*, p. 8.

2. Ibid., p. 9.

3. Frank Smith, *Reading without Nonsense* (New York: Teachers College Press, 1997), p. 6.

4. Deborah Meier, whose career began as a kindergarten teacher and who has established several K–12 experimental public schools based upon such a desire, has often written about this.

5. Robert Coles, *The Moral Intelligence of Children: How to Raise a Moral Child* (New York: Penguin Putnam, 1988), pp. 177–78.

2. The Chasm: How the Promise Gets Broken

1. I think, for example, of the lure of the social milieu as a distraction from schoolwork, the lack of an agreeable balance between physical activity and seat work, forced adherence to the teacher's agenda, frustrated desires to play or to work with one's hands. As a supervisor of a student teacher, several years ago, I sat in the back of a first grade classroom in an elementary school with almost exclusively African-American children. From where I sat, I could easily identify with several children, also located near the back of the room, for whom what was happening on the blackboard was but a pale screen compared to the dynamism of the social interactions around them— those they observed and those they instigated. It was no contest. What the white, middle-aged teacher was doing "up in front" was dry, abstract, joyless, while around them was the amazing world of their peers, kids who were neither babies who couldn't play right nor older siblings who could push you around or exclude you. Here was a first grader's paradise, an exclusive club. They were members, and they wanted to play!

2. A number of years ago, when I was an elementary school principal, I had one student who would do her homework with a pencil in her right hand and an eraser in her left, erasing everything she wrote, because she feared it wasn't good enough.

3. Upon visiting a predominately Hispanic high school in California a number of years ago, I noticed that none of the boys volunteered to respond to questions from the teacher. When I queried the teacher about this, she matter-of-factly told me, "Oh, the boys like to show what they can do when they're on the ball field. They don't participate in class."

3. What Teachers Can Do to Reclaim the Promise

1. Jeff Howard's work in the Efficacy Movement (Lexington, Mass.) is a good resource, particularly his article "Getting Smart:

The Social Construction of Intelligence," excerpted in *Network News Notes* 6(1): 1–8.

2. In one sixth grade class I work with, the students spontaneously applaud, gently, when somebody expresses an especially useful or interesting thought.

3. My student teachers tell me they can tell immediately if they are in a place where a sense of decency and friendship prevail, as opposed to a social anarchy or dictatorship.

4. Harry K. Wong and Rosemary T. Wong, in *The First Days of School* (Harry K. Wong Publications, 1998), have some useful ideas about such procedures.

5. Frank Smith comments on the modernization of the one-room schoolhouse: "What is still called 'grouping students by age and ability' really means segregating them according to inexperience and inability, as if the aim were to make it impossible for students to help or to learn from each other." (Smith, *Book of Learning and Forgetting*, p. 47).

6. In a school in rural New Hampshire, on "Career Day," one shy girl invited her parents to drive up in the huge truck they both drove for a living. She was the "star" of the day, and her esteem in the eyes of her classmates rose dramatically.

7. A successful experimental high school in Providence, R.I., called the "Met" employs this approach as a fundamental part of its curricular strategy. Known as LTI (Learning Through Internships), this dynamic technique is well explained in Eliot Levine's *One Kid at a Time: A Visionary High School Transforms Education* (New York: Teachers College Press, 2001).

8. An elementary bilingual teacher I know regularly waits at the schoolhouse door as neighborhood parents come to pick up their kids. He finds these brief interactions to be of great value in building a sense of trust and partnership with parents, so that when big problems arise, the relationship is already in place.

4. Revisiting the Chasm:
Misbehaving Kids, Boredom, and Wasting Time

1. Smith, *Book of Learning and Forgetting*, p. 60.
2. Evans Clinchy, in conversation.

5. What Parents Can Do to Reclaim the Promise

1. Smith, *Book of Learning and Forgetting*, p. 19.
2. There is a story about a little boy who surprised his mother by cheerily going off to school on his first day of kindergarten. The mother had expected anxiety, resistance, even tears. But, no, Nathan seemed quite willing to go. Later that day he told his mother that "it was fun." The next morning, when she came to wake him up for school, Nathan burst into tears. "I already *did* that," he cried. "I want to do something *else* today."

6. What Schools and Systems Can Do to Reclaim the Promise

1. The Institute for Responsive Education, headquartered at Northeastern University, has for decades been a strong national advocate for parent, family, and neighborhood partnerships with schools.

7. Curriculum as Relationships

1. "Exhibition" of knowledge is one of the "common principles" of the Coalition of Essential Skills, pioneered by Theodore Sizer.
2. Melissa Parent, in conversation. My interview with her can be found in *The Passionate Teacher*, rev. ed., chapter 19, "Is Passionate Teaching for New Teachers, Too?"
3. Frank Smith points out that the same kids who, when playing a video game, will challenge themselves with the highest level of difficulty they think they can do, in classroom or homework seek the easiest, least challenging route. We cannot explain away such a phenomenon by saying that "Of course, when they do video games, they are just playing, whereas with school work, real skills are demanded."
4. I am reminded of a story, in a book of horror tales, about a brilliant but socially paralyzed musician, a Professor Pfaff, who when seated at a piano would instantly translate printed words into music.

When the words were poetic or philosophical, the resulting music was hauntingly original. But the poor man had no control; his evil manager would torment him by placing a thick telephone book in front of him for hours. Sometimes I think teachers find themselves in Professor Pfaff's predicament, compelled to pore over and interpret student work that may have had little thought put into its production.

5. Frank McCourt, *'Tis* (New York: Scribner, 1999), pp. 241–43.

8. Curriculum? Who *Cares?*

1. It is also one of the chief arguments in my previous book, *The Passionate Teacher* (Boston: Beacon, 1995).

2. I used this scale during a summer graduate seminar on curriculum, when I had first drafted it. Surprisingly to me, the students saw me as significantly less impassioned about the topic than I felt I was. It was a sobering and useful exercise because it made me rethink how I was coming across to them regarding an issue that I am so very involved with as a writer.

3. Part 3, chapters 8–11, of *The Passionate Teacher* is devoted to a discussion of the teacher's stance.

4. A friend of my parents, now deceased, was such a teacher, and he wrote about his experiences in a book he entitled *Pearls before Swine.*

9. Parents and Curriculum:
A Partnership with Students and Teachers

1. "Report Cards Are Due, Only This Time for Parents," *New York Times,* November 23, 2000, p. 34A.

10. Words of Power

1. Smith, *Book of Learning and Forgetting,* pp. 25ff.

2. Paulo Freire, *The Paulo Freire Reader* (Continuum, 1998), p. 173.

3. Jim Trelease, *The Read Aloud Handbook* (New York: Penguin, 1995).

4. I recently shared this series of points with my college class on

children's literacy, and several students said it was the most important thing I had presented to them all semester.

5. Eleanor Duckworth, *The Having of Wonderful Ideas and Other Essays on Teaching and Learning* (New York: Teachers College Press, 1996).

11. A "Good Enough" Literacy Program

1. Bruno Bettelheim, *A Good Enough Parent* (New York: Knopf, 1987). Bettelheim acknowledges borrowing the notion from psychoanalyst D. W. Winnicott's earlier concept of the "good enough" mother (p. ix).

12. Lift Every Voice

1. Kenneth Koch, *Rose, Where Did You Get That Red?* (New York: Vintage Books, 1974)

2. Alfred North Whitehead, *The Aims of Education* (New York: Free Press, 1964), p. 16.

3. Oakland Board of Education, resolution of December 18, 1996, as amended in May 1997.

4. Theresa Perry and Lisa Delpit, *The Real Ebonics Debate: Power, Language, and the Education of African American Children* (Boston: Beacon, 1998).

5. John Dewey, *The School and Society* (Chicago: University of Chicago Press, 1990), pp. 55–56.

6. From Thomas LeClair, "A Conversation with Toni Morrison: 'The Language Must Not Sweat,'" *New Republic*, March 21, 1981, pp. 25–29, cited in John Russell Rickford and Russell John Rickford, *Spoken Soul: The Story of Black English* (New York: Wiley, 2000).

7. Lisa Delpit, *Other People's Children* (New York: New Press, 1995), p. 53.

8. Ibid., p. 67.

9. Theresa Perry, coauthor of *The Real Ebonics Debate*, in conversation.

10. Dewey, *School and Society*, p. 56.

13. A Passion for Excellence—and How We Undermine It

1. Deborah Meier tells me that her son, a teacher, has a favorite phrase: "Anything worth doing is even worth doing *badly.*" People who can't dance well should still dance.

14. Celebrating "Inconsistent Excellence"

1. Alfie Kohn makes a brilliant case against grading and other "external" motivators in *Punished by Rewards.*

2. See *Passionate Teacher,* chapter 17.

3 One other pernicious effect of our traditional grading system is that students in their twenties or thirties who apply for graduate school admission may be handicapped by a grade point average that includes their freshman year grades—which, for some, was a time of partying or bewilderment. They may have done very well afterward, returning to college after dropping out for a while, or getting their footing after a few semesters of goofing off. But those old Ds and Fs or even Cs haunt them still, projecting the impact of their youthful folly into middle age and, in fact, keeping some otherwise very worthy people from applying to graduate school. I have sat in meetings of a university's graduate admissions committee and seen otherwise qualified people—students whose work we knew to be of good quality—admitted only on a probationary basis because their grade point average (freshman follies included) didn't meet our standards. I knew others who just would not apply, out of shame or a desire to avoid the humiliation of having to answer for their freshman grades.

4. Alfred North Whitehead, *The Aims of Education and Other Essays,* (New York: Free Press, 1985), p. 2.

5. Ibid., p. 11.

15. Education at the Millennium: The Bad and the Good

1. See Alfie Kohn "Only for My Kid: How Privileged Parents Undermine School Reform," *Phi Delta Kappan* (April 1998): 568–77; Robert L. Fried, "Parental Anxiety and School Reform: When Inter-

ests Collide, Whose Needs Come First?" *Phi Delta Kappan* (December 1998): 265–71.

2. Evans Clinchy, in conversation.

16. Passionate Teaching and Learning in an Era of Standardization

1. Alfie Kohn, *The Schools Our Children Deserve* (Boston: Houghton Mifflin, 1999); Deborah Meier, *Will Standards Save Public Education?* (Boston: Beacon, 2000).

2. Alfie Kohn, *New York Times*, December 9, 1999.

3. Deborah Meier, *Boston Globe*, November 27, 2000.

4. I heard such a statement quite often in my visits to urban schools in the years before standardized testing began. And I hear it much less now that test results show that in some cities as many as 94 percent of the children fail to reach the proficiency level in reading, writing, and arithmetic.

5. Readers of *The Passionate Teacher* will remember educator Alfredo Fuentes, then a high school math teacher, now a high school principal.

6. For example, "FairTest" in Cambridge, Massachusetts, is an organization of educators and parents devoted to opposing "high-stakes" standardized tests (FairTest, 342 Broadway, Cambridge, MA 02139; 617–864–4810).

7. See, especially, *The Passionate Teacher,* and my *Kappan* article, "Parent Anxiety and School Reform."

A Few Thoughts and

Acknowledgments

Having written my first book, *The Passionate Teacher,* when I was about fifty, and having put just about everything I thought I knew into it, I figured I could comfortably wait another forty or so years for a sequel to germinate. This was not, however, to be.

The Passionate Learner emerged much faster than I'd have thought, little more than a year in the making. My questions— What do our diverse children bring to the teaching/learning experience that all the grown-ups in their life would do well to consider? How can parents and teachers be thoughtful coaches for children's learning? What does passionate teaching look like from a student's point of view?—demanded answers. The search for those answers produced other, even deeper questions. But it also brought me into conversation with parents of toddlers and teenagers, with elementary and secondary school teachers, with university colleagues, and with students of all ages. The reader has, I hope, found these vignettes, interviews, and stories inspiring, but they are typical of the everyday miracles wrought by skilled, thoughtful adults in schools and homes everywhere. Anyone who observes devoted teachers and parents working with children will see such amazing things. New and powerful examples kept flooding me as I prepared this book for publication; I kept wanting to add more.

Part of the reason the book came together relatively quickly is that I was privileged to be a scholar in residence, for a month, at the Rockefeller Foundation's Bellagio Study and Conference Center in Italy. The beautiful surroundings and ideal accommodations permitted me to devote hours each day to writing, knowing that a group of wonderful artists and scholars would be there at mealtimes for my wife and me to share our thoughts and experiences with, hosted by the kind staff of the center. When I returned to Northeastern University, I was able to continue my writing along with my teaching and fieldwork responsibilities, and I am grateful to my colleagues for their forbearance and support.

As I began to work with several Boston schools, I soon found that I was learning invaluable lessons from the teachers and students whose classes I visited. In particular, I appreciate the hospitality of Bak Fun Wong, principal of the Josiah Quincy Upper School, of faculty and staff members David Crane, Jim Heffron, Malcolm Mitchell, and Opal Hines-Fisher, who appear in the book, and the hospitality of other staff and students who made me feel so welcome there.

Inevitably, as I worked on this book, I became aware of my limitations. I have not written about students with serious disabilities, whether developmental or emotional. I leave it to other researchers and scholars to define and categorize the various "learning styles" of children. I deal with such differences here only anecdotally. While I recognize that the phenomenon of homeschooling is a legitimate response to parents' desires to keep the spirit of passionate learning alive in their children, I am an unabashed advocate for public education—untracked and inclusive—where children can encounter a full range of diversity and grow in appreciation of multicultural perspectives.

As a white male from a cosmopolitan background, I am removed from the daily experience of students and families who live with prejudice and poverty and whose learning and schooling are fraught with the inequities and injustices of our society. My grasp of these issues, as with issues of race, gender, and sexual identity, is limited by my experience.

I am deeply indebted to a number of people who have lent their time and thoughtful comments to me as I wrote. Readers of early drafts whose critiques helped shape my thoughts were Evans Clinchy, Seymour Sarason, Randy Wisehart, and Beth Ferholt. More recently, Donn Weinholtz and Jennifer Lee shared their impressions and suggestions, in time to help me complete the manuscript. Deborah Meier not only read and reacted to chapter drafts as I composed them but engaged me in long conversations over the course of the year. The book reflects only a part of what I have learned from her, and I am extremely grateful for her wisdom.

Other contributors whose words and thoughts are reflected herein include Christine Teague, Lea Johnson, Pattie Knight, Michele Gabor, Marya Van't Hul, Alfredo Fuentes, Susan Covert, and Susan Cooney Hagner. My thanks to all of them for making this book so much more alive than it would otherwise have been.

My association with the book's editor, Andy Hrycyna, began with *The Passionate Teacher,* and I consider myself privileged to have been able again to work with him on this book. He has helped me immeasurably at every stage with his insights and his feel for the book as a whole. I also want to acknowledge the excellent copyediting of Mary Ray Worley and the support of everyone at Beacon Press.

Finally, I owe my wife, Patricia Wilczynski, a level of appreciation that cannot adequately be put into words. She has been my reader, my partner, my lover, and my mainstay during the entire time.

Index

ability grouping of students,
239, 241, 268
accountability
resulting from public perception of inadequacy, 246–
247
of teachers and schools, 5,
233, 257
achievement gap between affluent and disadvantaged students, 232–233, 239–244
Achieving against the Odds (E.
Kingston-Mann & R.
Sieber), 271
Adams, Richard, 28
adults
helping children empower
themselves as learners, 230
helping children find answers
to their own questions, 42
nurturing children's learning
without directing or pre-
scribing it, 432
students' lack of trust in, 34

trying to make children learn,
9, 243
vs. kids; *see* kids vs. grown–
ups
Aims of Teaching, The (A. N.
Whitehead), 276, 277
anecdotes
Alfredo Fuentes on analyzing
math test results, 256–257
college students writing children's books on memories,
44–45
demanding my son's cooperation in unpacking the car, 68
"five little monkeys jumpin'
on the bed," 177–178
head lice and biology teaching, 235–238
"the lion is big; the lion is
brown," 140–141
Luisa, Maria and Antonio,
and John and Michelle: grading dilemmas, 213–214,
217–218

misbehaving and defiant middle school students, 61–62

"My Harry Potter Epiphany," 143–144

my sons' experiences with public schooling, 83–84

Scott, ten-year-old boy who resists school learning, 28–29

sixth grade class researching "unsung family heroes," 262–270

sunflowers in preschool, 41–43

teaching literacy in a New England factory town, 162–171

teaching phonics to child at home, 156–157

Tiffany (poetry can keep you out of trouble), 174–175

two-year-old Asian girl on bus, 18–19

assessment of learning. *See* grades and grading

attitudes

in relation to "The Chasm," 32–33, 37–38

in curriculum planning, 106–107

in literacy instruction, 160

negative shift by students in school toward learning, 35

as obstacles to learning, 32–33

parents and teachers, working together to influence children, 235

Bacon, Mary Montle, 128

behavior and misbehavior by students, 57–65

children accepting responsibility for own behavior, 63

coercion vs. cooperation and consent, 68–69

behavior management, 5

Bettelheim, Bruno, 161, 276

Blake, William, 176

blame, cycle of, for parents, 36

Book of Learning and Forgetting, The (F. Smith), 78, 138–139, 271, 273, 274, 275

boredom, 66–70

balance of powers needed, 70

as common complaint of students, 57

defined, 66

learning associated with, 30

mutuality and power-sharing, as antidotes, 67

parental dismissal of, 31

as part of students' distraction from classwork, 32

as a serious issue that requires a cooperative solution, 66–67

students' own analysis of causes and solutions, 70

Brown, Claude, 185

caring

as essential element in curriculum, 115

as threshold for student assignments, 121–122

charter schools, 98

chasm
four guides to overcoming, 37–38, 48
as indicator of relationships gone wrong, 47
as preventable phenomenon, 31
"How the Promise Gets Broken," 28–38
signs and origins of, 32–36
children. *See also* students
behaving well vs. learning, 2
being "good" vs. "bad," 2, 3
competition among, 33
disconnect between learning on one's own and in school, 75–76
disposition toward learning; *see* learning
forced to choose between loyalty to home and school, 92
hating school, 37
helping empower them as learners, 230
independent spirit of learning, 26, 73, 76–77, 84, 86, 136, 138, 254
inherent enthusiasm for learning, 3, 37
intellectual development of, ix
interests, not related to school, 33
learning from "the company they keep," 78
learning more actively outside of school than in class, 28–29, 78–81

as natural scientists, 18–20
parents and teachers celebrating their learning, 258–259
reading on their own, importance of, 46
unprepared for school, 35
victims of school culture, 3
vulnerable as students, 4
wanting to learn, importance of, 46
who learn more out of school than in, 5–9
children's literature course, 210–212, 223–226
choice in public schools, 234, 242
Clinchy, Evans, 69–70, 242, 271, 273, 277
Coalition of Essential Schools, 241
Coles, Robert, 26–27, 272
collaboration
vs. coercion, 68–69
students, parents, and teachers, 38, 48, 261
teachers with colleagues, 38
common core of learning, 248–250
community residents evaluating student academic work, 53
community settings and student performance, 53, 260
competitiveness as obstacle to passionate learning, 33
Concord, NH, mission and outcome statements, 248–249
conservatives and traditionalists, 239–244

constructivist approach to learning, 93–94
"Conversation with Toni Morrison, A" (T. LeClair), 276
cooperative learning, 177
Copernican vs. Ptolemaic view
of teaching, 126–127
Crane, David, 159–160, 176
culture of school and classroom,
30, 52
curriculum
content-focused vs. child-
centered, 11–12
cringe factor, 101
as daily work requirement,
104, 110
defined, 112
defined not as "content and
skills," 105–106
embedded in a web of relationships, 105, 108, 112–
114
guides for parents, 89–92,
105
inseparable from social milieu
of school, 105
linked to neighborhood and
family, 106
as mystery to parents, 104
as myth, 103
overshadowed by relation-
ships, 105–108
partnership between teacher
and students, 127–128
six contrasting definitions of,
101–103
unit on researching family
heroes, 262–270
unit outline for, 209–212
who cares?, 115–129
curriculum as relationships,
101–114
curriculum frameworks and
standardized testing, 251
curriculum units
emerging from children's
ideas, 41, 107
family heroes, 262–270

D'Arcangelo, Marcia, 271
Delpit, Lisa, 185–188, 276
Dewey, John, 112, 185, 191, 276
diagnostic tests and quizzes, uses
of, 118, 172, 219, 256, 258
disadvantaged students; students
from under-resourced
neighborhoods
educational inequity of, 240
low expectations for, 268
need of curriculum guides
for, 89
school success not expected
of, 3
and standardized testing, 246,
253–254
discipline of students. *See* behavior management
district graduation outcomes,
248–250
Duckworth, Eleanor, 155, 275
dummy groups, students' awareness of, 33

ebonics, 185–189
"Education at the Millennium:

The Bad and the Good,"
232–244
equity and inequity in education,
239–244
evolution and learning, 5, 30
excellence, 239–244. *See also*
quality and excellence

FairTest, 278
family-friendly curriculum
guide, 89–92, 105, 260
family heroes, sixth grade curric-
ulum unit, 262–270
First Days of School, The (H.
Wong & R. Wong), 273
Freire, Paolo, 139, 275
Fried, R., 277
Fried household, battles over
eating, 8–11
Fuentes, Alfredo, 256–257

Gabor, Michele, 143–144
Gardner, Howard, 50, 126
gender, students being treated
unfairly because of, 34
"Getting Smart, the Social Construction of Intelligence"
(J. Howard), 272
Golden Compass, The (P. Pullman),
28
Good Enough Parent, A (B. Bettelheim), 161, 276
grades and grading
allowing students and teachers to derive maximum benefit from, 223
based on a 120- or 125-point
scale, 219

celebrating inconsistent excellence in student work, 216–
231
closer look at grading, 220–
227
common ground for students
and teachers re: standards
and grading, 218–219
consistency of results as unrealistic goal, 216–217
defensive grading, unacceptable costs of, 215
discouragement of students,
stemming from, 32
dumbing down standards for
grading, 217
effect on students' love of
learning, 30
generosity of teachers, desirable, 217
limiting to A, B, C, and Incomplete, 221
negative impact on wide
range of students, 226
as occasion for vital teacher/
student conversation, 221
pleasing the teacher—the
right way, 227
precision and fairness as enemy of excellence, 212–
215
teachers refusing to grade
work students don't care
about, 122
trap of grading; *see* teachers:
trapped by grading practices
for a typical course, 202
validity of, 220

Hagner, Susan Cooney, 41–43
Harry Potter, 28, 143
Hartford, CT
    curriculum guide for parents
        and students, 89–91
    third grade students' views,
        2, 5
Having of Wonderful Ideas, The
    (E. Duckworth), 275
Heffron, Jim, 119–121, 160
high school, viewed as penance
    for unknown sin, 6
Howard, Jeff, 272

"I Can Do It" curriculum
    guides, 89–92, 98
Institute of Responsive Educa-
    tion, 274
intellectual freedom of preschool
    children, 44
internships of students in com-
    munity settings, 53
interviewees. *See* Opal (and
    Sydney); Mary (and Kate);
    Teague, Christine; Hagner,
    Susan Cooney

Johnson, Lea, 235–238
Josiah Quincy Upper School
    (Boston), 119, 159, 263

kids vs. grown-ups, as phenome-
    non in schools, 29, 58, 127
kindergarten, 22, 55
    lack of apathy by children in,
        25
Kingston-Mann, Esther, and
    R. Sieber, 271
knowledge as power, 259

Koch, Kenneth, approach to
    teaching poetry, 174, 176,
    276
Kohn, Alfie, 247, 252–253, 271,
    276, 277, 278

learner-centered vs. teacher-
    centered cosmology, 126–
    127
learning
    agendas in conflict, 74–81
    appetite for, 7, 10
    caring, as the heart of learn-
        ing, 117
    collaborative, 52
    constructivist approach
        needed, 93–94
    as continuous and joyful, 17
    despite schooling, 31
    disposition toward, by stu-
        dents, 26, 107, 109, 117,
        235
    and evolution, 30
    exciting and rewarding for
        all, 6
    forcing children to learn, 9
    as a function of relationships,
        47
    independent spirit of; *see* chil-
        dren: independent spirit of
        learning
    love of, measured on a scale,
        122
    maintaining early spirit
        through school, 26
    as a natural and universal
        desire, 7, 11
    as an onerous chore, 35

outside of school, 6, 37, 46, 49, 77–78, 259–260
positive signs that child is learning on his own, 79–80
promise of, as renewable warranty, 26
resistance of children toward viewed as "normal," 29–30
and schooling, comparison, 1
as social, collaborative process, 259–261
learning partnership among students and teachers, 127–128
learning styles among diverse children, 75–76
LeClair, Thomas, 276
Levine, Eliot, 273
life experiences, influence of in renewing passion for learning, 46
"Lift Every Voice," 176–193
literacy, 138–175. *See also* literacy instruction
African–American students' fear of "acting white," 153–154
assessment of, 171
cannot be taught in isolation, 145
children who can read but choose not to, 156–158
as a club, 138–139, 158
among college students, 142
creating a risk-free environment for, 169
and the "culture of school," 142
debate over how much of

school day it should consume, 144–146
despair over its current status, 141
as elite club for top students, 147
as extension of students' cultural identity, 145
in first grade, 140–141
and intellectual power, 138, 145
parents' role at home, 156–158
as self-motivated activity, 149
as social and community enterprise, 146
student literacy portfolios displayed in communities, 173
as students' "ticket to the world," 154
teachers, parents and students jointly promoting, 144
as tool of emancipation, 140, 145
vision of a literate society, 142
well taught and joyfully learned, 138
what school should be about, 140, 142
literacy is intellectual power, 138, 139, 145, 158
8 talking points for, 147–149
literacy instruction
approaches that diverse teachers might agree on, 154–155, 170
assessment in, 171
bringing in college books for sixth grade class, 151–152

community connection, 153–154

creating a risk-free environment, 169

defined for students and teachers, 145

engaging kids vs. instructing them, 168

evolving into a whole school focus, 166–170

favorite author for each student, 172

full participation of all students, 166

a "good enough" literacy program, 159–175

grammar lessons, 153, 172

heterogeneous approach, 165, 167

homework, changes in, 170–171

how we teach it is more important than what we teach, 146

for kids of middle ability levels, 150

literacy lab, as experimental idea, 146, 171–174

oral literacy and making speeches, 173, 188–189, 192

phonics, 156–157, 167, 169, 243

in poetry; *see* poetry

reading as a social experience, 165

storytelling and the oral tradition, 188–189, 192

students as literacy tutors, 173

students seeing connection between print and sense of self, 163

"writing workshop" approach, 164

looping of teachers, 87–89

Manchild in the Promised Land (C. Brown), 185

Mary and preschool daughter Kate, 20–25

math, teachers analyzing test results, 256

McCourt, Frank, 110–112, 275

Meier, Deborah, 52, 56, 61–64, 184, 247, 253, 271, 276, 277, 278

Meltzoff, Andrew, 18, 19–20, 271

misbehavior of students, 57–65

Mission Hill Elementary School (Boston), 61–64, 94

Mitchell, Malcolm, 149–154, 179, 263–269

Moffet, Donna, 60–61

Moral Intelligence of Children, The (R. Coles), 272

Morrison, Toni, 154, 186–187, 276

Mowat, Farley, 29

multigrade classrooms, 94

networking for new teachers, 95–96

Northeastern University, 114, 132, 145, 153, 274

Oakland Board of Education,
276
One Kid at a Time (E. Levine), 273
"Only for My Kid" (A. Kohn),
277
Opal, school nurse and mother
of preschooler Sydney, 20–
25
ostracism, of students who appear "different," 34
Other People's Children (T. Perry),
187, 276

Paolo Freire Reader, The, 275
Parent, Melissa, 107, 274
parent-and-child-friendly curriculum guide, 89–92
parental anxiety about school,
4–5, 20
"Parental Anxiety and School
Reform" (R. Fried), 277
parents
as active players in promoting
children's love of learning,
135–136
as curriculum partners with
teachers and students, 131–
136
documenting children's learning outside of school, 55
as full partners in teaching
and learning, 7, 97–98,
131–136
helping teachers adjust to
their child's learning style,
76
how and when to intervene in

child's school problems,
81–83
how to think about quality
learning before school year
begins, 227–231
intervening to help child with
literacy, 156–157
as members of partnership
triangle with teachers and
students, 54
modeling independent learning for their children, 80
paid leave to spend time in
school, 93
predicament regarding children who dislike school,
36–38
recognizing passionate learning in their child, 73–85
report cards for, 134–135
resistance to sharing responsibility for teaching, 54
responding to child who feels
defeated as a learner, 79–83
shame and humiliation felt by,
36
success-oriented, competitive, 6
supporting children's learning, 76
parent-friendly curriculum
guides, 89–92
parents and teachers working together, 6, 7, 38, 48, 92–93,
98, 235, 257–261
parent-teacher conferences,
student role in, 260
partnership in learning. *See also*

collaboration, 127–128,
    131–136
"Passion for Excellence—and
    How We Undermine It, A,"
    197–215
passionate learning
    attitudes of children, 37–38,
        72, 107
    as best response to critics of
        public schools, 247
    boredom and, 66–70
    caring and, 117–130
    collaboration vs. isolation of
        teachers as a factor in pro-
        moting, 7, 87–88, 94–95
    declines as students move
        through school, 2, 29, 32–
        37, 76, 231
    equity, impact on, 239–244
    as function of relationships,
        47, 107–109, 112–113
    grades and grading, impact
        on, 204, 208, 212–215,
        220, 231
    higher standards, compatible
        with, 218–219
    as key to children's future as
        lifelong learners, 198–199
    learner-centered classroom,
        126–127
    literacy and, 138–139, 146
    multigrade classrooms and,
        94–95
    as natural and universal trait
        of children, 1, 11, 14, 27,
        73, 270
    obstacles to, 32–37, 57, 70,
        74, 138

parents as nurturers of, 6, 37,
    73–85, 227–230
preschools and, 41–44
requires diversity of schools,
    242
right of every student, 240
schools' resistance to and role
    in advocating, 12, 86–98
standardized testing, impact
    on, 234, 244, 245–261
students' voices and, 177,
    180, 185
Passionate Teacher, The (R. Fried),
    ix, xi, 208, 221, 256, 264,
    275, 278
passionate teachers compared
    with "good teachers," 130
passionate teaching and learning
    in era of specialization,
    245–261
passionate teaching reflected in
    goals for a course, 201
peer culture and academic suc-
    cess, 5
peer pressure, as negative or posi-
    tive influence on learning,
    34
performance expectations for stu-
    dents, outlined, 209–212
Perry, Theresa, 185, 188–189,
    276
phonics. *See* literacy instruction
poetry
    "I am depressed" poem,
        174–175
    literacy instruction, 165–
        166, 174–176
    "unicorn" poem, 176

power
of adults "not-telling" and
allowing students to dis-
cover, 42–43
connection between learning
and personal power, 243,
244
students becoming powerful
in humanities class, 268
progressive vs. traditional approaches to schooling, 239–
244
the promise of passionate learning, 26
reclaiming the promise, parents, 73–85
reclaiming the promise,
school systems, 86–98
reclaiming the promise,
teachers, 41–56
Pullman, Philip, 28
Punished by Rewards (A. Kohn),
271, 276

quality and excellence, 197–215
active pursuit of meaning by
students, 198
building quality into the
teaching plan, 208–210
clash between teacher goals
and student response, 207,
231
confused with perfection and
completion of tasks, 198,
206
confusing messages parents
receive, 197
defined—what it is, and what
it isn't, 228–229
describing excellence in the
work of diverse learners,
198–199
different ways of students
demonstrating, 217–
218
excellence defined as "quality
of engagement over time,"
198
finding a way out of the trap,
205–208
as goals for student learning,
197
how student receptivity to
quality atrophies, 204
"less is more," 219
linking quality goals to grading policies, 204
parents' crucial role, 229–
230
pie charts for excellence in
course goals and grading,
200–202, 205
practical steps for teachers regarding quality standards
and grading, 219
precision and fairness in grading as enemy of excellence,
212–215
problems with conventional
ways of assessing students,
198–206
quality learning, defined,
228–229
quality learning, ways to
think about, 227–231

reflected in grading criteria,
222
straight-A students, problems
of, 218
structural disharmony, contradictions in goals and grading, 198, 206
student self-assessment re:
quality of own work, 219
students reaching desired proficiency levels, 222
for students who need extra
time or help, 199
teachers ignoring their most
important goals, 199, 203
traps teachers set for themselves, 199–204
young learners and excel-
lence, a quandary, 198–199

racism and social class prejudice,
34, 59
Read Aloud Handbook, The (J. Trelease), 275
Reading Without Nonsense (F.
Smith), 271
Real Ebonics Debate, The (L. Delpit and T. Perry), 276
recruiting teachers for passionate
learners, 92–93
report cards, 54, 231
non-comparative and non-
competitive, 55
for parents, 134–135
resources vs. responsibility, pro-
gressivism vs. tradition, national debate
(liberals vs. conservatives, re-

formers vs. traditionalists),
239–244
Rickford, John Russell and Rus-
sell John, 185, 276
Rose, Where Did You Get That Red?
(K. Koch), 74, 276

Salem High School, Conyers,
GA (student graduation
speeches), 193
Sarason, Seymour, ix–xi, 7, 30,
207
scales for measuring student/
teacher/parent attitudes to
schoolwork, 118–125
parents, students, teachers,
regarding academic work,
133
students regarding curriculum, 118
students regarding their
teachers, 124
students regarding writing,
119
teachers regarding curriculum, 123
teachers regarding students,
125
School and Society, The (J. Dewey),
276
school success necessary in society, 31
schools linked within a district,
94–95
Schools Our Children Deserve, The
(A. Kohn), 277
Scientist in the Crib, The (A. Meltzoff), 18

silence, power of in teaching and learning, 42–43
Sizer, Theodore, 241
Smith, Frank, 20, 66, 78, 138–139, 140, 158, 271, 273, 274, 275
soccer compared with schooling, 11–13
Spoken Soul (J. R. & R. J. Rickford), 185, 276
stance, teachers' toward students, 119, 129, 238, 263
standardized or high-stakes tests and testing, 5, 245–261
   the case against, 251–254
   as diagnostic tool, 256, 258
   emergence of "The Test," 248–251
   greatest current challenge to passionate learning and teaching, 244, 254
   how teachers and parents can confront threat for children, twelve steps, 257–261
   Kohn, Alfie, on, 252–253
   MCAS (Massachusetts tests), 246
   Meier, Deborah, on, 253
   as political cover for experimental programs, 258
   politicized climate, 233
   positive aspects of, 254–257
   teachers "under the gun" to produce test results, 234
standards in teaching and learning
   high standards for all students, 233

teachers and students coming to an understanding on, 219
strategies
   for building or enhancing a sense of community in the classroom, 50–52
   for communicating with parents about a child's progress, 54–55
   for linking the classroom to a wider supportive community, 52–53
   to promote oral literacy and self-confidence among students, 191–193
   for showcasing children's in-school and out-of-school learning, 49–50
students. *See also* children
   accepting responsibility for own misbehavior, 63
   disposition toward learning, 26, 107, 109, 117, 235
   interest in learning declines as they advance in school, x, 2, 3, 5, 6, 26
   internships in community settings, 54
   lack of trust in adults in school, 34
   learning outside of school, 47
   as participants in parent/teacher conferences, 55, 260
   as partners in problem solving, 38, 55
   preoccupation with finding the right answer, 110

resisting/submitting to adult
  authority, 218
right to be consulted about
  the purpose of an assignment, 67, 108–109
self-assessment in grading,
  219
sorting and labeling of, 46
as troublemakers, 57, 65
who stop reading for pleasure, 140
who want to learn, necessity
  of creating conditions for,
  46
styles of learning, 75, 76
systems of education, systemic
  change in schools and school
  districts, 86–98

talking. *See also* ebonics
brainstorming and spontaneous speaking, 184
four kinds of talking problems, 180–191:
  aggressiveness, 182–185;
  cultural and other differences, 185–189;
  resistance/peer influence,
  190–191;
  shyness, 181–182
as a function of relationships
  within the classroom, 191
listening and speaking, classroom rules for, 181, 184
need to promote, 177–179
"teacher-pleasing" vs. "teacher-
  bashing," 32
teachers

celebrating students' in-
  school and out-of-school
  learning, 49–51
collegiality among, 97
and the culture of the classroom, 52
discussing behavioral issues
  with students, 51
districts hiring only teachers
  who communicate well with
  parents, 92–93
getting the relationship
  "right" with students, 107–
  108
helping students be better listeners, 51
interested in students as
  whole persons, 48
inviting parents and residents
  into class, 53
isolation and loneliness, 7,
  87, 94–96
knowing students well, 238
looping, 87
negotiating with students
  about curriculum, 108–109
network-building for new
  teachers, 94–95
new teachers and behavior
  management, 59–60
refusing to grade work students don't care about,
  122
self-assessment regarding curriculum material (scale),
  123–124
showcasing diversity of student learning styles, 50

trapped by grading practices,
199–204, 212–215
unschooled minds, regarding
student-centered classroom,
126
vibrancy as a factor in student
learning, 166
viewing students as adversaries, 35, 65
working as a team of three,
over three years, 87–89
teaching
passionate teaching and learning as needed to overcome
public skepticism, 247
as profession "on probation,"
245–247, 257
Teague, Christine, 161–171
time
lack of as obstacle to change,
57, 71
waste of; *see* wasting time
'Tis (F. McCourt), 110–112,
275
Trelease, Jim, 141, 275

voice mail, as tool for teacher/
parent communication, 93

voices, need for students to open
their minds to new voices,
151

wasting time, as obstacle to passionate learning, 70–72
Watership Down (R. Adams), 28,
158
Whitehead, Alfred North, 179–
180, 229, 276, 277
*Will Standards Save Public Educa-
tion?* (D. Meier), 277
Wong, Harry and Rosemary, *The
First Days of School*, 273
Wordsworth, William, 1, 31
writing
as a punishment, 140
students figuring out how to
make it more interesting,
120
students writing stories for
younger kids, 94
survey scale of student attitudes on, 119–120

Yan Li Xu (sixth grade student
poet), 176–177
Yeats, William B., 26